Frontiers of Tax Reform

The Hoover Institution
gratefully acknowledges generous support from

TAD TAUBE
TAUBE FAMILY FOUNDATION

Founders of the Program on
American Institutions and Economic Performance

and Cornerstone gifts from

JOANNE AND JOHAN BLOKKER
SARAH SCAIFE FOUNDATION

Frontiers of
Tax Reform

Edited with an Introduction by
MICHAEL J. BOSKIN

HOOVER INSTITUTION PRESS
Stanford University
Stanford, California

Hoover Institution Press Publication No. 435

Copyright © 1996 by the Board of Trustees of the
Leland Stanford Junior University

First printing, 1996
02   01   00   99   98   97   96   9   8   7   6   5   4   3   2   1
Simultaneous first paperback printing, 1996
02   01   00   99   98   97   96   9   8   7   6   5   4   3   2   1

Manufactured in the United States of America

⊗ The paper used in this publication meets the minimum requirements
of American National Standard for Information Sciences—Permanence
of Paper for Printed Library Materials, ANSI Z39.48–1984.

Library of Congress Cataloging-in-Publication Data

Frontiers of Tax Reform / edited with an introduction by
Michael J. Boskin.

      p.   cm.

   Papers presented at a conference held in Washington, D.C.,
in May 1995, sponsored by the Hoover Institution.

   Includes index.

   ISBN 0-8179-9431-9 (alk. paper). — ISBN 0-8179-9432-7 (pbk.)

    1. Taxation—United States—Congresses.   2. Value-added tax.—
United States—Congresses.   I. Boskin, Michael J.   II. Hoover
Institution on War, Revolution, and Peace.

HJ2381.F76   1996
336.2'05'0973 — dc20   95-48858
                                       CIP

Contents

Contributors

The Honorable WILLIAM ARCHER is chairman of the Ways and Means Committee of the U.S. House of Representatives, as well as a member of the Joint Committee on Taxation. Archer has been a member of the United States Congress since 1971, representing the 7th Congressional District of Texas. His work in Congress has included initiatives such as the Balanced Budget Amendment and the line-item veto. Archer has long been a champion of lower taxes, less governmental intervention, and cutting government spending. He has also been a supporter of a "broad-based" consumption tax.

MICHAEL J. BOSKIN is a senior fellow at the Hoover Institution and Tully M. Friedman Professor of Economics at Stanford University. He is also adjunct scholar at the American Enterprise Institute and research associate at the National Bureau of Economic Research. From 1989 to 1993 Boskin was chairman of the President's Council of Economic Advisers. Boskin is currently chairman of the Advisory Commission to Study the Consumer Price Index appointed by the United States Senate, a member of the Advisory Committee of the Joint Committee on Taxation of the U.S. Congress, the Panel of Advisers to the Congressional Budget Office, and the Economic Advisory Council to the governor of California. Boskin is curently working on two books entitled *Post-War Economic Growth in the G-7 Countries* and *Consumption and Saving Patterns in the United States* (coauthored with L. Lau).

DAVID F. BRADFORD is a professor of economics and public affairs at Princeton University and an adjunct professor, New York University School of Law. He is also research associate at the National Bureau of Economic Research and adjunct scholar at the American Enterprise Institute. Bradford's roles in public service have included being a member of the President's Council of Economic Advisers from 1991 to 1993 and being the deputy assistant secretary for tax policy from 1975 to 1976. While at the Department of the Treasury, he directed a study resulting in a published volume, *Blueprints for Basic Tax Reform* (2d ed. Tax Analysts, 1984), that is widely regarded as the forerunner of the major U.S. income tax reform enacted in 1986. Bradford's book *Untangling the Income Tax* (Harvard University Press, 1986) provides a comprehensive review of income taxes and their alternatives, including consumption taxes.

ROBERT E. HALL is a senior fellow at the Hoover Institution and a professor of economics at Stanford University. Before joining Hoover and Stanford, Hall was professor of economics at the Massachusetts Institute of Technology and assistant professor at the University of California at Berkeley. Along with Hoover colleague Alvin Rabushka, Hall is an active proponent of the flat tax. Their article in the *Wall Street Journal* in December 1981 was the starting point for an upsurge of interest in the flat tax. This movement culminated in a dramatic flattening of tax rates in the Tax Reform Act of 1986. Their book, *The Flat Tax*, was originally published by the Hoover Institution Press in 1985 and was rereleased this year.

DALE W. JORGENSON is chairman of the Department of Economics and Frederic Eaton Abbe Professor of Economics at Harvard University. He has been on the economics faculty at Harvard since 1969 and has been director of the Program on Technology and Economic Policy at the Kennedy School of Government since 1984. From 1959 to 1969, Jorgenson was a professor of economics at the University of California at Berkeley and has been a visiting professor of economics at Stanford University and the Hebrew University of Jerusalem and visiting professor of statistics at Oxford University. He has also served as Ford Foundation Research Professor of Economics at the University of Chicago. Jorgenson is currently a member of the Advisory Commission to Study the Consumer Price Index appointed by the U.S. Senate. His most recent books, *Postwar U.S. Economic Growth* and *International Comparisons of Economic Growth*, were published by the MIT Press in 1995.

The Honorable KENNETH KIES was appointed chief of staff of the Joint Committee on Taxation on January 4, 1995. Before joining the committee he was a partner in Baker & Hostetler's Washington, D.C., office where he served as firmwide chair of the firm's tax practice. Kies has been tax counsel for numerous associations and task forces and has testified before the Senate Finance Committee, the Ways and Means Committee, and the Internal Revenue Service. From

1982 until 1987, Kies served as chief minority tax counsel on the Ways and Means Committee of the United States House of Representatives. While in that capacity, he was involved in such major legislative accomplishments as the Economic Recovery Tax Act of 1981, the Tax Equity and Fiscal Responsibility Act of 1982, the Tax Reform Act of 1984, and the Tax Reform Act of 1986.

LAURENCE J. KOTLIKOFF is a professor of economics at Boston University. Previously, he was on the faculties of economics at the University of California at Los Angeles and Yale University. Kotlikoff was a senior economist with the President's Council of Economic Advisers form 1981 to 1982. He has served as a consultant to numerous domestic and foreign governmental agencies and testified before congressional committees, including the House Ways and Means Committee, the Joint Economic Committee, and the Senate Finance Committee on issues of deficits, generational accounting, the tax structure, Social Security, pensions, saving, and insurance. Recent publications include *Generational Accounting*, *What Determines Savings?* and (with A. Auerbach) *Dynamic Fiscal Policy*.

CHARLES E. MCLURE JR. is a senior fellow at the Hoover Institution at Stanford University. McLure's accomplishments before joining the Hoover Institution include service as deputy assistant secretary of the Treasury for tax analysis from 1983 to 1985, as vice president of the National Bureau of Economic Research from 1977 to 1981, and as Cline Professor of Economics at Rice University from 1965 to 1977. His work at the Treasury included developing the department's proposals to President Ronald Reagan that became the basis of the Tax Reform Act of 1986. McLure is author of *The Value Added Tax: Key to Deficit Reduction* and *Must Corporate Income Be Taxed Twice?* His current research focuses on tax policy and intergovernmental fiscal relations in countries in transition from socialism and on consumption-based taxes.

GILBERT E. METCALF is an assistant professor of economics at Tufts University and a faculty research fellow at the National Bureau of Economics Research. Before joining the faculty at Tufts, Metcalf was assistant professor of economics at Princeton University. He recently published "Value Added Taxation: A Tax Whose Time Has Come?" in the *Journal of Economic Perspectives*. His research interests include consumption taxation, investment and uncertainty, energy taxation, and state and local public finance.

STEPHEN MOORE is director of fiscal policy studies at the Cato Institute. Before joining Cato, Moore was a senior economist at the Joint Economic Committee as an assistant to Representative Dick Armey, where he advised Armey on budget, tax, and competitiveness issues. Moore has served on two presidential commissions, in 1988 as a special consultant to the National Economic Commission and in 1987 as research director of President Ronald Reagan's Commission on Privatization. Moore is a regular contributor to the *Wall Street Journal, Human Events,* and *National Review,* as well as frequently published in the *Los Angeles Times, Christian Science Monitor,* and *Public Interest.*

ALVIN RABUSHKA, a senior fellow at the Hoover Institution of Stanford University, specializes in the public areas of taxation, constitutional limitations on taxing and spending, and economic development, with special attention to East and Southeast Asia and Israel. He is the author or coauthor of more than twenty books in the areas of race and ethnicity, aging, taxation, state and local government finances, the economic development of Hong Kong and "the Asian tigers" of Taiwan, Korea, and Singapore, and Israel's economy. He has also published a number of articles in both scholarly journals and more popular outlets such as the *Wall Street Journal,* the *New York Times, Fortune,* and the *Jerusalem Post.* He has consulted for or testified before a number of public agencies including the Joint Economic Committee of the Congress, House Ways and Means Committee, and Senate Finance Committee. His books and articles on the flat tax provided the intellectual foundation for several flat tax bills that were introduced in Congress during the 1980s, and he was recognized in *Money* magazine's twentieth anniversary issue for the importance of his flat tax proposal in bringing about passage of the Tax Reform Act of 1986.

MURRAY WEIDENBAUM is director of the Center for the Study of American Business and holds the Mallinckrodt Distinguished Professorship at Washington University in Saint Louis. From 1982 until 1989, Weidenbaum was a member of the President's Economic Policy Advisory Board. He served as President Ronald Reagan's chairman of the Council of Economic Advisers from 1981 to 1982. Other positions he has held in government and business include assistant secretary of the Treasury for economic policy, fiscal economist in the U.S. Bureau of the Budget, and corporate economist at Boeing Company. Weidenbaum's latest book is entitled *Business and Government in the Global Marketplace.*

GEORGE R. ZODROW is professor of economics at Rice University and a member of the Editorial Advisory Board of the *National Tax Journal.* Zodrow was a staff economist at the U.S. Treasury Office of tax analysis in 1984–1985 and participated in the preparation of "Treasury I," the study that was the precursor to the Tax Reform Act of 1986. He has also consulted with the World Bank and the Agency for International Development, examining taxation issues in numerous countries. He is coauthor of *The Taxation of Income from Business and Capital in Colombia,* which examined the feasibility of implementing a consumption-based direct tax in Colombia. Zodrow's research has included tax reform in the United States and in developing countries and state and local public finance.

Introduction

MICHAEL J. BOSKIN

Few are willing to speak out in favor of the current tax system. To be sure, there are defenders of virtually every specific provision, but, from the tax-paying public to politicians to academic tax policy experts, everyone excoriates the current tax system for what they see as its serious problems.

Many argue that taxes are too high, especially marginal effective tax rates. Others argue that the tax base is wrong, that it should focus more on consumption (or income that is consumed) than on current income. Still others decry the actual and perceived complexity of the tax code and the huge compliance and administrative costs it imposes. Others deplore the lack of fairness in the tax code, although different definitions of fairness come from different quarters. Perhaps most important, the tax code is viewed by many, myself included, as one of the culprits in the United States' unsatisfactory long-term economic growth performance.

Not surprisingly, then, tax reform is in the air. Tax reform is hardly a new phenomenon; the federal tax system underwent major or complete overhauls in 1978, 1981, 1982, 1983, 1985, 1986, 1990, and 1993. Additional tax cuts and reforms are being debated and negotiated in late 1995 as this book goes to press. But there does seem to be something different about this round of tax reform debate and discussion; the calls are for something fundamental and express an exasperation not felt since the late 1970s, when a combination of high tax rates and double-digit inflation pushed millions of Americans into higher tax brackets, even though their earnings were not keeping pace with inflation. That led to the

Kemp-Roth proposal for dramatic reductions in marginal tax rates, which was implemented in President Ronald Reagan's 1981 Economic Recovery and Tax Act. Most of the "reforms" since, with the notable exception of 1986, were designed primarily to deal with persistent large federal government budget deficits (i.e., to raise revenue). The 1986 reform, in contrast, was to be revenue neutral but to reform the tax code to achieve "fairness, simplicity, and growth." Most objective observers give the 1986 tax reform high marks for the dramatic reduction in marginal tax rates but poor marks for simplicity and those features of the tax system, other than statutory marginal rates, that most affect growth. But the implicit 1986 contract for a broader base and lower rates has been dramatically reversed—first in 1990, with a modest increase in effective tax rates (but a whopping break of a political pledge!), and substantially in 1993, when top marginal tax rates were increased by about one-third!

Another important feature of the series of tax reforms—in addition to recycling various tax features such as investment credits, capital gains differentials, moving the rates up and down, and the like—was sequentially removing a large fraction of the population from the base of the federal income tax. Today the top 5 percent of taxpayers pays almost half of all federal income taxes, and the bottom 50 percent, only 5 percent. Many millions of Americans have been removed from the tax rolls. In addition, the earned-income tax credit, a device that transfers income to relatively low-income wage earners, a sort of negative income tax, has become a large and rapidly growing federal entitlement program.

The complexities of the tax code mostly revolve around business taxes and personal taxation of capital income. For example, the tax rules regarding pension contributions and withdrawals now include stiff penalties for contributing too much or too little or withdrawing too early or too late. This form of micromanagement, which extends well beyond the pension arena, is part of the frustration felt by innumerable taxpayers in their everyday financial affairs.

The complexities do not confine themselves to the well-off or businesses. About half the taxpayers who file on the 1040EZ Form—the simple income tax return—use a professional tax preparer to figure out their taxes! Independent audits suggest that taxpayer inquiries of the IRS result in a correct answer less than two-thirds of the time. It offends a fundamental sense of fairness to be charged fines or interest for following IRS instructions that ex post prove to be wrong.

From the billions of man-hours and hundreds of billions of dollars of administrative and compliance costs to the large potential drag on overall economic growth, there seems ample opportunity to improve the tax system. But the tax system must be understood in a broader context; for example, the United States is a federal system, and devolution of authority, responsibility, and resources to state and local governments is desirable. Understanding the eventual impact of tax reform involves evaluating its impact on federalism. Taxes are also the primary vehicle by which federal spending is financed. Many would argue for a tight relation between taxes and spending, not just in the sense of balancing the budget but in making it obvious to taxpayers that their taxes finance government spending. This has even led to proposals to abolish withholding so that the taxpayers would have to pay every month. Obviously, this would greatly increase the administrative and compliance costs, but it would also make citizens think carefully about what government spending is truly desirable. All this occurs in the context, as discussed above, of a dramatic reduction in the fraction of the population paying federal income taxes. The rise in the ratio of people receiving payments from the government to those paying taxes to the government (netting all transactions) is disturbing even today. But given dramatic increases in life expectancy and the looming retirement of the baby boomers, demography will drive that ratio upward. On both the spending and the tax side of the budget, everyone must be made aware of the cost of government.

With so many tax reforms in the last decade and a half, one goal might be to have a tax system that can endure for many years. In many ways the simplest tax system would be one that was the same year after year after year, facilitating planning and diffusing understanding. That may well imply structural restrictions on tax changes, making it more difficult for Congress to pass frequent major changes.

Perhaps most important, given the apparent long-term growth anemia in the U.S. economy, is whether a fundamental tax reform could substantially boost the economy's performance, leading to a rise in real incomes. Most economists believe that the major way in which tax reform can boost economic performances is by altering the tax system's deleterious impact on incentives to work, save, invest, and innovate. A pure income tax, for example, taxes saving twice: first when it is earned as part of income and again when interest and dividends are earned on savings. Worse yet, if that saving is plowed into corporate equities, a third tax (the separate corporate tax) is paid. Of course, the tax system taxes nominal capital gains and sometimes thereby imposes enormous rates of tax on real gains. In a world where technological obsolescence is becoming evermore important relative to traditional "wear and tear," in numerous industries depreciation, while called accelerated, falls well short of what is necessary to recoup full capital costs.

Several major tax reform proposals that have been developed in recent years are now finding strong proponents in the political leadership in Congress. All tax legislation must originate in the Ways and Means Committee in the House of Representatives. The powerful chairman of the House Ways and Means Committee, Congressman Bill Archer of Texas, has declared that he wants to "pull the income tax out by its roots so it can never grow back again." Congressman Archer, who favors a broad-based consumption tax, has spoken in favor of fundamental tax reform based on several principles. His essay in this volume discusses the principles he believes should form the guideposts to evaluate tax reform proposals and explains why a broad-based consumption tax is his preferred alternative.

My essay discusses several goals of tax reform and compares the alternatives along these dimensions. It points to important similarities among the various reform proposals, for example, reducing the heavy (double) taxation of saving. Indeed, while they get there from different routes and would have vastly different administrative, compliance, transition, and other features, all the proposals end up with a tax base approximating consumption rather than income. (I focus on the need to encourage economic growth and the desirability of low marginal effective tax rates.)

House majority leader Dick Armey and others have proposed a variant of the so-called flat tax, developed by Robert Hall and Alvin Rabushka of the Hoover Institution. In their essay, Hall and Rabushka lay out the features of their flat tax and in so doing expose a variety of problems in the existing tax system and some misinterpretations of their tax proposal. In the end, Hall-Rabushka is a tax on consumption, net of a large personal exemption, which makes the tax somewhat progressive. They believe their tax system is simple enough that it can be filed on a postcard. Their tax proposal winds up taxing capital income, with immediate expensing for investment in the business tax and labor income in the personal tax. Hence, between the two taxes, it taxes total income minus investment, which is consumption in the economy.

An important but less fundamental reform proposal has been developed by Senators Sam Nunn and Pete Domenici, the so-called USA (unlimited savings allowance) Tax. It most resembles the existing income tax but has an allowance for *all* net saving not limited by category and use. Murray Weidenbaum discusses the Nunn-Domenici proposal and its advantages and disadvantages relative to other reforms. It would affect the distribution of tax burdens less than other more fundamental reforms and also contains credits in the business and personal income tax for payroll taxes. It also has a special way to treat old capital that has been accumulated by citizens that may have been taxed or tax preferenced in the past. The Nunn-Domenici proposal, however, has the highest marginal tax rates of all the proposals. Combining the 11 percent value-added-type business tax with the top 40 percent marginal tax rate in the personal tax, the top marginal tax rate under Nunn-Domenici becomes substantial—something explicitly rejected by the more fundamental reform proposals that call for a broad-based value-added tax or retail sales tax or flat-rate "income" tax.

Value-added taxes (VATs) work by taxing the contribution to the value of a product at each point along the chain of production. Conceptually, a value-added tax could approximate the taxation of consumption or gross income in the economy, depending on its allowance for deducting capital expenditures. The discussions in the United States surround a consumption-type VAT. Gib Metcalf in his essay discusses various approaches to value-added taxation and its pros and cons. Value-added taxes are in widespread use in many other countries. They are often justified as helping a nation's competitiveness because the VAT is rebatable at the border, although economists generally believe other economic adjustments will offset some or all of this advantage. Two serious issues confronting proponents of value-added taxes are, first, that in other countries they have primarily been used to augment the revenue base, which has allowed the financing of an expansion of government. That is not a popular idea today and indeed is anathema to most proponents of broad-based consumption taxes as a vehicle for tax reform, who would like to see a good, clean VAT replace personal and corporate income taxes.

A second issue surrounding a VAT is how to deal with low-income taxpayers, whose consumption may be high relative to their income. One could exempt commodities consumed disproportionately by low-income people—food, for example—but it would be hard to exempt the food of low-income people as opposed to food consumed by the wealthy or the middle class. Thus, a refundable credit system would likely have to be included as part of the VAT proposal, and although this would be far less intrusive than the existing tax system, it would be an administrative and compliance concern, especially given the widespread fraud and abuse that apparently surrounds the earned-income tax credit.

Steve Moore discusses the economic and civil liberties advantages of a retail sales tax as a substitute for the income tax. He places great weight not just on the immense compliance and administrative cost of the income tax but on the intrusiveness into private lives of the tax collection process.

Charles McLure and George Zodrow offer an as yet not widely disseminated alternative to Hall-Rabushka and Nunn-Domenici. Their "pick-and-choose" approach lays out a strong case for a hybrid combination of business and personal taxes that takes the best features of the various proposals. They emphasize how difficult it is to measure, and therefore tax, income; inflation, depreciation, and inventory accounting are all huge complications in the income tax. Their case is strong, but the debate has not yet focused on the issues they stress. At some point, would-be reformers will have to confront these issues and may well find the McLure-Zodrow answers appealing.

Any move from one tax system to another involves major transition issues. Changes in the taxation of various assets will involve, by necessity, capital gains and losses on those assets, as can be readily seen by the wild swings in the tax treatment of real estate, from underdepreciated before 1981 to overdepreciated after 1981 to the swing back in the other direction in 1986. Enormous sectoral disruption can occur with substantial correlative economic costs, not just for the owners of the assets but in terms of regional unemployment, for example. *Thus, major tax reforms should not be undertaken lightly.* Moving from the current federal corporate and personal tax system to an idealized reform may provide substantial benefits in the long run, but what will be the nature of the transition costs and will it be worth it? Will we end up with the ideal tax reform or a partial reform that vitiates many or most of the benefits to simplicity and growth?

In his essay, David Bradford tackles these questions with penetrating insight. No one has thought more deeply or carefully about the transition from our current tax system to a consumption-based system than has Bradford. These issues are important to all of us, not just those technically involved with the tax laws, as they form a fundamental part of the evaluation of the desirability of any reform proposal and of transition rules and periods.

In his discussion, Ken Kies focuses on the informational demands for providing the input to intelligent decision making by Congress on tax reform. Although many issues are similar to those encountered in minor reforms, others are much more complex. The types of major changes being espoused by Chairman Archer or Majority Leader Armey would cause major reductions in marginal tax rates that will likely have substantial effects on economic behavior well beyond those that might be expected from small changes. The whole notion of how the tax community, the public, and the press think about the distributional impacts of a tax system lags decades behind academic thinking on the matter. During the Eisenhower administration, when six out of every seven dollars of government spending was for purchases of goods and services, it may have made sense to think about the distribution of tax burdens in isolation. But now that a majority of federal spending, net of interest on the debt, is on transfer payments to people, the vast majority of income support and redistribution occurs on the outlay side of the budget. Thus, at a minimum, one should look at the distribution of the tax *and* the transfer system, not just the tax system alone.

Another fundamental issue involves the time frame. Many people smooth their consumption to bring it more in line with their average, or permanent, income. Thus, distribution tables in any given year, when the distribution of income is far more dispersed than it would be over a longer period of time for the same families or households, can be misleading. Indeed, many would argue that the distribution tables should be presented in terms of consumption, rather than income, as that is what ultimately determines the standard of living. Finally, if there is a lot of consumption smoothing, current consumption may be a better measure of ability to pay than is current income because consumption more closely tracks average or permanent income. These and other issues will place demands on the informational input to the public policy process, from distribution tables to growth effects.

Finally, is tax reform worth the candle? If the world is complex, is a simple tax appropriate? Or is a complex tax worth the trouble and economic cost? Dale Jorgenson and Larry Kotlikoff present two powerful analyses, from complementary but different perspectives, on the likely economic benefits of moving from the current tax system to a lower-rate broad-based consumption tax. Their results suggest that the economic impact would be substantial. Kotlikoff's estimate is that output would increase by 5 to 10 percent. Jorgenson makes a present-value calculation that the net benefits would be $1 trillion to the U.S. economy. Other evaluations, including my own and those of Bob Lucas, likewise suggest large potential effects on income and output over the long run. If these results are correct, these are very sizable rewards. They strongly support the notion that, if it can be kept in place for many years, it would be worth undergoing serious transition and adjustment costs to achieve a fundamental tax reform.

I urge all who are interested in tax reform to read, indeed study, these essays. This volume, which is the result of a May 1995 conference in Washington, D.C., sponsored by the Hoover Institution, brings together some of the world's leading scholars and policymakers to discuss various tax reform alternatives, pros and cons of various approaches, potential benefits from tax reform, and serious issues raised in considering tax reform.

The nation will be debating fundamental tax reform for at least the next two years. If a fundamental tax reform gains enough momentum to be legislated, the impacts on our economy and society will be enormous. It is therefore everyone's business whether and how the tax system will be reformed. We hope this volume becomes a valuable resource, not only to those who will be engaged in the tax reform debate but to the larger audience of interested citizens who will be affected by it.

PART ONE

PERSPECTIVES ON TAX REFORM

1

Goals of Fundamental Tax Reform

BILL ARCHER

Each of us has grown up in this country assuming that the income tax would always be with us. After the last election, I believe many of us realize that we can take new, visionary, bold, and creative ideas into the arena and that we do not have to accept as a given that the income tax will always be with us. I for one believe that it has outlived its usefulness as a helpful tool to accomplish the goals that this country should be attempting to reach. I believe it is now time for us to look in a visionary way for an agenda for the next century and to begin to launch the debate in a serious way at this point in our country's history.

I went through the major tax reform of 1985–86, and I was very hopeful then because Ronald Reagan had done an outstanding job of telling us why the current income tax system was not good and how we would end up with a product that we could be proud of. But during the course of tax reform deliberations in the Ways and Means Committee, I realized that we were going to end up with something that was only a further complication of what we had already criticized, and I fell off the bandwagon of tax reform and led the opposition to the 1986 Tax Reform Act. I think it was one of the best things that I have ever done. I think that history has proved that what I said on the floor of the House in the debate was accurate. We have a worse tax code today than we did before we entered tax reform in 1986. We must do better. It would be my goal for our revenue-raising system in this country to meet five objectives:

- *1. Simplify enforcement and compliance*

We have seen studies today that show that the current income tax system is costing our economy a minimum of $300 billion dollars in compliance costs. And that is the conservative, bottom-line figure. Many say that it could be approaching $500–$600 billion dollars a year. That is simply a destruction of wealth, not wealth creating. Figure into the equation of compliance costs— whether it's a tax consultant, a tax preparer—the work that is done in keeping the records, the time spent in preparing the tax returns.

I am the first chairman of the Ways and Means Committee to do his own tax return year after year, and I have said that I am either going to fix it or that I am going to suffer through it personally along with everyone else. It would be a good idea for every congressperson to have to do his or her own tax return; perhaps we would see a better tax code. I roughly estimate that it takes me, in bits and pieces of time, somewhere close to sixteen hours to do my own tax return. Once you begin to consider all of what is involved, the litigation, the uncertainty, it is truly time for us to think of a simpler method of raising revenues.

In addition, the intrusiveness of the Internal Revenue Service (IRS) into our individual lives is a matter of greater and greater concern on the part of the American people. And I think we should attempt to find a system of taxation that will get the IRS completely out of our individual lives—I mean completely and totally out of our individual lives. From the standpoint of individual freedom, the intrusiveness of government, I don't know how you place a value on that, but it has to be massive.

- *2. Give the greatest possible incentive to savings*

Economists ranging from Michael Boskin and Murray Weidenbaum to those of a liberal persuasion or in-between, Republicans or Democrats, that appear before the Ways and Means Committee, every single one of them agrees that the dearth in our economy is savings. And yet we have pursued a course since 1981 that continues year after year to change the code, to pinch back on incentives for savings.

- *3. Give the greatest opportunity to get at the underground economy*

Again, the estimates have to be rough because, obviously, if you're not paying taxes you're not going to get out and tell people you're not paying taxes. The estimates of the revenue that we lose to the underground economy range from $100 to $200 billion dollars a year. For everyone of us who conscientiously pays our own taxes, that's an off-load onto each one of us of an additional burden to maintain the cost of government.

Goals 4 and 5 are items that I attach perhaps the greatest importance to in an agenda for the next century.

- *4. Remove taxes from the price of our exported products and services*
- *5. Charge taxes on incoming foreign products so that they bear their fair share of our cost of government*

Now if in fact these five goals are important (and I believe them to be), then we can score various forms of taxation on a scale of one to ten; in all five categories the current income tax scores zero. We can begin from there to talk about alternative methods to raise money for this country.

Let me give you a little bit of my own development in thinking on these issues. In 1985, I was for a flat tax. I begged Ronald Reagan, Don Regan, and my friend Jimmy Baker to put a flat tax into their proposal. They elected not to do so. But at that time I was focusing, as most all of us were, domestically, inwardly, believing that our market being the biggest in the world was perhaps all that we needed to be concerned about. But ten years later I recognize, and I think a majority of the American people recognize, that we must focus externally. Although we can hope and pray that we will not settle differences on military battlefields in the next century, we cannot fail to win the competitive battle in the international commercial global marketplace.

Because we will see our society either economically decline in its standard of living or continue to move ahead, with American workers being able to believe that their dream of greater real family income and their children having an opportunity to do better than they can be achieved. If we are to be able to continue that dream as a realistic factor in our lives, we must win the battle in the global marketplace or wither economically. So since 1985–1986 I think I have matured and now believe that a flat tax cannot give us that. I have said a number of times that I want to tear the income tax system out by its roots and totally replace it with another form of taxation.

If we can achieve the goals that I have mentioned, I think we will propel America into becoming the economic juggernaut of the world in the next century. Although we don't have accurate estimates yet, we can think roughly in terms of 16 percent of some type of broad-based consumption tax as achieving the goals that I mentioned. When you remove that 16 percent from the price of our products exported and charge that 16 percent to incoming foreign products, you have a differential of 32 percent compared with our current situation, and I submit to you that we will beat our competition all over the world. I had one colleague say several years ago to me, "I'm a very fair individual. All I ever want is a fair advantage." That is all I want for the United States of America—a fair advantage. In achieving these last two items, removal of the tax at the border on our products, charging the tax on foreign products when they come in, they must be legal according to the General Agreement on Tariffs and Trade because if we start a trade war, the world loses.

Going back to the five items, how does the flat tax score versus the consumption tax? In the area of simplicity, certainly the flat tax is a great advantage over the current tax system; I would score it probably somewhere between seven and eight on a scale of one to ten. But it does not get the IRS completely out of our individual lives, which is why I don't give it a ten. We must keep the records that become the basis for the aggregate number that we send in each year to the IRS, and we are still subject individually to audit at any time by the IRS. Other aspects of the flat tax that get away from simplicity include how to treat corporations and business income. What formula will be used to assign the percentage for taxation if it is to apply to businesses as well as individuals (different people have different ideas about that)?

In the area of savings, the flat tax scores much better than the current income tax. Although my good friend Dick Armey, for whom I have great respect, says that his flat tax can bring in equal amounts of revenue to the current system at a rate of 17 percent, others have told me that it falls as much as $140 billion dollars a year short of being revenue neutral. Bob Packwood says it would take a rate of 19 percent or 20 percent on a flat tax to generate income equal to what we are currently accruing under the current system. That is far better than an effective top marginal tax rate of 43 percent or 44 percent under the current income tax code insofar as its impact on savings. But it is still a 19 percent to 20 percent potential negative impact on savings relative to current earnings But I would score it somewhere around six to eight in that category.

In the area of getting at the underground economy, I would score the flat tax a zero, maybe a one. Human nature is one thing that doesn't change. Conditions change, circumstances change, but human nature continues to be with us. I submit to you that if I am in the underground economy and paying a zero tax today and you come to me and tell me you've lowered my top marginal rate from 43 percent to 20 percent and ask, "Don't you want to come in and pay your taxes?" I would say that you have got to be joking! Zero is better than nineteen or twenty; besides, if I am in an illegal activity, I'm surely not going to come up and say, "Well, you've lowered the rates so now I want the IRS to know everything about what I am doing." The flat tax, in my opinion, will not get at the underground economy.

On the issue of whether the tax can be removed from the price of our products at the border, it cannot. Can it be charged to incoming foreign products so that they pay a fair share of the cost of our government? It cannot. It scores a zero on each of the last three categories.

A consumption tax scores between eight and ten in the first category. It certainly can get the IRS out of our individual lives, depending on the design. In the area of savings, I think it scores a ten because it gives everyone the complete earnings that they make and the discretion to do what they want with them. Although it's a bizarre example that is not going to be duplicated in real life, if you wanted to take all your earnings and live in a cave and eat berries and wear a loincloth, you could save 100 percent of what you earned under a consumption tax. You will pay tax only when you purchase something in the marketplace. As for category three, the underground economy, if you're in the illegal drug business and want to buy a Mercedes with your ill-gotten gains, you're going to pay your share of the cost of government. You cannot escape it. So I would score a properly designed consumption tax somewhere between eight and ten in the underground economy. Certainly it scores a ten in being subject to removal from the price of the products at the border, and it scores a ten in being able to be charged to incoming foreign products. So when we begin to start drawing the comparative analyses between what are we going to do if we are going to truly overhaul, I would hope to replace completely the current income tax system, both corporate and individual, with another method of raising money for the federal government.

Finally, when I use the metaphor of pulling the income tax out by its roots, I think there is a dramatic difference between a broad-based consumption tax and the flat tax because the flat tax leaves the roots of the income tax in the ground. Once again, human nature, which doesn't change and which determines history, tells us that, once you have the roots in the ground, the pressure of the roots will most surely push the tree into growth again. We've already seen that happen in this country, initially with a flat income tax at the beginning of our history. And it grew. Then we pruned it dramatically in 1985–1986 and got down to a low rate, which was claimed to be 28 percent (actually 31 percent but nevertheless claimed to be 28 percent by the proponents in 1986), and now what is it again, an effective rate of somewhere between 43 percent and 44 percent. It went up within four years in 1990, under a Republican administration, and then it dramatically went up again in 1993. And I submit to you that it will only be a matter of a few years before the flat tax begins to grow into the type of tree that we have today on the books.

I have not yet settled on a design or vehicle that I am satisfied gives us the greatest degree of advantage and the least degree of disadvantage. This will be exceedingly difficult. The winds of change are blowing, but we must be able to defend the details of whatever proposal we come up with. And there are problems in whatever we do. You can't get from here to where I would like to get without having to climb some pretty big mountains. So it's one thing to talk about goals, and it's another thing to have a product or a design or a vehicle that will get you to those goals.

We're going to begin hearings in the Ways and Means Committee the first week of June [1995] for three consecutive days in the full committee, and we're going to listen to all types of approaches as to what we can do to have a better tax system in this country. I think we can believe that it is realistic, finally, perhaps for the first time in our lives, to abandon the current income tax system and to do something that serves each of us better in the future. I am glad to be a part of it. I think the conference is a healthy beginning to what I believe will develop into a true national debate, the end of which, I hope, will be a consensus to do away with the current income tax system.

Q&A

Q: I was wondering if your vision of a broad-based consumption tax would apply to services?

A: I think it would have to, otherwise it would not comply with the broad-based part of the definition.

Q: So it would apply to legal bills and medical bills as well, or have you made a decision on that yet?

A: That again gets back to the specifics of a design that I'm not yet prepared to put my name on. I've got a lot of people working to advise me as to various approaches. I do think, preliminarily, that the one area that would be exempt would be medical services. I think it would be counterproductive to start increasing the price of medical services in the environment that we have today.

Q: One of the conference papers suggested that you are about to introduce a national sales tax bill with your name on it. I'm wondering if you could talk just for a moment about your comparison of a value-added tax with a national sales tax.

A: I have not yet decided what approach I believe is the best. This is important to each of us, and it should be done very, very thoughtfully. There are certain advantages to a value-added tax, and there are certain advantages to a sales tax. It might also be possible that there is another design, neither of those two, that in the end I will believe will be in the best interest of this country. So right now I have an open mind on it. All I want to do is find something that will comply with the five goals that I mentioned. I think it is exceedingly important to the future of this country. When we have some of the best brains in the United States spending all their time figuring out ways to transfer wealth instead of produce wealth, we should do something about that. When we have the opportunity to improve dramatically the competitive pricing of our products in a world market place, we should do something about that. And I believe it is possible to do it, and I think that perhaps either one of those vehicles would do it. But on a relative basis which would have an advantage over the other? That is what I am looking at right now.

Q: How do you get over the fairness issue that is sanctioned between the wealthy family that has accumulated goods versus the young family that's in the early stages of needing to acquire goods?

A: Well, there are several answers to that. One is that we do have to examine how we are going to take care of low-income people. The price of products, if it is a 16 percent figure, would go up 16 percent immediately in the marketplace, and there would be an immediate spike to the consumer price index of 16 percent. It would be a one-time spike, but it would occur. And so we've got to try to come to grips about how we handle the fairness to people in low-income categories, which means we've got to examine waivers or credits or rebates. One thing that would have to happen is that the cost of food stamps would go up as an item in the federal budget because you would have to accommodate the increase in the price of food for those who are unable to help themselves and on some sort of a food subsidy program. The question is, can you do it strictly through the government help programs on the spending side that are already out there or do you need some additional credit or waiver or rebate? I think we've got to think in those terms.

Beyond that, however, I believe it will score as being more progressive than the flat tax because, as people get into higher incomes, it's going to be more than an arithmetic formula, it's going to be a geometric formula as to the increase of their consumption of more expensive items and paying a bigger part of the cost of government. So you have an automatic progressive escalator that's built in. In addition, the thing that we can't ignore is the overall economic impact that is going to create more jobs and more real earnings for Americans across the board, which ultimately will determine how well we do as a society. If we begin to argue about who is going to get a bigger piece of a pie that is either shrinking or remaining the same size, we certainly end up in a blind alley. But if we're going to be able to increase the pie, then all Americans have a greater opportunity to have a higher standard of living and, in addition, to be able to bear the burden that is going to grow dramatically when the baby boomers retire in the next century. Whatever we are able to produce and create in the way of wealth is going to be essential to be able to accommodate taking care of our elderly senior citizens in the next century.

2

A Framework for the Tax Reform Debate

MICHAEL J. BOSKIN

There is a tremendous opportunity to greatly improve the federal system of corporate and personal income taxation in a manner that will both significantly improve economic performance and substantially reduce the compliance and administrative burden on America's families and firms. Estimates of the annual compliance burden range from more than $100 billion to almost $600 billion, with well over 5 billion hours of human effort devoted to that task. The cost in distortions of economic decisions is also enormous. And the Internal Revenue Service apparently gives correct answers to taxpayer inquiries only about 63 percent of the time. *The tax system is clearly too complex.* Remarkably, the system of voluntary compliance yields a very high percentage of tax liabilities actually due, especially when viewed relative to other countries. That speaks well of Americans' basic values. But there is widespread concern that the system of voluntary compliance will be decreasingly effective over time unless tax rates are reduced and the tax system made far less complex.

Tax Reform and Economic Policy

Tax policy is imbedded in the overall economic system and the overall system of public policy instruments. Taxes—current or future—are how government spending is financed. The tax system affects and is affected by other areas of policy.

The current tax system as well as government spending, deficits, and regulation are the subject of intense legislative political debate currently and are widely viewed, according to all public opinion polls, as out of control. *Taxes are too high and complex; the government spends too much; it is too centralized and too inefficient; the government borrows too much and regulates too much private activity too inflexibly.* Thus an improved tax system has the potential to improve the economy significantly. But it must be accompanied by slower spending growth to balance the budget, devolution of some federal functions to the states and localities, less and more-flexible regulation, and sound money.

The current tax reform debate focuses on personal and corporate federal income taxes. These amount to about 10 percent of gross domestic product (GDP) and about a quarter of all explicit and implicit taxes. Total federal, state, and local government spending is about 40 percent of GDP. Current explicit taxes are somewhat less than that, the difference being budget deficits. The current reform debate generally does not focus on the payroll taxes or excise taxes. Nor is it explicitly directed at state and local taxes, although some proposals would affect them.

Recall also that there are two partially hidden taxes that we generally do not list as taxes in our budgets. One is the hidden tax imposed by our regulatory and legal system. (Some of those regulations and part of our legal system work reasonably well, but some do not, imposing unnecessary additional costs on families and firms.) The costs are very much like a tax. Estimates range all over the place but recently have been in the $400 to $500 billion range per year. That is the yield of the payroll tax and a large fraction of the yield of the income tax.

There are also large future tax liabilities implied (but not terribly well measured) by the budget deficit. America was born in a revolution against taxation without representation; who are less represented than the future generations who will bear this burden?

There is a general feeling that we have increasingly seen the point of tax and the point and purpose of expenditure diverge. That is one of the reasons there is so much discontent with government. In 1958, during the Eisenhower administration, six out of every seven dollars the then much smaller federal government spent was on purchases of goods and services such as national defense and roads. Only one out of every seven dollars was spent on transfer payments. Today, net of interest on the debt, transfer payments are the bulk of the absolutely and relatively much larger federal spending. So one can no longer speak of the tax side of the budget by itself. At the very least, taxes and transfers must be considered simultaneously, better yet, taxes and spending more generally.

Tax policy interacts with trade and trade policy. In an era of large and expanding trade in goods and services and investment, more foreign-source income flows across national borders.

Finally, tax policy interacts with monetary policy. Tax brackets were indexed in the early 1980s but not the definition of income. Nominal capital gains and nominal interest are taxed, nominal interest is deducted, historic cost depreciation is used, and so on. So inflation still affects effective tax rates.

Although all these other areas of policy must also be improved to spur economic growth, the tax reforms currently under discussion would go a long way toward improving the economy. *That is because, although the tax collections themselves are only a modest part of overall GDP, the current tax system systematically affects private sector (household and firm) behavior affecting the bulk of GDP. The result is behavior that is heavily tilted toward the present against the future.* For example, the current corporate and personal income tax system heavily taxes saving, investment, and entrepreneurship. Indeed, some types of saving are doubly or triply taxed. Our tax system is one reason America's net national saving—the amount the nation has available to invest in a more productive future—is very low relative to other advanced economies.

Five Tests for Tax Reform

I have five standards or tests that I apply to tax reform proposals.

- *1. Will tax reform improve the performance of the economy?*

By far the most important aspect of economic performance is the rate of economic growth because that growth determines future living standards. The most important way the tax system affects economic growth is through the rate of saving, investment, entrepreneurship and work effort.

- *2. Will tax reform affect the size of government?*

Tax reforms that more closely tie the payment of taxes to expenditures and get the individual citizen and taxpayer focusing on the fact that their taxes are being used to finance expenditure will ensure a more effective and efficient government. Also, any new tax—a broad-based consumption tax, for example—should completely replace the income tax. Otherwise, there is a risk that the new tax will just be piled on the old and used to raise revenue to grow government—the European disease that has so damaged their economies.

- *3. Will a new tax structure affect federalism?*

Closely tied to item 2, I believe it is important to strengthen the federal system. Tax reforms can affect the federal system in many ways, and we should favor those that strengthen it and devolve authority to state and local government and private institutions to the extent possible.

- *4. Will a new tax structure likely endure?*

We have had major tax reforms or fundamental tax reforms in each of the follow- ing years: 1978, 1981, 1982, 1983, 1985, 1986, 1990, and 1993. We should be concerned that we could move to a better tax system only to undo it shortly thereafter. In 1986, the trade-off was lower rates for a broader base. That was undone in 1990 and dramatically worsened in 1993.

- *5. Over time, will tax reform contribute to a prosperous, stable democracy?*

I have emphasized prosperity above. Now I want to emphasize stable democracy in the following sense: Are we likely to see over time a change relative to what is currently projected in the ratio of taxpayers to people receiving income from government? We now have a much higher ratio of people who are net income recipients to people who are taxpayers than in any previous time in our history. Fortunately, that number is still well under 50 percent. But as we move through time, as the retired population grows, the baby boom generation approaches retirement and then retires, the fraction of the population in any given year who are receiving more than they are paying will grow. We must deal with this both on the tax side (underground economy, perhaps too many off the tax rolls) and, especially, on the transfer payment side (the entitlements programs) and do so soon, or we will get into a spiral of higher benefits, higher tax rates, a weaker economy, and intergenerational conflict.

Before discussing alternative reforms and how they relate to these standards, a simple parable will distill much economic knowledge on the subject of the economic cost of taxation. Suppose the government takes a dollar away from the taxpayer to finance spending. To collect that dollar, the government has to distort the allocation of resources. The tax will affect private decisions: It is well known that an income tax doubly or triply taxes saving and thus distorts the incentive to consume versus save or, alternatively, to consume in the present versus the future. Both income and payroll taxes distort the incentive to work in the market ver- sus the home and/or of employers to hire permanent or temporary workers and so on.

The severity of these distortions depends on two things: first, the size of the tax wedge. How high is the real effective marginal tax rate that drives a wedge between doing one of the activities versus the other, between consuming and saving, between working in the market and working in the home, and so on? Second, how sensitive or elastic is the activity to changes in tax rates? Through numerous studies, some activities are well known to be quite sensitive to tax rates, for example, the realization of capital gains and the labor supply of second earners in families. The combination of the size of the wedge and the sensitivity of the activity to it determines the severity of the tax distortion.

Generally, *the overall total burden that these tax distortions impose on the economy goes up with the square of marginal tax rates. The marginal cost goes up proportionally with tax rates. Thus, high marginal tax rates are bad for the economy.* Thus the income tax distorts many decisions. Workers switch between taxable income and fringe benefits; investors, between low-dividend and high-dividend stocks; and so on. The cost to the economy of each additional tax dollar is about $1.40 to $1.50.

Now the tax dollar (which costs us $1.40 or $1.50) is put into a bucket. Some of it leaks out in overhead, waste, and so on. In a well-managed program, the government may spend $.80 or $.90 of that dollar on achieving its goals. Inefficient programs would be much lower, $.30 or $.40 on the dollar. This immediately tells us that a key to the quality of the tax system—how badly it distorts the economy, hinders growth, misallocates resources—is the level of *effective* marginal tax rates. *The lower the effective marginal tax rates, the smaller the distortion of private decisions.*

Unfortunately, some examine just the statutory rates rather than the effective marginal tax rates. *The effective tax rates on private activity can be quite different from statutory rates because they interact with the tax base and can cascade across several taxes. For example, there are people who, despite a statutory rate of 28 percent, pay tax rates in excess of 100 percent on real capital gains because they have nominal gains but real losses.*

Perhaps nowhere is the current income tax system more harmful than in the taxation of saving, investment, and entrepreneurship. One of the nation's most serious problems is that we have a very low rate of national saving. It is low relative to the nations with which we compete. It is low relative to our own historical average. If it was the result of a tax, budget, regulatory, and legal system that was neutral with respect to whether people and firms consumed or saved and invested, I would not necessarily see much problem with it. *But the overwhelming evidence is that these public policies wind up favoring current consumption and penalizing saving and investment.*

Our net national saving rate in the 1990s has been about 2 percent. That rate has been declining and is low relative to that in other rich industrial countries (see figures 1 and 2). That is the sum of what households, businesses, and governmental units add, net of depreciation, to our nation's ability to grow in the future. Two percent is remarkably low. Fortunately, we have been an attractive enough place to invest that our net investment rate has been higher than that, the difference being financed by importing capital.

There are two reasons the nation's saving rate is so low. Most people focus

Figure 1   Private Saving in the United States (1970–1994)

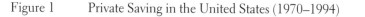

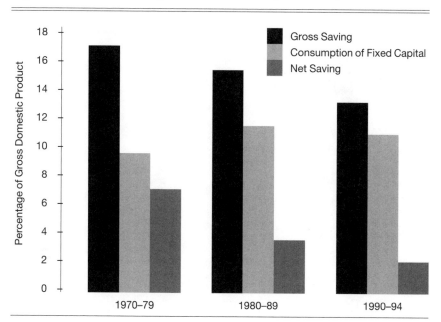

SOURCE: Bureau of Economic Analysis

on the budget deficit (see figure 3), which is clearly one reason. But just as important has been a decline in the private saving rate (see figure 1). *Those who have argued that the best thing we can do to raise the nation's saving rate is to reduce the budget deficit are only correct if they add the following proviso: in a manner that does not reduce private saving.*

The 1993 tax increases, for example, clobbered private saving. In addition to the direct limits on 401(k) plans and so on, the rate increases apply to those groups with the highest propensity to save: well-off households, middle-income two-earner households in their peak earning and saving years, and small businesses. Eighty percent of American businesses are unincorporated; 42 percent of corporations are sub-S corporations. These businesses pay taxes as individuals, and many had large increases in their effective tax rates on profits available for reinvestment. Not surprisingly, personal saving declined at about a $60 billion annual rate. *So even if the tax increases collect the projected revenues—and my guess is they will not—they had little net effect on national saving. The smaller deficit is being matched by less saving. This is at best circular.*

I favor tax policies that reduce or redress the disincentives to save, invest, and innovate in our current tax system, as well as policies to reduce the federal budget

Figure 2   International Comparison of Saving and Investment Rates

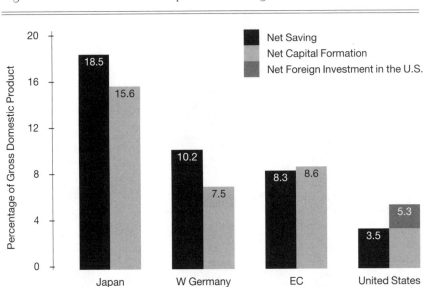

SOURCE: OECD *National Accounts: Main Aggregates*, 1995 Edition

deficit. Indeed, that is how I tie the current debate together on whether it makes sense to have tax cuts as well as spending cuts given the budget deficit. *My answer is yes when those tax reductions will increase private saving to complement the reduction in government borrowing from the spending cuts.*

WHAT DOES ALL THIS IMPLY FOR FUNDAMENTAL TAX REFORM?

As Congress moves forward to debate legislation on various piecemeal tax proposals this year—such as capital gains rate reduction, individual retirement accounts (IRAs), and other tax cuts—a useful way to think about these reforms, as well as the more fundamental reforms, is that they are designed to redress the severe distortion of saving and capital formation caused by the current system of income taxation. Most other countries rely much more heavily on taxes on consumption—so-called indirect consumption taxes such as sales taxes and value-added taxes and income tax systems that exempt large amounts of saving from the tax base—thereby leaving most households' tax base as income minus all saving (i.e., only that part of income that is consumed). Most of their corporate taxes have various features that allow more rapid write-off of investment than does

Figure 3   Effect of Public Deficits on Saving

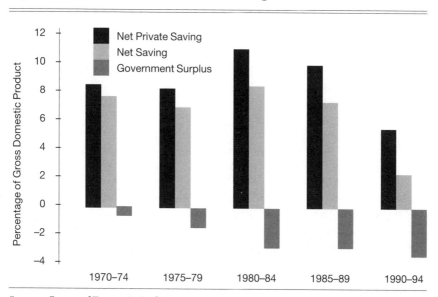

SOURCE: Bureau of Economic Analysis

the U.S. corporate tax; some have features by which they integrate the corporate and personal tax; others, such as Japan, have corporations that have much higher leverage and therefore finance a much larger fraction of investment through tax-advantaged debt.

The U.S. corporate and personal income taxes (and other taxes at both the federal and state level) tax some types of saving once, others twice, some three times, and in some instances even four times. To set concepts, *it is generally understood that a pure income tax would tax saving twice: first when it is earned as part of income and again when it earns a return in the form of interest or dividends.* An alternative way to think about this is that present consumption is taxed once while future consumption is taxed twice because the bulk of saving is done for the purpose of future consumption, for example, during retirement.

Now consider the separate corporate and personal income tax and a family putting their saving in corporate equities. The family first pays taxes on their own income (perhaps their wages). That is tax one. They save some of that after-tax income in the form of corporate equities. But the corporation pays corporate taxes (on behalf of the family as a shareholder). That is a second tax. Then the family pays taxes again when it receives dividends or capital gains (in this case one has to net out inflation, deferral, the possibly slightly lower tax rate, incomplete loss offset, and so on to determine the true effective tax rate). That is a third tax on the saving. If the family is fortunate enough to accumulate, even at a few thousand dollars a year compounded over a lifetime, enough to leave a taxable estate, the saving is taxed a fourth time.

Of course, there are numerous exceptions to this rule. For example, employer-provided pensions, 401(k) plans, IRAs, and so on are forms of tax deferral (not tax forgiveness) that eliminate one layer of the taxation of saving. But going through the entire complexity of the tax code still *produces the overall conclusion that capital formation is taxed especially heavily in the United States, relative to other uses of income and relative to our competitors.*

There are numerous ways to simplify the tax system and remove the distortion between the present and the future, between consumption and saving of households, and among types of investments. That is, there are numerous ways to tax consumption in the economy. We can generally divide these into two approaches—direct and indirect. So-called indirect taxes include a national retail sales tax, various types of value-added taxes, and so on. So-called direct taxes would tax households and firms on the part of income that was consumed. Those taxes are sometimes called consumed income taxes. *It is important to examine the combination of the business-level tax and the personal-level tax to determine what the final tax base will be.*

Economists use a concept called the circular flow of income and product to describe the economy. Business firms use capital and labor, which they pay wages and interest or other forms of capital income, to produce products, which they sell to obtain revenues out of which the payments to labor and capital are made. One can look at the total value of the production of the firms or the total income received by households as two equivalent sides of the nation's accounts. Thus, households can be taxed at the personal level by taxing their total income, or various components of it such as wages, interest, dividends, and so on. Alternatively, households can be taxed by taxing firms on the capital and labor they employ, or on their output. The taxes thus collected would reduce the flow of payments back to households. In this sense, *a tax at the business level should be thought of as a withholding tax on households.* To repeat the old saying, corporations do not pay taxes, people do. Taxes collected at the business level are paid by shareholders, owners of capital in general, workers, or consumers.

Thus, a tax on output sold by firms is equivalent to an equal-rate tax on the wage income and capital income paid by the firm from the sales of the output. Alternatively, households could be taxed when they use the income they receive from the firms to purchase goods and services or to save, the two broad uses that are made of income. Alternatively, because saving equals investment (ignoring complexities of the international economy for the moment), income can also be taxed by taxing consumption plus investment in the economy.

Turning from taxing output or income to taxing consumption, the government can do so in a variety of ways. The most obvious is taxing the purchase of goods as through a retail sales tax. A second option is to tax income of households but allow them to deduct net saving, leaving a tax base of consumed income. An alternative is to tax wage income at the personal level but to tax capital income at the business level (a withholding tax on the capital income of the shareholders); to make the tax a consumption tax, we would allow immediate expensing (i.e., a business tax deduction for investment in the year made).

Tax neutrality, a level playing field, toward investment must be defined in two dimensions: between investment and consumption (intertemporal neutrality) and among types of investment (atemporal neutrality). Think of intertemporal neutrality as a level playing field goalpost to goalpost and atemporal neutrality as level from sideline to sideline. Even a perfect income tax would only achieve atemporal neutrality, not the more important intertemporal neutrality. A pure consumption tax, however levied, would guarantee neutrality both with respect to investment versus consumption *and* among types of investment. The attempt to achieve neutrality among types of investment in an income tax is almost guaranteed to fail as problems such as inflation accounting, measuring true economic depreciation, and so on are insurmountable (e.g., technological obsolescence is increasingly more important than traditional "wear and tear" for economic depreciation).

It is sometimes argued that taxing consumption is unfair; income, the argument goes, is a better measure of ability to pay. Thomas Hobbes first made the case for taxing what is taken out of the economy (roughly measured by consumption) rather than contributed to it (approximated by income). Such philosophical arguments aside, modern economics recognizes that households smooth their consumption when income fluctuates and that most households have a longer time horizon and consume out of permanent or expected average income. Thus, consumption in any year may well be a better proxy for permanent income than is income in that year.

Although these are very different approaches to consumption taxation, with very different attributes, it is important to stress the conceptual equivalence of these approaches to taxing consumption. Consumption equals income minus saving; thus the Nunn-Domenici–type tax with an unlimited net saving deduction is a consumed income tax (in the case of Nunn-Domenici, levied at progressive rates). Consumption taxes can be levied directly as a retail sales tax on the purchases of goods *and* services. But consumption is also equal to income less investment and therefore labor income plus capital income less investment. Hence, a tax such as the so-called flat tax of Majority Leader Armey (which owes much to my Hoover colleagues Bob Hall and Alvin Rabushka), which taxes wages at the personal level and capital income less expensed investment at the business level, also winds up with consumption as the tax base. The main features of the alternative reform proposals, and of current law, are presented in table 1.

I noted above the importance of low tax rates: the broader the base, the lower

Table 1   Comparison of Current Law and Major Reform Proposals

	Present Law	Value-Added Tax (VAT) and/or National Retail Sales Tax (Chairman Archer and Others)	Armey Flat Tax (Hall-Rabushka)	Nunn-Domenici USA Tax
Summary	Theoretically, a progressive tax on corporate and personal income. Numerous special features (e.g., exemptions and deductions). Some income taxed only when consumed (e.g., pensions). Fringes (e.g., health insurance) and owner-occupied housing favored relative to ordinary income. Complex depreciation, inventory accounting. Inflation still a big problem. Progressive rate structure.	Separately, or in combination, replaces corporate and personal income tax with broad-based consumption tax. With a VAT, businesses taxed on difference between gross revenue and input costs including purchases of capital goods. With a retail sales tax, a flat percentage added on retail price of goods *and* services.	Replaces corporate and personal income taxes with two related taxes: a single (flat) rate on personal labor income (including pension income) only. Businesses pay same rate on gross revenue minus costs of inputs, capital goods, wages, and pension contributions. Large personal exemptions in personal tax.	Replaces corporate and personal income tax with a personal progressive-rate consumed income tax applied to income minus (net) saving. Single-rate VAT imposed on business income. Both taxes have a credit for payroll taxes.
Personal Tax	Numerous special provisions make tax a complex hybrid of income and consumption bases. Biggest items not taxed as income accrues are tax-deferred pensions, mortgage interest deductions, employer-paid health care, and property tax deductions.	VAT: No direct tax on individuals, but consumers pay through higher prices. Retail Sales Tax: Consumers pay tax added to price, as is common with state sales taxes.	Individuals are taxed on all compensation and pension distributions but *not* other sources of income (e.g., interest and dividends). Large exemption plus per dependent deduction. Family of four would start paying only on compensation above about $36,000 in current plan. Tax rate is subject of controversy.	Individuals taxed on all income except fringes and tax-exempt interest. Unlimited deductions for net saving, some education costs, mortgage interest, and charitable contributions. Payroll tax credit and exemptions and dependent deduction amounting to about $12,500 for a family of four. Progressive

			Hall-Rabushka estimate 19 percent. Armey starts at 20 percent, declines to 17 percent as assumes spending cut. Others estimate rate would have to be 22 percent to avoid increase in deficit (using static scoring analysis).	rates rise quickly from 8 percent to 40 percent as (consumed) income increases.
Corporate Tax	Thirty-five percent rate on corporate income (special rates apply to small incomes). Business depreciates capital cost over asset life. Debt favored relative to equity.	VAT: tax on value added or cash flow and wages. Retail sales tax, flat rate added to price of *final* goods and services. Special exemptions or lower rates for "necessities" such as food have been proposed by some. Rates not yet specified, likely in 15–16 percent range unless there is extensive erosion of the base.	Business tax on gross income minus cost of inputs, wages, pension contributions, and corporate capital (e.g., expensed immediately). Other fringes not deductible. Rate 20 percent to start decreases to 17 percent as spending is cut. But some question numbers, claiming may have to be 22 percent to avoid deficit increasing (under static scoring).	Tax, like VAT, on gross revenues minus cost of inputs, capital purchases (i.e., capital is immediately consumed). Compensation *not* deductible. Rate = 11 percent.
Most Controversial Points	Complexity; high rates; huge administrative and compliance costs; changed every few years; inflation, depreciation, present immense problems. Considered large drag on economy relative to pure forms of alternatives.	Taxing services; dealing with low-income households; tax on old capital. Worry will be new tax to expand spending rather than replacement for income tax.	Separately taxing labor and capital income may be hard to explain to public used to current system; requires renegotiation of foreign tax treaties; distributional arguments; eliminating charitable deductions and mortgage interest deductions. Some versions abolish withholding.	High tax rates; not simple.

the rate or rates. Thus, a national retail sales tax on all consumption goods, including services, replacing the current corporate and personal income tax, would reduce the drag on saving, investment, entrepreneurship, and economic growth. It could be implemented in a manner that is far less intrusive and burdensome on taxpayers. It would, however, be a proportional tax on consumption. If greater progressivity is desired, a refundable tax credit, or exempting commodities consumed disproportionately by the poor, would be the two approaches. The latter is inefficient in the sense of exempting, for example, food for rich and poor alike. The former would require some cumbersome administrative apparatus and, as we have seen with the earned-income tax credit, open up opportunities for abuse. I believe each of these problems is surmountable. Also, although it would not completely eliminate the underground economy, this approach probably would get at more of the underground economy than any other.

The approach of allowing an unlimited saving deduction (sort of a super net IRA) in a system similar to the current income tax system, offered recently by Senators Nunn and Domenici, is a progressive-rate consumed income tax. Although it has many admirable features (such as offsetting the payroll tax), as currently configured it winds up with marginal tax rates that are quite high (a top rate of 51 percent). A serious complexity issue is the need to track all preexisting assets.

The possibility of taxing capital that was previously accumulated but already taxed a second time when it is used to finance consumption, however, is a particularly important issue, especially for the elderly who, on balance, consume out of their assets. Also, because a huge part of the complexity of the tax system is in the treatment of capital income, I believe the alternative of taxing labor income at the personal level while taxing capital income minus investment (business cash flow) at the business level would be administratively simpler. David Bradford has designed such a tax, with lower progressive rates, which he calls the X tax.

This approach to the tax base, with a flat rate, is the so-called flat tax. Although common usage calls it a flat-rate income tax, as proposed by Majority Leader Armey, the flat tax taxes labor income or wages at the personal level and capital income minus investment at the business level at the same proportional rate. Some of the simplicity is a result of the single rate, as various transactions just net out, such as a business deducting interest paid and a household paying taxes on interest received, because these would be at the same rate. Some progressivity is introduced into the flat tax with high personal exemptions that remove many households from the income tax rolls. Whereas the tax rate is constant, the ratio of taxes to income rises with income until it gradually approaches the flat rate. For example, if the exemption level for a family of four were set at $25,000, a family earning $25,000 would have an average tax rate of zero; one earning $50,000 would have an average tax rate of 10 percent if the flat rate is 20 percent (20 percent on the $50,000 minus the $25,000 exemption); a family earning $100,000 would have an average tax rate of 15 percent (20 percent on $100,000 minus $25,000); at extremely high earnings, the average tax rate gets very close to the marginal rate of 20 percent.

The value-added tax (VAT), which is in widespread use in other countries (although as mentioned above is often viewed as the way to finance the much larger government spending), also taxes income minus investment. It does so for each good and service by taxing income minus investment at each stage of production. Adding up across stages of production and across all goods and services leaves the tax base as aggregate income minus investment, or aggregate consumption in the economy. As a technical matter, among types of VATs, a subtraction method VAT with destination-principle border tax adjustments on balance would be better than the other types of VATs.

Each type of tax will require far greater examination from the polity and the public, as they are not yet well understood. Each of these alternatives has its pluses and minuses. I can only begin to mention a few here, using the criteria above. If it could completely replace the corporate and personal income tax, a national retail sales tax probably in the end would be the simplest to administer and do the best job at getting at the underground economy. It would also tie taxes and spending more closely. Some argue it would encroach on the states' revenue source. With no income tax, there would be no deductibility of state and local taxes and no tax-exempt bonds (the same would be true in a pure flat tax with no deductions), although lower interest rates would partly offset this effect. A broad-based indirect consumption tax would be rebatable at the border under General Agreement on Tariffs and Trade (GATT) rules. To the extent refundable credits and/or exemptions were necessary, tax rates would have to be higher and the advantages of a low-rate broad-based consumption tax would be diminished.

The same is true of a value-added tax, which, although it has a self-policing feature, is somewhat more complex than the retail sales tax but still relatively simple compared with income taxes. A VAT, however, unlike a retail sales tax, *may* loosen the tie between taxes and spending from the standpoint of the tax-payer consciously "feeling the pain" of taxation. *In either case, I personally could support such an approach only if it were used to replace income taxes fully, lest it be used to expand the scope of government.*

The flat-rate tax would be a major improvement over the existing income tax system, but again, to the extent that exemptions, deductions, and so on were left in place or crept back in over time, some of its advantages would be eroded. And, as with a broad-based sales tax or VAT, I would be concerned that small increases in the rate would raise lots of revenue and that, over time, we would evolve back toward a higher-rate system *unless spending was strictly controlled.*

Every deduction in the income tax has its supporters—including the direct beneficiaries—and an apparent rationale. But the general interest in lower rates and a healthier economy overwhelms most, perhaps all, such arguments.

The two I would be most concerned about are the mortgage interest deduction and the charitable deduction. The United States does favor investment in housing relative to corporate plant and equipment compared to most other countries. The equity in their home is the largest asset for a majority of American families, and home values reflect the value of the mortgage interest deduction. Perhaps a gradual transition could mitigate this effect. I believe charities strengthen a pluralistic democracy, and the evidence (including work for the Filer Commission by Martin Feldstein and myself) is that the charitable deduction yields *more* for charities than it "loses the Treasury" (i.e., it is an efficient way to finance charities). I would rather have thousands of charities doing their good deeds than have government bureaucracies try to do them. Note that these deductions also vanish with a retail sales tax or VAT. Some of the same federalism issues arise if there is no deduction for state and local taxes and local government bonds lose their tax-free advantage. Finally, to strengthen or make more obvious the tie between taxation and government spending, withholding could be abolished or amended, as suggested in the Armey plan, but this would add additional administrative and compliance costs.

The progressive consumed income tax, whether of the saving deduction Nunn-Domenici variety or the Bradford X tax (a progressive tax on labor income at the personal level plus taxing capital income minus expensed investment, business cash flow, at the *highest* tax rate at the business level), would be an improvement over the current system but not nearly so much as the other approaches. I do believe there is a stronger case for the Bradford approach than the Nunn-Domenici approach for compliance and administrative reasons, but again, recall the general statement made above that *from the standpoint of economic performance, lower effective marginal tax rates are best.* Although the tax rates on consumed income get quite high under Nunn-Domenici, it is the only approach that attempts to integrate payroll tax credits to reduce the marginal impact of the payroll tax on labor supply and employment.

What is likely to be gained by moving to one of these tax systems? Will it be worth the substantial political capital and transition costs to various families, firms, industries, and economic disruption that accompany any major tax change? The answer, in my opinion, is that the gains are *potentially* quite large. My review of the literature plus my own modeling reveal estimates of long-run GDP up to 10 percent higher per year by replacing the current corporate and personal income taxes with a broad-based, direct, or indirect tax on consumption or consumed income. Perhaps a conservative estimate would be 5 percent per year, which, however, is gained partly by forgoing some consumption. This occurs because the increased saving and capital formation increase wages and future income. *These are large potential gains, large enough, in my opinion, to begin a serious dialogue and discussion, indeed national debate, on the desirability and feasibility of fundamental tax reform, which in turn might develop the support for legislation in the near future.*

PART TWO

ALTERNATIVE
TAX REFORM
PROPOSALS

3

The Flat Tax:
A Simple, Progressive
Consumption Tax

ROBERT E. HALL and
ALVIN RABUSHKA

Tax forms truly can fit on postcards. A cleanly designed tax system takes only a few elementary calculations, in contrast to the hopeless complexity of today's income taxes. We have developed a complete plan for a whole new tax system. Our system puts a low tax rate on a comprehensive definition of income. Because its base is so broad, the tax rate is an astonishingly low 19 percent but raises the same revenue as does the current tax system. The tax on families is fair and progressive — the poor pay no tax at all, and the fraction of income that a family pays rises with income. The system is simple and easy to understand. And the tax operates on the consumption tax principle — families are taxed on what they take out of the economy, not what they put into it.

Our system rests on a basic administrative principle: income should be taxed exactly once, as close as possible to its source. Today's tax system violates this principle in all kinds of ways. Some kinds of income — like fringe benefits — are never taxed at all. Other kinds, like dividends and capital gains, are taxed twice. And interest income, which is supposed to be taxed once, escapes taxation completely in all too many cases where clever taxpayers arrange to receive interest beyond the reach of the IRS.

Under our plan, all income is taxed at the same rate. Equality of tax rates is

Major portions of this paper are drawn from *The Flat Tax*, second edition (Hoover Institution Press, 1995).

a basic concept of the flat tax whose logic is much more profound than just the simplicity of calculation with a single tax rate. Whenever different forms of income are taxed at different rates or different taxpayers face different rates, the public figures out how to take advantage of the differential.

Progressivity, Efficiency, and Simplicity

Limiting the burden of taxes on the poor is a central principle of tax reform. Some ideas for tax simplification and reform flout this principle—neither a federal sales tax nor a value-added tax is progressive. Instead, all citizens, rich and poor alike, pay essentially the same fraction of their spending in taxes. We reject sales and value-added taxes for this reason. The current federal tax system avoids taxing the poor, and we think it should stay that way.

Exempting the poor from taxes does not require graduated tax rates rising to high levels for upper-income taxpayers. A flat rate, applied to all income above a generous personal allowance, provides progressivity without creating important differences in tax rates. Graduated taxes automatically create differences in tax rates among taxpayers, with all the attendant opportunities for leakage. Because it is high-income taxpayers who have the biggest incentive and the best opportunity to use special tricks to exploit tax-rate differentials, applying the same tax rate to these taxpayers for all of their income in all years is the most important goal of flat-rate taxation.

Our proposal is based squarely on the principle of consumption taxation. Saving is untaxed, thus solving the problem that has perplexed the designers of the current tax system, which contains an incredible hodgepodge of saving and investment incentives. As a general matter, the current system puts substantial taxes on the earnings from savings. On that account, the economy is biased toward too little saving and too much consumption. But Congress has inserted a number of special provisions to spur saving. Most important, saving for retirement is excused from current taxation. Workers are not taxed on the amount their employers contribute to pension funds, and the employers can deduct those contributions. The self-employed can take advantage of the same opportunity with Keogh and individual retirement account (IRA) plans. The overall effect of the existing incentives is spotty—there are excessive incentives for some saving-investment channels and inadequate incentives for others. In our system, there is a single, coherent provision for taxing the return to saving. All income is taxed, but the earnings from saved income are not taxed further.

We believe that the simplicity of our system is a central feature. Complex tax forms and tax laws do more harm that just deforesting America. Complicated taxes require expensive advisers for taxpayers and equally expensive reviews and audits by the government. A complex tax invites the taxpayer to search for a special feature to exploit to the disadvantage of the rest of us. And complex taxes diminish confidence in government, inviting a breakdown in cooperation with the tax system and the spread of outright evasion.

An Integrated Flat Tax

Our flat tax applies to both businesses and individuals. Although our system has two separate tax forms—one for business income and the other for wages and salaries—it is an integrated system. When we speak of its virtues, such as its equal taxation of all types of income, we mean the system, not one of its two parts. As we will explain, the business tax is not just a replacement for the existing corporate income tax. It covers all businesses, not just corporations. And it covers interest income, which is currently taxed under the personal income tax.

In our system, all income is classified as either business income or wages (including salaries and retirement benefits). The system is airtight. Taxes on both types of income are equal. The wage tax has features to make the overall system progressive. Both taxes have postcard forms. The low tax rate of 19 percent is enough to match the revenue of the federal tax system as it existed in 1993.

Here is the logic of our system, stripped to basics: We want to tax consumption. Families do one of two things with income—spend it or invest it. We can measure consumption as income minus investment. A truly simple tax would just have each firm pay tax on the total amount of income generated by the firm less that firm's investment in plant and equipment. The value-added tax works just that way. But the value-added tax is unfair because it is not progressive. That's why we break the tax in two. The firm pays tax on all the income generated at the firm except the income paid to its workers. The workers themselves pay tax on what they earn, and the tax they pay is progressive.

To measure the total amount of income generated at a business, the best approach is to take the total receipts of the firm over the year and subtract the payments the firm has made to its workers and suppliers. This approach guarantees a comprehensive tax base. Value-added taxes in Europe work just this way. The base for the business tax is the following:

Total revenue from sales of goods and services
less
purchases of inputs from other firms
less
wages, salaries, and pensions paid to workers

less
purchases of plant and equipment

The other piece is the wage tax. Each family pays 19 percent of its wages, salary, and pension income over a family allowance. The allowance makes the system progressive. The base for the compensation tax is total wages, salaries, and retirement benefits less the total amount of family allowances.

We calculate flat tax revenue from the U.S. National Income and Product Accounts for 1993 (see table 1). The first line shows gross domestic product (GDP), the most comprehensive measure of income throughout the economy. The next two lines are items that are included in GDP but would not be taxed under the flat tax, such as sales and excise taxes. Line three, income included in GDP but not in the tax base, is mostly the value of the services of houses owned and lived in by families; this income does not go through the market. Wages, salaries, and pensions, line four, would be reported by the firm's workers on their wage tax forms and would be deducted by businesses. Investment, line five, is the amount spent by businesses on purchases of new plant and equipment (each business could also deduct its purchases of used plant and equipment, but these would be included in the taxable income of the selling business and would net out in the aggregate). Line six shows the taxable income of all businesses after they have deducted their wages and investment. The revenue from the business tax, line seven, is 19 percent of the tax base on line six. Line eight shows the amount of family allowances that would be deducted. The wage tax base on line nine shows the amount of wages, salaries, and pensions left after deducting all family allowances from the amount on line four. The wage tax revenue on line ten is 19 percent of the base. Total flat tax revenue on line eleven is $627 billion. Lines twelve and thirteen show the actual revenue from the personal and corporate income tax. The total actual revenue on line fourteen is also $627 billion. The flat tax revenue and the actual revenue are the same, by design. Our proposal is to reproduce the revenue of the actual income tax system, not to raise or lower it.

These computations show that in 1993 the revenue from the corporate income tax, with a tax rate of 34 percent, was $118 billion. The revenue from our business tax at a rate of only 19 percent would have been $362 billion, just over three times as much, even though the tax rate is not much more than half the current corporate rate. The flat business tax yields more revenue than does the existing corporate tax for two main reasons: First, slightly more than half of business income is from noncorporate businesses—professional partnerships, proprietorships, and the like. Second, the business tax puts a tax on fringe benefits, which escape taxation in the current system.

The substantial revenue the government would derive from the flat business tax is the key to the fairness of our tax system. Because most business income

Table 1   Flat Tax Revenues Compared with Current Revenues

Line	Income or Revenue	Billions of Dollars
1	Gross domestic product	$6,374
2	Indirect business tax	431
3	Income included in GDP but not in tax base	217
4	Wages, salaries, and pensions	3,100
5	Investment	723
6	Business tax base (line one minus lines two through five)	1,903
7	Business tax revenue (19 percent of line six)	362
8	Family allowances	1,705
9	Wage tax base (line four less line eight)	1,395
10	Wage tax revenue (19 percent of line nine)	265
11	Total flat tax revenue (line seven plus line ten)	627
12	Actual personal income tax	510
13	Actual corporate income tax	118
14	Total actual revenue (line twelve plus line thirteen)	627

goes to the rich, putting an airtight tax of 19 percent on that income permits tax rates on working people to be lowered.

The other side of the coin, of course, is that our wage tax would yield less revenue than does the current personal income tax—$265 billion in 1993 as against $510 billion. We are not proposing a massive shift in taxes from wages to capital income. Our wage tax applies just to wages, salaries, and private pensions, whereas today's personal income tax includes unincorporated business income, dividends, interest, rent, and many other kinds of income that we tax as part of business income. The switch to the more reliable principle of taxing business income at the source, rather than hoping to catch the income at the destination, is the main reason that the business tax yields so much more revenue than does the corporate tax.

THE INDIVIDUAL WAGE TAX

The individual wage tax has a single purpose—to tax the large fraction of total income that employers pay as cash to their workers. It is not a tax system by itself but one of two major parts of the complete system. The base of the tax is defined narrowly and precisely as actual payments of wages, salaries, and pensions. Pension contributions (as opposed to benefits) and other fringe benefits paid by employers are not counted as part of wages. In other words, the tax on pension income is paid when the retired worker actually receives the pension, not when the employer sets aside the money to pay the future pension. This

Form 1	**Individual Wage Tax**	**1995**

Your first name and initial (if joint return, also give spouse's name and inital)   Last name | Your social security number

Present home address (number and street including apartment number or rural route) | Spouse's social security no.

City, town, or post office, state, and ZIP code | Your occupation➤

Spouse's occupation➤

1	Wages and salary	1	
2	Pension and retirement benefits	2	
3	Total compensation (line 1 plus line 2)	3	
4	Personal allowance		
	(a) ❑ $16,500 for married filing jointly	4(a)	
	(b) ❑ $9,500 for single	4(b)	
	(c) ❑ $14,000 for single head of household	4(c)	
5	Number of dependents, not including spouse	5	
6	Personal allowances for dependents (line 5 multiplied by $4,500)	6	
7	Total personal allowances (line 4 plus line 6)	7	
8	Taxable compensation (line 3 less line 7, if positive; otherwise zero)	8	
9	Tax (19% of line 8)	9	
10	Tax withheld by employer	10	
11	Tax due (line 9 less line 10, if positive)	11	
12	Refund due (line 10 less line 9, if positive)	12	

principle applies even if the employer pays into a completely separate pension fund, if the worker makes a voluntary contribution to a 401(k) program, or if the worker contributes to a Keogh, IRA, or SEP fund.

The tax form for our wage tax is self-explanatory. To make the tax system progressive, only earnings over a personal or family allowance are taxed. The allowance is $25,500 for a family of four in 1995 but would rise along with the cost of living in later years. All the taxpayer has to do is report total wages, salaries, and pensions at the top, compute the family allowance based on marital status and number of dependents, subtract the allowance, multiply by 19 percent to compute the tax, take account of withholding, and pay the difference or apply for a refund (see form 1). For about 80 percent of the population, filling out this postcard once a year would be the only effort needed to satisfy the Internal Revenue Service. What a change from the many pages of schedules the typical frustrated taxpayer fills out today!

For the 80 percent of taxpayers who don't run businesses, the individual wage tax would be the only tax to worry about. Many features of current taxes would disappear, including charitable deductions, mortgage interest deductions, capital gains taxes, dividend taxes, and interest taxes.

Anyone who is self-employed or pays expenses directly in connection with making a living will need to file the business tax in order to get the proper deduction for expenses. Fortunately, the business tax form is even simpler than the wage tax form.

THE BUSINESS TAX

It's not the purpose of the business tax to tax businesses. Fundamentally, people pay taxes, not businesses. The idea of the business tax is to collect the tax that the owners of a business owe on the income produced by the business. Collecting business income tax at the source of the income avoids one of the biggest causes of leakage in the tax system today: Interest can pass through many layers, where it is invariably deducted when it is paid out but not so frequently reported as income.

Airtight taxation of individual business income at the source is possible because we already know the tax rate of all of the owners of the business—it is the common flat rate paid by all taxpayers. If the tax system has graduated rates, taxation at the source becomes a problem. If each owner is to be taxed at that owner's rate, the business would have to find out the tax rate applicable to each owner and apply that rate to the income produced in the business for that owner. But this is only the beginning of the problem. The IRS would have to audit a business and its owners together in order to see that the owners were reporting the correct tax rates to the business. Further, suppose one of the owners made a mistake and was later discovered to be in a higher tax bracket. Then the business would have to refile its tax form to collect the right tax. Obviously this wouldn't work. Business taxes have to be collected at the destination, from the owners, if graduated rates are to be applied. Source taxation is only practical when a single rate is applied to all owners. Because source taxation is so much more reliable and inexpensive, there is a powerful practical argument for using a single flat rate for all business income.

The business tax is a giant, comprehensive withholding tax on all types of income other than wages, salaries, and pensions. It is carefully designed to tax every bit of income outside of wages but to tax it only once. The business tax does not have deductions for interest payments, dividends, or any other type of payment to the owners of the business. As a result, all income that people receive from business activity has already been taxed. Because the tax has already been paid, the tax system does not need to worry about what happens to interest, dividends, or capital gains after these types of income leave the firm. The resulting simplification and improvement in the tax system are enormous. Today the IRS receives more than a billion Form 1099s, which keep track of interest and dividends, and must make an overwhelming effort to match these forms to the 1040s filed by the recipients. The only reason for a Form 1099 is to track income as it makes its way from the business where it originated to the ultimate recipient. Not a single Form 1099 would be needed under a flat tax with business income taxed at the source.

The way that we have chosen to set up the business tax is not arbitrary—on

Form 2	Business Tax	1995
Business Name		Employer identification Number
Street Address		County
City, State, and ZIP Code		Principal Product

1	Gross revenue from sales	**1**	
2	Allowable costs		
	(a) Purchases of goods, services, and materials	**2(a)**	
	(b) Wages, salaries, and pensions	**2(b)**	
	(c) Purchases of capital equipment, structures, and land	**2(c)**	
3	Total allowable costs (sum of lines 2(a), 2(b), 2(c)	**3**	
4	Taxable income (line 1 less line 3)...	**4**	
5	Tax (19% of line 4)	**5**	
6	Carry-forward from 1994	**6**	
7	Interest on carry-forward (6% of line 6)	**7**	
8	Carry-forward into 1995 (line 6 plus line 7)	**8**	
9	Tax due (line 5 less line 8, if positive)	**9**	
10	Carry-forward to 1996 (line 8 less line 5, if positive)	**10**	

the contrary, it is dictated by the principles we set forth at the beginning of this chapter. The tax would be assessed on all the income originating in a business but not on any income that originates in other businesses, nor would it tax the wages, salaries, and pensions paid to employees. The types of income taxed by the business tax would include

- Profits from the use of plant and equipment
- Profits from ideas embodied in copyrights, patents, trade secrets, and the like
- Profits from past organization-building, marketing, and advertising efforts
- Earnings of key executives and others who are owners as well as employees and who are paid less than they contribute to the business
- Earnings of doctors, lawyers, and other professionals who have businesses organized as proprietorships or partnerships
- Rent earned from apartments and other real estate
- Fringe benefits provided to workers

All a business's income derives from the sale of its products and services. On the top line of the business tax form (see our form 2) goes the gross sales of the business—its proceeds from the sale of all of its products. But some of the proceeds come from the resale of inputs and parts the firm purchased; the tax has already been paid on these items because the seller also has to pay the business tax. Thus, the firm can deduct the cost of all the goods, materials, and services it purchases for the purpose of making the product it sells. In addition, it can deduct its wages, salaries, and pensions, for, under our wage tax, the taxes on these will be paid by the workers receiving them. Finally, the business can deduct all its outlays for plant, equipment, and land. Later we will explain why this investment incentive is just the right one.

Everything left from this calculation is the income originating in the firm and is taxed at the flat rate of 19 percent. In most businesses, a lot is left, so the prospective revenue from the business tax is the $362 billion we computed earlier. Many deductions allowed to businesses under current laws are eliminated in our plan, including interest payments and fringe benefits. But our exclusion of these deductions is not an arbitrary move to increase the tax base. In all cases, the elimination of deductions, when combined with the other features of our system, moves toward the goal of taxing all income once at a common, low rate and to achieve a broad consumption tax.

Eliminating the deduction for interest paid by businesses is a central part of our general plan to tax business income at the source. It makes sense because we propose not to tax interest received by individuals. The tax that the government now hopes (sometimes in vain) that individuals will pay will assuredly be paid by the business itself.

We sweep away the whole complicated apparatus of depreciation deductions, but we replace it with something more favorable for capital formation, an immediate 100 percent first-year tax write-off of all investment spending. Sometimes this approach is called *expensing* of investment; it is standard in the value-added approach to consumption taxation. In other words, we don't deny depreciation deductions, we enhance them. More on this shortly.

Fringe benefits are outside the current tax system entirely, which makes no sense. The cost of fringes is deductible by businesses, but workers are not taxed on the value of the fringes. Consequently, fringes have a big advantage over cash wages. As taxation has become heavier and heavier, fringes have become more and more important in the total package offered by employers to workers—fringes were only 1.2 percent of total compensation in 1929, when income taxes were unimportant, but reached almost 18 percent in 1993. The explosion of fringes is strictly an artifact of taxation, and fringes are an economically inefficient way to pay workers. Were the tax system neutral, with equal taxes on fringes and cash, workers would rather take their income in cash and make their own decisions about health and life insurance, parking, exercise facilities, and all the other things they now get from their employers without much choice. Further, failing to tax fringes means taxes on other types of income are all the higher. Bringing all types of income under the tax system is essential for low rates.

Under our system, each business would file a simple form. Even the largest business—the General Motors Corporation in 1993, with $138 billion in sales— would fill out our simple postcard form. Every line on the form is a well-defined number obtained directly from the business's accounting records. Line one, gross revenue from sales, is the actual number of dollars received from the sales of all the products and services sold by the business, plus the proceeds from the sale of plant, equipment, and land. Line two(a) is the actual amount paid for all the inputs bought from other businesses necessary for the operation of the business (that is, not passed on to its workers or owners). The firm could report any purchase actually needed for the business's operations and not part of the compensation of workers or owners. Line two(b) is the actual cash put in the hands of workers and former workers. All the dollars deducted on this line will have to be reported by the workers on their form 1 wage tax returns. Line two(c) reports purchases of new and used capital equipment, buildings, and land. Note that the firm won't have to agonize over whether a screwdriver is a capital investment or a current input—both are deductible, and the IRS won't care which line it appears on.

The taxable income computed on line four bears little resemblance to anyone's notion of profit. The business tax is not a profit tax. When a firm is having an outstanding year in sales and profits but is building new factories to handle rapid growth, it may well have a low or even negative taxable income. That's fine—later, when expansion slows but sales are at a high level, the income generated at the firm will be taxed at 19 percent.

Because the business tax treats investment in plant, equipment, and land as an expense, companies in the start-up period will have negative taxable income. But the government will not write a check for the negative tax on the negative income. Whenever the government has a policy of writing checks, clever people abuse the opportunity. Instead, the negative tax would be carried forward to future years, when the business should have positive taxable income. There is no limit to the number of years of carry-forward. Moreover, balances carried forward will earn the market rate of interest (6 percent in 1995). Lines six through ten show the mechanics of the carry-forward process.

Investment Incentives

The high rates of the current tax system significantly impede capital formation. On this point almost all experts agree. The government's solution to the problem has been to pile one special investment or saving incentive on top of another, creating a complex and unworkable maze of regulations and tax forms. Existing incentives are appallingly uneven. Capital projects taking full advantage of depreciation deductions and the deductibility of interest paid to organizations exempt from income tax may actually receive subsidies from the government, rather than being taxed. But equity-financed projects are taxed heavily. Investment incentives severely distort the flow of capital into projects eligible for debt finance.

Our idea is to start over—throwing away all the present incentives and replacing them with a simple, uniform principle—treating the total amount of investment as an expense in the year it was made. The entire incentive for capital formation is on the investment side, instead of the badly fitting split in the current tax system between investment incentives and saving incentives. The first virtue of this reform is simplicity. Businesses and government need not quarrel, as they do now, over what is an investment and what is a current expense. The distinction doesn't matter for the tax. Complicated depreciation calculations carrying over from one year to the next, driving the small business owner to distraction, will vanish from the tax form. The even more complicated provisions for recapturing depreciation when a piece of equipment or a building is sold will vanish as well, to everyone's relief.

Expensing of investment has a much deeper rationale than simplicity. Every act of investment in the economy ultimately traces back to an act of saving. A tax on income with an exemption for saving is in effect a tax on consumption, for consumption is the difference between income and saving. Consumption is what people take out of the economy; income is what people contribute. A consumption tax is the exact embodiment of the principle that people should be taxed on what they take out, not what they put in. The flat tax, with expensing of investment, is precisely a consumption tax.

Expensing investment eliminates the double taxation of saving; this is another way to express the most economically significant feature of expensing. Under an income tax, people pay tax once when they earn and save and again when the savings earn a return. With expensing, the first tax is abolished. Saving is, in effect, deducted in computing the tax. Later, the return to savings is taxed through the business tax. Although economists have dreamt up a number of other ways to eliminate double taxation of saving (involving complicated record keeping and reporting by individuals), the technique exploited in our flat tax is by far the most straightforward.

The easiest case for showing that expensing of investment is a consumption tax arises when someone invests directly in a personally owned business. Suppose a taxpayer receives $1,000 in earnings and turns around and buys a piece of business equipment for $1,000. There is a tax of $190 on the earnings but also a deduction worth $190 in reduced taxes for the equipment purchase. On net, there is no tax. The taxpayer has not consumed any of the original $1,000 either. Later, the taxpayer will receive business income representing the earnings of the machine. This income will be taxed at 19 percent. If the taxpayer chooses to consume rather than invest again, there will be a 19 percent tax on the consumption. So the overall effect is a 19 percent consumption tax.

Most people don't invest directly by purchasing machines themselves. The

U.S. economy has wonderfully developed financial markets for channeling savings from individual savers, on the one hand, and businesses who have good investment opportunities, on the other hand. Individuals invest in firms by purchasing shares or bonds, and then the firms purchase plant and equipment. The tax system we propose taxes the consumption of individuals in this environment as well. Suppose the same taxpayer pays the $190 tax on the same $1,000 and puts the remaining $810 into the stock market. For simplicity, suppose that the share pays out to its owner all of the after-tax earnings on equipment costing $1,000. That assumption makes sense because the firm could buy $1,000 worth of equipment with the $810 from our taxpayer plus the tax write-off worth $190 that would come with the equipment purchase. Our taxpayer gets the advantage of the investment write-off even though there is no deduction for the purchase of the share. The market passes through the incentive from the firm to the individual investor.

Another possibility for the taxpayer is to buy a bond for $810. Again, the firm issuing the bond can buy a $1,000 machine with the $810, after taking advantage of the tax deduction. To compete with the returns available in the stock market, however, the bond must pay the same returns as does a stock selling for the same price, which in turn is equal to the after-tax earnings of the machine, so it won't matter how the taxpayer invests the $810. In all cases, there is effectively no tax for saved income; the tax is only payable when the income is consumed.

In our system, any investment, in effect, would have the same economic advantage that a 401(k), IRA, or Keogh account has in the current tax system. And we achieve this desirable goal by *reducing* the amount of record keeping and reporting. Today, taxpayers have to deduct their Keogh-IRA contributions on their Form 1040s, and then they have to report the distributions from the funds as income when they retire. Moreover, proponents of the "cash-flow" consumption tax would extend these requirements to all forms of saving. Our system would accomplish the same goal without any forms or record keeping.

Capital Gains

Capital gains on rental property, plant, and equipment would be taxed under the business tax. The purchase price would be deducted at the time of purchase, and the sale price would be taxed at the time of the sale. Every owner of rental real estate would be required to fill out the simple business tax return, form 2.

Capital gains would be taxed exclusively at the business level, not at the personal level. Thus, our system would eliminate the double taxation of capital gains inherent in the current tax system. To see how this works, consider the case of the common stock of a corporation. The market value of the stock is the capitalization of its future earnings. Because the owners of the stock will receive their earnings after the corporation has paid the business tax, the market capitalizes after-tax earnings. A capital gain occurs when the market perceives that prospective after-tax earnings have risen. When the higher earnings materialize in the future, they will be correspondingly taxed. In a tax system like the current one, with both an income tax and a capital gains tax, there is double taxation. To achieve the goal of taxing all income exactly once, the best answer is to place an airtight tax on the income at the source. With taxation at the source, it is inappropriate and inefficient to tax capital gains as they occur at the destination.

Another way to see that capital gains should not be taxed separately under the flat tax is to look at the national income accounts. Gross domestic product, the most comprehensive measure of the nation's command over resources, does not include capital gains. The base of the flat tax is GDP minus investment, that is, consumption. To include capital gains in the flat tax base would depart from the principle that it is a tax on consumption.

Capital gains on owner-occupied houses are not taxed under our proposal. Very few capital gains on houses are actually taxed under the current system— gains can be rolled over, there is an exclusion for older home sellers, and gains are never taxed at death. Exclusion of capital gains on houses makes sense because state and local governments put substantial property taxes on houses in relation to their values. Adding a capital gains tax on top of property taxes is double taxation in the same way that adding a capital gains tax on top of an income tax is double taxation of business income.

Imports, Exports, and Multinational Business

With the North American Free Trade Agreement and the growth of trade throughout the world, U.S. companies are doing more and more business in other countries, and foreign companies are increasingly active here. Should the U.S. government try to tax American business operations in other countries? And should it tax foreign operations in the United States? These are increasingly controversial questions. Under the current tax system, foreign operations of U.S. companies are taxed in principle, but the taxpayer receives a credit against U.S. taxes for taxes paid to the country where the business operates. Because the current tax system is based on a confused combination of taxing some income at the origin and some at the destination, taxation of foreign operations is messy.

Under the consistent application of taxing all business income at the source, the flat tax embodies a clean solution to the problems of multinational operations. The flat tax applies only to the domestic operations of all businesses, whether of domestic, foreign, or mixed ownership. Only the revenue from the sales of products within the United States plus the value of products as they are exported would be reported on line one of the business tax form 2. Only the costs of labor, materials, and other inputs purchased in the United States or imported to the United States would be allowable on line two as deductions for the business tax. Physical presence in the United States is the simple rule that determines whether a purchase or sale is included in taxable revenue or allowable cost.

To see how the business tax would apply to foreign trade, consider first an importer selling its wares within the United States. Its costs would include the actual amount it paid for its imports, valued as they entered the country—this would generally be the actual amount paid for them in the country of their origin. Its revenue would be the actual receipts from sales in the United States. Second, consider an exporter selling goods produced here to foreigners. Its costs would be all the inputs and compensation paid in the United States, and its revenue would be the amount received from sales to foreigners, provided that the firm did not add to the product after it departed the country. Third, consider a firm that sends parts to Mexico for assembly and brings back the final product for sale in the United States. The value of the parts as they leave here would count as part of the revenue of the firm, and the value of the assembled product as it was returned would be an expense. The firm would not deduct the actual costs of its Mexican assembly plant.

Under the principle of taxing only domestic activities, the U.S. tax system would mesh neatly with the tax systems of our major trading partners. If every nation used the flat tax, all income throughout the world would be taxed once and only once. Because the basic principle of the flat tax is already in use in the many nations with value-added taxes, a U.S. flat tax would harmonize nicely with those foreign tax systems.

Application of the wage tax, form 1, in the world economy would follow the same principle. All earnings from work in the United States would be taxed, irrespective of the worker's citizenship, but the tax would not apply to the foreign earnings of Americans.

Choices about the international location of businesses and employment are influenced by differences in tax rates. The United States, with a low tax rate of 19 percent, would be much the most attractive location among major industrial nations from the point of view of taxation. Although the flat tax would not tax the overseas earnings of American workers and businesses, there is no reason to fear an exodus of economic activity. On the contrary, the favorable tax climate in the United States would draw in new business from everywhere in the world.

The Transition

In our advocacy of the flat tax, we are spending the bulk of our effort in laying out a good, practical tax system. We have not made concessions to the political pressures that may well force the nation to accept an improved tax system that falls short of the ideal we have in mind. One area where the political process is likely to complicate our simple proposal is the transition from the current tax to the flat tax. The transition issues that are likely to draw the most attention are depreciation and interest deductions. In both cases, taxpayers who made plans and commitments before the tax reform will cry loudly for special provisions to continue the deductions.

Congress will face a choice between denying taxpayers the deductions they expected before tax reform or granting the deductions and raising the tax rate to make up for the lost revenue. Fortunately, this is a temporary problem. Once existing capital is fully depreciated and existing borrowing paid off, any special transitions provisions can be taken off the books.

DEPRECIATION DEDUCTIONS

Existing law lets businesses deduct the cost of an investment on a declining schedule over many years. From the point of view of the business, multiyear depreciation deductions are not as attractive as the first-year write-off prescribed in the flat tax. No business will complain about the flat tax as far as future investment is concerned. But businesses may well protest the unexpected elimination of the unused depreciation they thought they would be able to take on the plant and equipment they installed before the tax reform. Without special transition provisions, these deductions would simply be lost.

How much is at stake? In 1992, total depreciation deductions under the personal and corporate income taxes came to $597 billion. At the 34 percent rate for most corporations (which is close to the rate paid by the individuals who are likely to take deductions as proprietors or partners), those deductions were worth $192 billion. At the 19 percent flat rate, the deductions would be worth only $108 billion.

If Congress chose to honor all unused depreciation from investment predating tax reform, it would take about $597 billion out of the tax base for 1995. In order to raise the same amount of revenue as our original 19 percent rate, the tax rate would have to rise to about 20.1 percent.

Honoring past depreciation would mollify business interests, especially in industries with large amounts of unused depreciation for past investment but little prospect of large first-year write-offs for future investment. In addition, it would buttress the government's credibility in tax matters by carrying through on a past promise to give a tax incentive for investment. By contrast, the move would require a higher tax rate and a less efficient economy in the future.

If Congress did opt to honor past depreciation, it should recognize that the higher tax rate needed to make up for the lost revenue would be temporary. Within five years, the bulk of the existing capital would be depreciated and the tax rate brought back to 19 percent. From the outset, the tax rate should be committed to drop to 19 percent as soon as the transition depreciation is paid off.

INTEREST DEDUCTIONS

Loss of interest deductions and elimination of interest taxation are two of the most conspicuous features of our tax reform plan. Important economic changes would take place once interest is put on an after-tax basis. During the transition, there will be winners and losers from the change, and Congress is sure to hear from the losers. Congress may well decide to adopt a temporary transitional measure to help them. Such a measure need not compromise the principles of the flat tax or lessen its contribution to improved efficiency.

Our tax reform calls for the parallel removal of interest deduction and interest taxation. If a transitional measure allows the continuation of deductions for interest on outstanding debt, it should also require the continuation of taxation of that interest as income of the lender. If all deductions are completely matched with taxation on the other side, then a transition provision to protect existing interest deductions would have *no* effect on revenue. In that respect, interest deductions are easier to handle in the transition than are depreciation deductions.

If Congress decides that a transitional measure to protect interest deductions is needed, we suggest the following. Any borrower may choose to treat interest payments as a tax deduction. If the borrower so chooses, the lender *must* treat the interest as taxable income. But the borrower's deduction should be only 90 percent of the actual interest payment, while the lender's taxable income should include 100 percent of the interest receipts.

Under this transitional plan, borrowers would be protected for almost all of their existing deductions. Someone whose personal finances would become untenable if the mortgage-interest deduction were suddenly eliminated can surely get through with 90 percent of the earlier deduction. But the plan builds in an incentive for renegotiating the interest payments. Suppose a family is paying $10,000 in annual mortgage interest. It could stick with this payment and deduct $9,000 of it per year. Its net cost, after subtracting the value of its deduction with the 19 percent tax rate, would be $8,290. The net income to the bank, after subtracting the 19 percent tax it pays on the whole $10,000, would be $8,100. Alternatively, the family could accept a deal proposed by the bank: The interest payment would be lowered to $8,200 by rewriting the mortgage. The family would agree to forgo its right to deduct the interest, and the bank would no longer have to pay tax on the interest. Now the couple's cost will be $8,200 (instead of $8,290 without the deal), and the bank's income will be $8,200 (instead of $8,100 without the deal). The family will come out $90 ahead, and the bank will come out $100 ahead. The deal will be beneficial to both.

One of the nice features of this plan is that it does not have to make any distinctions between old borrowing, existing at the time of the tax reform, and new borrowing, arranged after the reform. Lenders would always require that new borrowers opt out of their deductions and thus offer a correspondingly lower interest rate. Otherwise, the lender would be saddled with a tax bill larger than the tax deduction received by the borrower.

As far as revenue is concerned, this plan would actually add a bit to federal revenue in comparison to the pure flat tax. Whenever a borrower exercised the right to deduct interest, the government would collect more revenue from the lender than it would lose from the borrower. As more and more deals were rewritten to eliminate deductions and lower interest, the excess revenue would disappear and we would be left with the pure flat tax.

Variants of the Flat Tax

In this chapter, we have set forth what we think is the best flat tax. But our ideas are more general than this specific proposal. The same principles could be applied with different choices about the key trade-offs. The two most important trade-offs are

- *Progressivity versus tax rate.* A higher personal allowance would put an even lower burden on low- and middle-income families. But it would require a higher tax rate.

- *Investment incentives versus tax rate.* If the business tax had less than full write-off for purchases of capital goods, the tax rate could be lower.

Here are some alternative combinations of allowances and tax rates that would all raise the same amount of revenue:

Allowance for family of four	Tax rate
$12,500	15%
22,500	19%
34,500	23%

The choice among these alternatives depends on beliefs about how the burden of taxes should be distributed and on the degree of inefficiency that will be brought into the economy by the corresponding tax rates.

Here are some alternative combinations of investment write-offs and tax rates that would all raise the same amount of revenue:

Equipment write-off	Structures write-off	Tax rate
100%	100%	19%
75	50	18
50	25	17

The choice among these alternatives depends on the sensitivity of investment-saving to incentives and on the degree of inefficiency brought by the tax rate.

Stimulus to Growth

The flat tax at a low, uniform rate of 19 percent will improve the performance of the U.S. economy. Improved incentives to work through increased take-home wages will stimulate work effort and raise total output. Rational investment incentives will raise the overall level of investment and channel it into the most productive areas. And sharply lower taxation of entrepreneurial effort will enhance this critical input to the economy.

WORK EFFORT

About two-thirds of today's taxpayers enjoy the low income tax rate of 15 percent enacted in 1986. Under the flat tax, more than half of these taxpayers would face zero tax rates because their total family earnings would fall short of the exemption amount ($22,500 for a family of four). The other half would face a slight increase in their tax rates on the margin, from 15 percent to 19 percent. In 1991, the remaining third of taxpayers were taxed at rates of 28 and 31 percent, and the addition of the 39.6 percent bracket in 1992 worsened incentives further. Heavily taxed people earn a disproportionate share of income: In 1991, 58 percent of all earnings were taxed at rates of 28 percent or higher. The net effect of the flat tax, with marginal rates of 0 and 19 percent, would be to improve incentives dramatically for almost everyone who is economically active.

One point we need to emphasize is that a family's marginal tax rate determines its incentives for all types of economic activity. There is much confusion on this point. For example, some authors have written that married women face a special disincentive because the marginal tax on the first dollar of her earnings is the same as the marginal tax on the last dollar of her husband's earnings. It is true that incentives to work for a woman with a well-paid husband are seriously eroded by high tax rates. But so are her husband's incentives. What matters for both of their decisions is how much of any extra dollar of earnings they will keep after taxes. Under the U.S. income tax, with joint filing, the fraction either of them takes home after taxes is always the same, no matter how their earnings are split between them.

Sheer hours of work make up one of the most important dimensions of productive effort and one that is known to be sensitive to incentives. At first, it may seem difficult for people to alter the amount of work they supply to the economy. Aren't most jobs forty hours a week, fifty-two weeks a year? It turns out that only a fraction of the workforce is restricted in that way. Most of us face genuine decisions about how much to work. Teenagers and young adults—in effect anyone before the responsibilities of parenthood—typically work much less than full time for the full year. Improving their incentives could easily make them switch from part-time to full-time work or cause them to spend less time taking it easy between jobs.

Married women remain one of the largest underutilized resources in the U.S. economy, although a growing fraction enters the labor market each year. In 1993, only 58 percent of all women over fifteen were at work or looking for work; the remaining 42 percent were spending their time at home or in school but could be drawn into the market if the incentives were right. There is no doubt about the sensitivity of married women to economic incentives. Studies show a systematic tendency for women with low after-tax wages and high-income husbands to work little. Those with high after-tax wages and lower incomes work a lot. It is thus reasonable to infer that sharply reduced marginal tax rates on married women's earnings will further stimulate their interest in the market.

Another remarkable source of unused labor power in the United States is men who have taken early retirement. Although 92 percent of men aged twenty-five to fifty-four are in the labor force, only 65 percent of those from fifty-five to sixty-four are at work or looking for work—just 17 percent of those over sixty-five. Again, retirement is very much a matter of incentives. High marginal taxation of earnings discourages many perfectly fit men from continuing to work. Because mature men are among the best paid in the economy, a great many of them face marginal tax rates of 28, 36, or even 40 percent. Reduction to a uniform 19 percent could significantly reduce early retirement and make better use of the skills of older men.

Economists have devoted a great deal of effort to measuring the potential stimulus to work from tax reform. The consensus is that all groups of workers would respond to the flat tax by raising their work effort. A few workers would reduce their hours either because the flat rate would exceed their current marginal rate or because reform would add so much to their incomes that they would feel that earning was less urgent. But the great majority would face much improved incentives. The smallest responses are from adult men and the largest from married women.

In the light of the research on labor supply, were we to switch from the current tax law to our proposed flat tax, a reasonable projection is an increase of about 4 percent in total hours of work in the U.S. economy. That increase would mean about 1.5 hours per week on the average but would take the form of second jobs for some workers, more weeks of work per year for others, as well as more hours per week for those working part time. The total annual output of goods and services in the U.S. economy would rise by about 3 percent, or almost $200 billion. That is nearly $750 per person, an astonishing sum. Of course, it might take some time for the full influence of improved incentives to have its effect. But the bottom line is unambiguous: Tax reform would have an important favorable effect on total work effort.

CAPITAL FORMATION

Economists are far from agreement on the impact of tax reform on investment. As we have stressed earlier, the existing system puts heavy tax rates on business income, even though the net revenue from the system is small. These rates seriously erode investment incentives. Generous but erratic investment provisions in the current law and lax enforcement of taxes on business income at the personal level, however, combine to limit the adverse impact. The current tax system subsidizes investment through tax-favored entities such as pension funds, while it taxes capital formation heavily if it takes the form of new business. The result has been to sustain capital formation at reasonably high levels but to channel the investment into inefficient uses.

The most important structural bias of the existing system is the double taxation of business income earned in corporations and paid out to shareholders. Double taxation dramatically reduces the incentive to create new businesses in risky lines where debt financing is not available. On the other side, the existing system places no current tax on investments that can be financed by debt and where the debt is held by pension funds or other nontaxed entities. The result is a huge twist in incentives, away from entrepreneurial activities and toward safe, debt-financed activities.

The flat tax would eliminate the harmful twist in the current tax system. The flat tax has a single, uniform incentive for investment of all types—businesses would treat all purchases of capital equipment and buildings as expenses. As we noted earlier, allowing immediate write-off of investment is the ideal investment incentive. A tax system that taxes all income evenly and allows expensing of investment is a tax on consumption. Public finance economists Alan Auerbach and Laurence Kotlikoff estimate that the use of a flat-rate consumption tax in place of an income tax would raise the ratio of capital stock to gross national product from 5.0 to 6.2. Other economists are less optimistic that the correction of the double taxation of saving would provide the resources for this large an increase in investment. But all would agree that there would be *some* favorable effect on capital formation.

In terms of added GDP, the increase in the capital stock projected by Auerbach and Kotlikoff would translate into 6 percent more goods and services. Not all of this extra growth would occur within the seven-year span we are looking at. But, even allowing for only partial attainment in seven years and for a possible overstatement in their work, it seems reasonable to predict a 2 to 4 percent increase in GDP on account of added capital formation within seven years.

Tax reform would improve the productivity of capital by directing investment to the most productive uses. Auerbach has demonstrated, in a paper published by the Brookings Institution, that the bias of the current tax system toward equipment and away from structures imposes a small but important burden on the economy. The flat tax would correct this bias. Auerbach estimates that the correction would be equivalent to a 3.2 percent increase in the capital stock. GDP would rise on this account by 0.8 percent.

ENTREPRENEURIAL INCENTIVES AND EFFORT

U.S. economic growth has slowed in the past two decades, and surely one reason is the confiscatory taxation of successful endeavors and the tax subsidy for safe, nonentrepreneurial undertakings. There aren't any scholarly studies with quantitative conclusions on the overall benefits from a fundamental shift, but they could be large.

Today's tax system punishes entrepreneurs. Part of the trouble comes from the interest deduction. The people in the driver's seat in the capital market, where money is loaned and borrowed, are those who lend out money on behalf of institutions and those individuals who have figured out how to avoid paying income tax on their interest. These people don't like insecure loans to new businesses based on great new ideas. They do like lending secured to readily marketable assets by mortgages or similar arrangements. It's easy to borrow from a pension fund to build an apartment building, buy a boxcar, put up a shopping center, or anything else where the fund can foreclose and sell the asset in case the borrower defaults. Funds won't lend money to entrepreneurs with new ideas because they are unable to evaluate what they could sell off in case of a default.

Entrepreneurs can and do raise money the hard way, by giving equity interests to investors. An active venture-capital market operates for exactly this purpose. But the cost to the entrepreneur is high — the ownership given to the financial backers deprives the entrepreneur of the full gain in case things work out well.

So far we have just described the harsh reality of trying to get other people to put money into a risky, innovative business. Even with the best tax system, or no taxes at all, entrepreneurs would not be able to borrow with ordinary bonds or loans and thus capture the entire future profits of a new business. Equity participation by investors is a fact of life. But it is the perverse tax system that greatly worsens the incentives for entrepreneurs. The combination of corporate and personal taxation of equity investments actually is close to confiscation. The owners of a successful new business are taxed first when the profits flow in, at 34 percent, and again when the returns make their way to the entrepreneur and the other owners. All of them are likely to be in the 40 percent bracket for the personal income tax, making the combined effective tax rate close to 60 percent. The entrepreneur first gives a large piece of the action to the inactive owners who put up the capital and then surrenders well over half of the remainder to the government.

The prospective entrepreneur will likely be attracted to the easier life of the investor who uses borrowed money. How much easier it is to put up a shopping center, borrow from a pension fund or insurance company, and deduct everything paid to the inactive investor.

Today's absurd system taxes entrepreneurial success at 60 percent, while it actually subsidizes leveraged investment. Our simple tax would put the same low rate on both activities. A huge redirection of national effort would follow. And the redirection could only be good for national income. There is nothing wrong with shopping centers, apartment buildings, airplanes, boxcars, medical equipment, or cattle; but tax advantages have made us invest far too much in them, and their contribution to income is correspondingly low. Real growth will come when effort and capital flow back into innovation and the development of new businesses, the areas where confiscatory taxation has discouraged investment. The contribution to income from new resources will be correspondingly high.

TOTAL POTENTIAL GROWTH FROM IMPROVED INCENTIVES

We project a 3 percent increase in output from increased total work in the U.S. economy and an additional increment to total output of 3 percent from added capital formation and dramatically improved entrepreneurial incentives. The sum of 6 percent is our best estimate of the improvement in real incomes after the economy has had seven years to assimilate the changed economic conditions brought about by the simple flat tax. Both the amount and the timing are conservative.

Even this limited claim for economic improvement represents enormous progress. By 2002, it would mean each American will have an income about $1,900 higher, in 1995 dollars, as a consequence of tax reform.

Interest Rates

The flat tax would pull down interest rates immediately. Today's high interest rates are sustained partly by the income tax deduction for interest paid and the tax on interest earned. The tax benefit ameliorates much of the pain of high interest, and the IRS takes part of the income from interest. Borrowers tolerate high interest rates, and lenders require them. The simple tax would permit no deduction for interest paid and put no tax on interest received. Interest payments throughout the economy will be flows of after-tax income, thanks to taxation of business income at the source.

With the flat tax, borrowers will no longer be so tolerant of interest payments and lenders will no longer be concerned about taxes. The meeting of minds in the credit market, where borrowing equals lending, will inevitably occur at a lower interest rate. Potentially, the fall could be spectacular. Much borrowing comes from corporations and wealthy individuals, who face marginal tax rates of 34 and 40 percent. The wealthy, however, almost by definition, are the big lenders in the economy. If every lender and every borrower were in the 40 percent bracket, a tax reform eliminating deduction and taxation of interest would cut interest rates by a factor of 0.4—for example, from 10 to 6 percent. But the leakage problem in the United States is so great that the actual drop in interest would be far short of this huge potential. So much lending comes through the devices by which the well to do get their interest income under low tax rates that a drop by a factor of 0.4 would be impossible. Lenders taxed at low rates would be worse off if taxation were eliminated but interest rates fell by half. In an economy with lenders enjoying low marginal rates before reform, the meeting of the minds would have to come at an interest rate well above 0.6 times the preform level. But the decline would be at least a fifth—say from 10 percent to 8 percent. Reform would bring a noticeable drop in interest rates.

One direct piece of evidence is municipal bonds, which yield interest not taxed under the federal income tax. Tax reform would make all bonds like tax-free municipals, so the current rates on municipals gives a hint about the level of all interest rates after reform. In 1994, municipals yielded about one-sixth less interest than comparable taxable bonds. But this is a conservative measure of the likely fall in interest rates after reform. Today, tax-free rates are kept high because there are so many opportunities to own taxable bonds in low-tax ways. Why own a bond from the city of Los Angeles paying 6 percent tax free when you can create a personal pension fund and hold a Pacific Telesis bond paying 7 percent? Interest rates could easily fall to three-quarters of their present levels after tax reform; rates on tax-free securities would then fall a little as well.

The decline in interest rates brought about by putting interest on an after-tax basis would not by itself change the economy very much. To Ford Motors, contemplating borrowing to finance a modern plant, the attraction of lower rates would be offset by the cost of lost interest deductions. But the flat tax will do much more than put interest on an after-tax basis. Tax rates on corporations will be slashed to a uniform 19 percent from the double taxation of a 34 percent corporate rate on top of a personal rate of up to 40 percent. And investment incentives will be improved through first-year write-off. All told, borrowing for investment purposes will become a better deal. As the likely investment boom develops, borrowing will rise and will tend to push up interest rates. In principle, interest rates could rise to their prereform levels but only if the boom is vigorous. We can't be sure what will happen to interest rates after tax reform, but we can be sure that high-interest, low-investment stagnation will not occur. Either interest rates will fall or investment will take off.

As a safe working hypothesis, we will assume that interest rates fall in the year after tax reform by about a fifth, say from 10 to 8 percent. We assume a quiescent underlying economy, not perturbed by sudden shifts in monetary policy, government spending, or oil prices. Now take a look at borrowing decisions made before and after reform. Suppose a prereform entrepreneur is considering an investment yielding $1 million a year in revenue and involving $800,000 in interest costs at 10 percent interest. Today the entrepreneur pays a 40 percent tax on the net income of $200,000, giving an after-tax flow of $120,000. After reform, the entrepreneur will earn the same $1 million and pay $640,000 interest on the same principal at 8 percent. There will be a 19 percent tax on the earnings without deducting interest; the amount of the tax is $190,000. After-tax income is $1,000,000−$615,000−$190,000=$170,000, well above the $120,000 before reform. Reform is to the entrepreneur's advantage and to the advantage of capital formation. Gains from the lower tax rate more than make up for losses from denial of the interest deduction.

How can it be that both the entrepreneur and the government come out ahead from the tax reform? They don't—there is one element missing from this accounting. Before the reform, the government collected some tax on the interest paid by the entrepreneur—potentially as much as 40 percent of the $800,000, but, as our stories about leakage make clear, the government is actually lucky to get a small fraction of that potential.

To summarize, the flat tax automatically lowers interest rates. Without an interest deduction, borrowers require lower costs. Without an interest tax, lenders are satisfied with lower payments. The simple flat tax will have an important effect on interest rates. Lower interest rates will also stimulate the housing market, a matter of great concern to almost everybody.

HOUSING

Everyone who hears about the flat tax, with no deductions for interest, worries about its effect on the housing market. Won't the elimination of the deduction depress the prices of existing houses and impoverish the homeowner who can only afford a house because of its interest deductions? Our answer to all of these questions is no, but we freely concede that there is a significant issue here.

In all but the long run, house prices are set by the demand for houses because the supply can only change slowly. If tax reform increases the cost of carrying a house of given value, then demand will fall and house prices will fall correspondingly. For this reason, we are going to look pretty intensively at what happens to carrying costs before and after tax reform.

If tax reform had no effects on interest rates, its adverse effect on carrying costs and house values would be a foregone conclusion. A $200,000 house with a $120,000 mortgage at 10 percent has interest costs of $12,000 per year before deductions and $8,640 after deductions (for someone in the 28 percent tax bracket). The monthly carrying cost is $720. Take away the deductions, and the carrying cost jumps to $12,000 per year, or $1,000 per month. Inevitably, the prospective purchaser faced with this change would have to settle for a cheaper house. Collectively, the reluctance of purchasers would bring house prices down so that the buyers could afford the houses on the market.

As we stressed earlier, our tax reform will immediately lower interest rates. And lower rates bring higher house prices, a point dramatically impressed on homeowners in the early 1980s when big increases in interest severely dampened the housing market. The total effect of reform will depend on the relative strengths of the contending forces—the value of the lost interest deduction against the value of lower interest. We have already indicated that there are good reasons to think interest rates would fall by about 2 percentage points—say from 10 to 8 percent for mortgages. The value of the lost deduction, by contrast, depends on just what fraction of a house a prospective purchaser intends to finance. First-time home buyers typically, but not always, finance three-quarters or more of the price of a house. Some of them have family money or other wealth and make large down payments. Families moving up by selling existing houses generally plan much larger equity positions in their new houses. Perhaps a down payment of 50 percent is the average, so families are paying interest (and deducting) on $500 per thousand dollars of house.

A second determinant of the carrying cost is the value of the deduction, set by the marginal tax rate. Among homeowners, a marginal rate of 28 percent is typical, corresponding to a taxable income of $37,000 to $89,000. Interest-carrying costs per thousand dollars of house are $50 per year before taxes ($500 borrowed at 10 percent interest) and $36 per year after taxes. When tax reform comes, the interest rate will fall to 8 percent and carrying costs will be $40 per year ($500 at 8 percent) both before and after taxes. Tax reform will put this buyer behind by $4 per thousand dollars of house per year, or $800 per year for the $100,000 house.

If this $800 per year were the end of the story, it would bring a modest decline in house prices. But there is another factor we haven't touched on yet.

The buyer's equity position—the down payment—must come from somewhere. By putting wealth into a house, the buyer sacrifices the return that wealth would have earned elsewhere. The alternative return from the equity in the house is another component of the carrying cost. Tax reform almost surely reduces that component. As just one example, take a prospective buyer who could put wealth into an untaxed retirement fund if he didn't put it into a house. The fund holds bonds; after reform, the interest rate on bonds would be perhaps 3 percentage points lower, and so the implicit cost of the equity would be lower by the same amount.

To take a conservative estimate, tax reform might lower the implicit cost of equity by 1 percentage point as interest rates fall. Then the carrying costs of the buyer's equity would decline by $5 ($500 at 1 percent) per thousand dollars of house per year. Recall that the buyer has come out behind by $4 on the mortgage-interest side. On net, tax reform would *lower* the carrying costs by $5−$4=$1 per thousand, or $200 per year for the $200,000 house. Then housing prices would actually rise under the impetus of tax reform.

We won't argue that tax reform will stimulate the housing market. But we do feel that the potential effects on house prices are small—small enough to be lost in the ups and downs of a volatile market. Basically, reform has two effects—to reduce interest rates and related costs of funds (and so to stimulate housing and other asset markets) and to deny interest deductions (and so to depress housing). To a reasonable approximation, these influences will cancel each other out.

If tax reform sets off a rip-roaring investment boom, interest rates might rise in the years following the immediate drop at the time of the reform. During this period, when corporations will be competing strongly with home buyers for available funds, house prices would lag behind an otherwise brisk economy. The same thing happened in the great investment boom of the late 1960s. But to get the strong economy and new jobs that go with an investment boom, minor disappointments in housing values would seem a reasonable price. In the long run, higher incomes will bring a stronger housing market.

What about the construction industry? Will a slump in new housing accompany a tax reform that banishes interest deductions, as the industry fears? The fate of the industry depends intimately on the price of existing housing. Were tax reform to depress housing by raising carrying costs, the public's interest in new houses would fall in parallel with its diminished enthusiasm for existing houses. Because tax reform will *not* dramatically alter carrying costs in one direction or another, it will not enrich or impoverish the construction industry.

So far, we have looked at the way prospective buyers might calculate what value of house they can afford. These calculations are the proximate determinants of house prices. But they have no bearing on the situation of an existing homeowner who has no intention of selling or buying. To the homeowner, loss of the tax deduction would be pure grief.

Our transition proposal takes care of the problem of existing mortgages without compromising the principles of the flat tax or diminishing its revenue. Homeowners would have the right to continue deducting 90 percent of their mortgage interest. Recall that the bank would then be required to pay tax on the interest it received, even though interest on new mortgages would be untaxed. Homeowners could expect to receive attractive propositions from their banks to rewrite their mortgages at an interest rate about three percentage points lower but without tax deductibility. Even if banks and homeowners could not get together to lower rates, the homeowner could still deduct 90 percent of what he deducted before.

Conclusions

The flat tax comes with strong recommendations. It would bring a drastic simplification of the tax system. It imposes an across-the-board consumption tax at the low rate of 19 percent. It raises enough revenue to replace the existing personal and corporate income taxes. Through consistent use of the source principle of taxation, it would drastically limit the leakage that pervades today's taxes based on the destination principle. The flat tax is progressive—it exempts the poor from paying any tax and imposes a tax that is a rising share of income for other taxpayers. The economy would thrive under the improved incentives that the flat tax would provide.

4

The Nunn-Domenici USA Tax: Analysis and Comparisons

MURRAY WEIDENBAUM

The Nunn-Domenici USA Tax is unique among the many attractive proposals for reforming the federal tax structure. It alone promotes economic growth and simplification without sacrificing fairness. Although each analyst and taxpayer may give different weight to these and other values, it is instructive to analyze the alternatives in the light of a standard set of goals.

In carrying out this objective, this chapter contains three sections: (1) a description of the USA Tax plan, (2) an analysis of its effects in terms of growth, simplification, and fairness, and (3) a comparison with alternative reforms.

Highlights of the Nunn-Domenici Proposal

The Nunn-Domenici USA Tax plan consists of two parts. The first converts the individual income tax into a progressive consumption tax. The second is a new business tax, which replaces the existing corporate tax as well as the individual tax on unincorporated businesses. The combined structure is designed to be "revenue neutral" in that it raises the same amount of revenue as the existing tax system. (This is so, at least initially, in its static form. In a dynamic

The author is indebted to Samuel Hughes for helpful research assistance and to Ernest Christian, Rudolph Penner, and Barry Rogstad for advice and counsel.

sense, the future revenue flow is likely to be higher than what the current tax law generates because of the positive effects on the economy, as explained later.)

THE TAX ON INDIVIDUALS AND FAMILIES

The USA individual income tax contains an unrestricted deduction for saving. (The term "unlimited savings allowance" [USA] refers to this feature.) Unlike the flat tax, the taxpayer saves out of pretax income.

Progressivity is achieved through a progressive rate table plus an enlarged zero bracket/family allowance and expanded use of earned-income credits. Simplicity is attained by eliminating a great variety of special treatments to certain transactions and taxpayers.

In contrast to the current individual income tax, the USA version possesses the following characteristics:

- It permits a full and unlimited deferral of the portion of income that is saved. The tax is paid only when the principal and earnings are withdrawn from savings and devoted to consumption.

- It treats all income equally for tax purposes. The distinction drawn is not on the source of income but between the portion consumed and the part saved.

- It allows wage earners a full credit for the 7.65 percent Federal Insurance Contributions Act (FICA) payroll tax (the employee portion of Social Security and Medicare taxes).

- It exempts the consumption out of previously taxed savings from taxation (these funds have already been included in taxable income). Thus, a retiree who is drawing down previously taxed savings, accumulated before the USA Tax plan, can draw down and live on that savings tax free.

In addition, individuals with less than $50,000 of previously taxed savings can elect to deduct these amounts against taxable income. This special, transitional deduction is allowed in equal parts over three years.

A fuller view of the revised individual income tax can be gained by showing how the tax is calculated. The following four steps contain the essence of the plan:

Step 1. Calculate gross income. Gross income is the sum of wages and salaries plus financial income such as interest, dividends, and amounts received from sales of stocks, bonds, and other assets. This step is similar to the current procedure.

Table 1   Initial Federal Individual Income Tax Schedule
               under Nunn-Domenici

Taxable Income ($)	Federal Tax Rate (%)
SINGLE	
0–3,200	19
3,200–4,400	27
14,400 and over	40
HEAD OF HOUSEHOLD	
0–4,750	19
4,750–21,100	27
21,100 and over	40
MARRIED	
0–5,400	19
5,400–24,000	27
24,000 and over	40

NOTE: In three subsequent years, the rates for the first two brackets are reduced to cover the transition from the current tax on saving plus consumption to the new tax base on consumption alone.

Step 2. Subtract deductions.

Step 2A. Deduct exemptions. First deduct a family allowance, which ranges from $4,400 for a single individual to $7,400 for a married couple filing jointly. Second, deduct $2,550 for each taxpayer, spouse, and dependent. Conceptually, this is similar to the current procedure. In practice, the deductions are more generous. For a family of four, the total exemption comes to $17,600.

Step 2B. Subtract unlimited savings allowance. Deduct the total amount of income saved during the year. Include deposits in savings accounts, purchases of stocks and bonds, and start-up capital contributed to one's own small business. This step, in effect, constitutes the creation of a universal and unlimited individual retirement account (IRA), without the current paperwork and restrictions.

Step 2C. Subtract higher education deduction. Deduct up to $2,000 for each taxpayer, spouse, and up to two dependents for college tuition and similar vocational education. The deduction is also allowed for remedial education of students under eighteen years of age. This innovative reform acknowledges the importance of investments in "human capital."

Step 2D. Subtract three existing deductions. Continue to deduct home mortgage interest, charitable contributions, and alimony paid. All other current deductions are eliminated, including state and local taxes.

Step 3. Calculate initial tax liability. After making all the subtractions allowed from gross income to compute taxable income, the taxpayer applies a

Table 2   Calculating the Business Tax under Nunn-Domenici

$$\begin{aligned}
&\quad \frac{\text{Gross Revenues from}}{\text{Sales of Goods and Services}} - \text{Export Sales} \\[6pt]
&= \frac{\text{Sales in the}}{\text{United States}} - \frac{\text{Cost of Equipment and Services}}{\text{(purchased from other businesses)}} - \text{Cost of Inventory} \\[6pt]
&= \text{Taxable Gross Receipts} \times \text{Tax Rate of } 11\% \\[4pt]
&= \text{Gross Tax Bill} - 7.65\% \text{ Payroll Tax Paid} \\[4pt]
&= \text{Tax Liability}
\end{aligned}$$

new rate table (see table 1) to compute the initial liability. The rates are designed to maintain roughly the same tax burden in each income class as imposed by the current system. Within each class, however, the high savers experience a lower tax and the low savers, a higher tax.

Step 4. Calculate net tax liability.   Finally, the total amount of Social Security and Medicare tax paid on wages and salaries (subject to a cap) is deducted from the initial tax liability to compute the taxpayer's net tax liability, the amount owed to the Treasury. This last deduction eliminates the most regressive feature of the existing federal revenue system. If the Social Security and Medicare tax exceeds the initial income tax liability, the excess will be refunded to the taxpayer, as will the earned-income tax credit for the working poor, which is maintained and expanded.

THE TAX ON BUSINESSES

In the Nunn-Domenici USA Tax plan, all businesses, whether incorporated or not, are taxed at the same flat rate of 11 percent on their gross profit. There is no tax advantage from shifting to or from the corporate form.

In calculating its gross profit, a business starts with its total revenues from the sale of goods and services in the United States. It then subtracts the amount paid to other firms for the goods and services bought from them, including plant and equipment as well as inventory, parts, supplies, outside services, and utilities (see table 2).

Immediate expensing of all investments in capital equipment is a tremendous simplification compared with the current system, and it also encourages investment in durable business assets. Coupled with the new saving incentive contained in the individual income tax, the result is a substantial boost to the entire capital formation process.

Financial transactions are excluded from the calculation of gross profits. The business neither includes interest and dividends received nor deducts interest and dividends paid. Furthermore, compensation of employees is not deductible from sales revenues. However, a credit is allowed for the 7.65 percent employer FICA payroll tax that businesses must pay on the wages paid to employees.

This new type of cash-flow tax on gross profits is superficially similar to a value-added tax (VAT): both use a tax base of sales minus purchases. However, the business cash-flow tax differs from the VAT in several important respects. First, the tax is intended to be a replacement of the corporate income tax, not an additional sales tax. Second, the cash-flow tax lacks the administrative complexities of a VAT, which requires firms to track on an invoice-to-invoice basis the amount of tax attributable to each transaction.

Indeed, the Nunn-Domenici cash-flow tax drastically simplifies the current business tax structure. Firms will devote fewer resources to complying with tax regulations (and to devising creative methods to minimize their tax burden) and more resources to productivity-increasing investment. For example, the Nunn-Domenici business tax eliminates bizarre, complicated tax provisions such as the "amortization of intangible expenditures," a procedure that depreciates purchases of patents, licenses, and other intangibles. Such complicated laws contribute to the high costs of tax compliance. The Tax Foundation estimates that business tax compliance costs in 1990 totaled $112 billion, a sum nearly equal to 75 percent of federal corporate income tax collections. The simplifications would particularly aid small businesses.

The USA Tax plan also introduces a new tax treatment of international trade. Amounts received from exports (sales of goods and services to a purchaser outside the United States) are excluded from the calculation of gross profit. Correspondingly, in the United States a special 11 percent import tax is imposed on the sale of goods and services from abroad. Thus, a foreign business that manufactures outside the United States but sells its products in the U.S. market will pay the 11 percent tax.

In tax parlance, the USA business tax is territorial. Businesses do not include in gross profits the proceeds from sales made or services provided outside the United States, and they cannot subtract amounts paid for the purchase of goods or the provision of services outside the United States. Nor will businesses be taxed on dividends paid by foreign subsidiaries. Foreign businesses include in reportable gross profit only the amounts they receive for goods and services provided in the United States. For a comparison of the key elements of the new business tax with the existing corporate income tax, see table 3.

Table 3   Comparison of USA Business Tax with
               Existing Corporate Income Tax

Item	USA Business Tax	Current Corporate Income Tax
Rate	11%	35%
Cost of plant and equipment	Expensed	Depreciated over years
Export sales	Excluded; not taxed	Generally included and taxed
Goods directly competing in foreign markets	Not taxed	Taxed
Dividends paid for services of capital	Not deducted	Not deducted
Interest paid for services of debt capital	Not deducted	Deducted
Wages and salaries paid for services of employees	Not deducted	Deducted
Employer payroll tax on wages paid	Yes	Yes
Credit for employer payroll tax on wages paid for services of employees	Full credit allowed	No credit

Analysis of Impacts

ENCOURAGING SAVING AND INVESTMENT

A major objective of the Nunn-Domenici USA Tax is to reduce the tax burden on saving and investment. The intent is to encourage a higher rate of capital formation. This, in turn, will lead to a more rapidly growing economy and an improved standard of living for the American people.

In addition, public finance economists over the years have offered several basic justifications for shifting the primary base of taxation from income to consumption in an effort to achieve greater equity as well as economic efficiency. Consumption-based taxes put the fiscal burden on what people take from society—the goods and services they consume—rather than on what they contribute by working and saving, as do income taxes. Thus, under a consumption-based tax system, saving and long-term investment are encouraged at the expense of current consumption. Over a period of time, society is likely to achieve higher levels of both saving and consumption because the added investment, by generating a faster growing economy, will lead to a bigger income "pie" to be divided among the various participants in economic activity.

Figure 1   International Comparisons of Saving and Investment

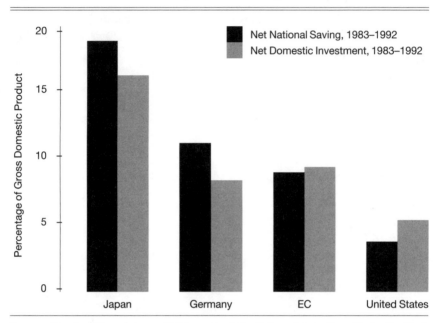

SOURCE: Bipartisan Commission on Entitlement and Tax Reform, Interim Report to the President, August 1994.

This argument becomes more compelling when we examine the historical record. The data convincingly show that the United States consistently devotes a smaller fraction of its national output to saving and investment than do the other major industrial nations (see figure 1). In addition, the correlation between the investment share of gross domestic product and the growth rate of the national economy is striking and positive. There is a close relationship between these two key economic variables for the major member nations of the Organization for Economic Cooperation and Development (OECD) over the past three decades(see figure 2).

The Nunn-Domenici tax plan responds to this situation directly. Under this reform, individual and family taxpayers (who do the great bulk of net saving) deduct *all* of their saving from their income in deriving their tax base.

Under this approach, the basic way for taxpayers to reduce their tax liability (legally) is for individuals and families to save more and companies to invest more. In contrast, to minimize tax liability under the existing tax system, taxpayers have to earn less, reducing the incentives to work, save, and invest. By increasing the amounts saved and invested, the proposed tax system augments the forces

Figure 2   Relationship of Investment to Economic Growth

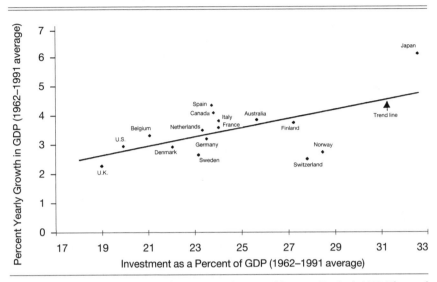

SOURCE: International Monetary Fund, *International Financial Statistics Yearbook*, 1993. The trend was obtained by performing an ordinary least squares regression of GDP on investment. The slope coefficient of 0.14 is significant at the 5 percent level.

that create the formation of capital. Moreover, there is considerable support in economic theory for the proposition that a consumption-based measure may better reflect the lifetime ability of households to pay taxes than a measure based on annual income.

It is useful to note what is absent from the Nunn-Domenici proposal. It does not select any specific sector of the economy to receive especially favorable tax treatment through traditional loopholes, nor does it discourage any category of activity through tax penalties. Thus, the proposed tax code is far more neutral than the present system or any other in modern times. An added benefit is the simplicity of the resultant tax system, a subject dealt with in the following section.

This chapter does not include any computations of the precise statistical effects that the enactment of Nunn-Domenici will have on the U.S. economy. That is a task best left to econometricians, who can examine the details in the light of their macroeconomic models. Yet there is no need to yield too much on that score. Surely, the direction of change is favorable. Eliminating the federal tax burden on saving encourages the formation of a larger pool of potential investment capital. Reducing the tax burden on investment likewise encourages the investment of that pool of saving.

The result, under most reasonable circumstances, is a faster rate of economic growth with an accompanying rise in employment and living standards. That highly desirable outcome, in turn, generates two favorable budgetary consequences. First, it enlarges the tax base without any change in the tax ground rules. This creates a faster flow of revenue into the Treasury, reducing the government's need to borrow. Likewise, a stronger economy means lower payments for unemployment benefits, welfare, and other transfer payments. The process just described is the most painless way of bringing down those continually high budget deficits.

PROMOTING SIMPLIFICATION

Economist—and tax reform skeptic—Robert Eisner of Northwestern University has provided the appropriate introduction to the subject of tax simplification:

> I am happy to stipulate that we waste many, many billions of person-hours and hundreds of billions of dollars in administering, complying with and seeking to avoid or evade current income taxes.

Empirical studies provide statistical support for Eisner's sweeping statement. The current individual tax code alone is estimated to cost taxpayers $50 billion in compliance costs. We may never again achieve the level of simplicity offered by the original 1913 income tax. Its Form 1040 was three pages long with one page of instructions. It was filed by only 1 percent of the population. In this spirit, the Nunn-Domenici plan eliminates about four-fifths of the current income tax provisions in the Internal Revenue Code. The resultant simplification of the federal tax system would be evident in many ways. The several thousands of pages of the tax code would be reduced to approximately three hundred.

By making saving generally deductible from gross income, there is no need for the paperwork and other overhead expenses now required to establish and maintain IRAs, Keoghs, and other "tax-favored" accounts. Nor need the taxpayer be concerned with staying within the arbitrary limits now required under these specialized savings incentives. Moreover, consumption-type taxes do not require complicated corrections for inflation because the tax base is inherently based on current cash flows.

Similarly, by expensing all business investment, the taxpayer no longer has to estimate the useful life of assets or choose from an array of complicated depreciation systems. Also, there is little incentive to fuss with the conversion of ordinary income into capital gains because only the income actually consumed winds up in the tax base. Tax is deferred on capital gains, dividends, interest, and other forms of income that remain in the pool of savings.

Because all businesses—whether they are incorporated or not—are subject to one and the same tax system, there is no longer any incentive to go through the expense and bother of repeatedly changing the legal form of the enterprise merely to take advantage of shifting differentials between individual and corporate income taxes.

Likewise, because interest and dividends are subject to the same tax treatment, there is no longer any tax incentive to leverage a company's financial structure or to convert dividend payments into interest payments. The result will not be an end to the current merger and acquisition boom. Rather, business decision makers will make such choices on the basis of underlying economic advantage rather than tax considerations.

However, this report does not deal with the many transitional effects that result whenever any major change is made in the tax system. A common example is the effects on the value of assets purchased under the assumption that they will be subject to the old tax system. Dealing with these important but usually limited concerns almost invariably requires some significant but usually temporary movement away from simplification.

MAINTAINING FAIRNESS

The fairness of a tax system, like beauty, is mainly in the eye of the beholder. Economists tend to view the subject in terms of horizontal equity and vertical equity. Horizontal equity is simply our jargon for "equal treatment of equals." The idea is that taxpayers with similar incomes should generally pay the same tax. Inevitably, qualifications are added when dealing with taxpayers in special circumstances. This, of course, opens the door to the introduction of all sorts of loopholes into the revenue structure.

The Nunn-Domenici USA Tax plan moves to greater horizontal equity in many ways. For individual and family taxpayers, virtually all types of income are treated the same. Likewise, virtually all forms of saving are treated identically. This is even more apparent in the case of businesses, where all enterprises— corporations, partnerships, and individual proprietorships—become subject to a single tax system. Likewise, virtually all capital investment is treated equally, as is the return on financial investment (e.g., interest versus dividends).

As for vertical equity, a progressive rate structure is usually—but not universally—chosen as the appropriate instrument for achieving this aspect of fairness. Some fairly esoteric assumptions underlie the proposition that it is fair for taxpayers with higher incomes to pay a higher *percentage* of their income than do those with lower incomes. A considerable literature is devoted to such questions as the diminishing marginal utility of income as the individual ascends the income scale and the difficulties in making interpersonal utility comparisons.

A significant number of public finance specialists, however, have concluded

Table 4   Comparison of Nunn-Domenici with the Status Quo
               (estimated change in the federal income tax burden)

Family Income Class ($)	Change in Tax Liability (%)
0–10,000	−75
10,000–20,000	−9
20,000–30,000	−14
30,000–50,000	−5
50,000–75,000	No change
75,000–100,000	No change
100,000–200,000	+3
Over 200,000	+4

that the case for a progressive income tax structure is questionable, or "uneasy." That line of reasoning supports a proportional tax system, whereby the government assesses all taxpayers the same percentage of their income. To my knowledge, there is no professional support for adopting a regressive tax structure whereby the upper brackets pay a smaller percentage than the lower brackets. If the case for progressive taxation is "uneasy," surely the case against regressive taxation remains "easy." In practice, of course, there are taxes that are regressive in terms of their effects.

As for the Nunn-Domenici proposal, the rate structure is clearly progressive because it is based on a table of graduated rates. None of the other tax reforms currently discussed contains a rate table. As noted earlier, the USA Tax plan contains three rates: 19 percent, 27 percent, and 40 percent. The designers of the plan have calculated the change in tax burdens by income class from the current tax structure. The tax liability declines substantially for the lowest income group, is stable for the middle of the income distribution, and rises somewhat for the top brackets (see table 4). The calculations underlying the table are based on the concept of "expanded family income." This notion is broader than the measure used by the Internal Revenue Service. For example, it includes transfer payments.

Comparison of Alternatives

The Nunn-Domenici USA Tax plan is one of an array of proposed reforms of the U.S. Internal Revenue Code currently under serious consideration. How does the USA Tax plan compare with those other tax proposals? The most popular alternative is Representative Dick Armey's flat tax, which is based on the scholarly work of Robert Hall and Alvin Rabushka of the Hoover Institu-

Table 5   Comparison of Federal Income Tax Rate Structures

Year or Proposal	Top Rate (%)	Bottom Rate (%)	Ratio of Top Rate to Bottom Rate
1980 (pre-Reagan)	70	14	5.0
1985 (mid-Reagan)	50	11	4.5
1987 (late Reagan)	38.5	11	3.5
1994 (current)	39.6	15	2.6
Nunn-Domenici	40	19	2.1
Armey H/R	19	19	1.0

tion at Stanford University (referred to here as Armey H/R). Other proposals under serious consideration include a national retail sales tax and a VAT.

NUNN-DOMENICI AND ARMEY-HALL/RABUSHKA

Although it is fashionable to focus on the important differences between Nunn-Domenici and Armey/HR, the careful reader is struck by their basic similarities. Both are revenue neutral. Both proposals promote economic growth by putting more of the tax burden on consumption, lightening it on saving, and expensing investment. Both simplify the tax system very substantially, although Armey/HR requires a new monthly tax return from each taxpayer. Neither requires an additional record-keeping apparatus or enforcement system because neither creates a new tax. Moreover, by avoiding a transactions-based sales tax or VAT, neither is regressive or inflationary.

Both are similar enough to the existing income tax to avoid the danger that accompanies a sales tax or VAT—the likelihood that Congress will wind up approving both (that was the case with Medicare and Medicaid, which originally were developed as alternatives rather than supplements to each other). Thus, it is not difficult to conclude that either Nunn-Domenici or Armey/HR would be a substantial improvement over the status quo.

There is a problem, however, with attempting to label the flat tax a progressive consumption tax, as do Hall and Rabushka. First of all, judging by Congressman Armey's version, the base of the flat tax is not consumption but wage and salary income—not all of which is consumed. Furthermore, the presence of a zero rate is not persuasive in addressing equity concerns. That common characteristic of all income taxes does not provide the graduation or progression from lower to higher rates that is the essence of a progressive structure.

A crude comparison of the progressivity of different federal income tax structures is seen in table 5. The ratios are based on the formal rate tables and do not take account of the many special provisions imbedded in the Internal Revenue

Code (the public finance literature contains more sophisticated measures requiring information not available to the author).

It can be seen that, by this standard, most of the move from a highly progressive rate structure to a flat tax has already occurred. For example, in 1980, the top rate of 70 percent was exactly five times as high as the bottom rate of 14 percent, indicating a rather progressive tax structure. By 1985, as a result of the enactment of the initial Reagan tax program, the ratio of the top rate to the bottom rate had declined very modestly, from 5.0 to 4.5. Following subsequent tax reform, by 1987 the ratio was down to 3.5 and by 1994 had fallen to 2.6.

Under Nunn-Domenici, this rough measurement of tax progressivity drops further, to 2.1. In comparison, the ratio for a flat tax is 1.0, indicating a proportional tax structure for all income above the baseline deduction.

SALES TAXES AND THE VAT

Sales taxes and value-added taxes represent a very different approach to raising revenue than either Nunn-Domenici or Armey/HR. Whereas the latter two proposals reform and simplify the existing income tax system, a national sales tax or VAT requires a new and very different form of revenue collection at the federal level. On the positive side, the attractions of sales-type taxation include the encouragement of saving in a major way and a reduction of the paperwork burden on taxpayers.

The basis of income taxes paid by individuals and organizations is an annual return that lists a variety of financial data and facilitates computations of tax liability. Sales taxes and VATs, in contrast, are levied on the value of individual purchases of goods and services. As a result, both a national sales tax and a value-added tax would require a new record-keeping apparatus for businesses and a new collection system for the federal government. Those proposals that provide refunds for low-income people also require continuing some variation of the present record-keeping and reporting arrangements. Despite the wishes of some of the proponents, under this variant, the Internal Revenue Service will not wither away.

Furthermore, because both the retail sales tax and the VAT are levied on individual transactions and, hence, included in the price of the good or service, the introduction of either one would trigger an upward movement in the consumer price index and other measures of inflation, as does any future increase in the rates of either tax. Secondary inflationary effects would result from the operation of escalator clauses in wage and supply agreements.

Sales taxes and VATs also alter the tax burden of varying income classes, raising equity concerns. Because consumption is a declining function of income (as people's income rises, they devote smaller proportions to consumption), both proportional-rate sales taxes and VATs are inherently regressive. Efforts to soften this regressivity require all sorts of complicated adjustments and may provide unintended loopholes to some taxpayers. For example, the common practice of exempting food, clothing, and medicine provides a windfall to many upper-income groups. Such exceptions also require that a higher rate be levied on the remaining tax base, introducing further distortions in consumer purchasing patterns.

There are important differences, of course, between general sales taxes and value-added taxes. Essentially, they involve a trade-off between simplicity (favoring the sales tax) and economic efficiency (favoring the VAT).

Perhaps of greatest impact is the concern that enacting either a national sales tax or a VAT could promote the expansion of the public sector. That is likely to occur as a result of giving the federal government an additional revenue source. Assurances to the contrary—that the new tax would merely replace a portion of the income tax—are not comforting. Based on historical experience, pressure would rise over the years to push up the rates of such "hidden" taxes.

The proponents of a VAT point to its widespread use overseas. Unlike current proposals in the United States, however, the adoption of a tax on value added was true structural reform in Western Europe. The VAT typically replaced an extremely inefficient form of consumption tax, a cascading sales or turnover revenue system, that was already in place. Those taxes applied to the total amount of a firm's sales rather than only to its value added. Thus, sales taxes were paid over and over again on the same items as they moved from firm to firm in the various stages of the production and distribution process, from raw material supplier to manufacturer to wholesaler to retailer to final customer. Such cascade-type taxes favored integrated firms that could legally avoid one or more stages of the tax. However, they severely discriminated against independent companies, each of which operated at only one phase of the production process.

Despite these advantages over a national sales tax, collecting the VAT is not simple. Exemptions are no minor matter in terms of the administrative complexity they generate. In France, a long and extensive debate occurred over whether Head and Shoulders antidandruff shampoo was a tax-exempt medicine or a cosmetic subject to the full VAT.

Conclusion

In their fundamentals, the Nunn-Domenici and Armey/HR approaches to comprehensive tax reform are closely related. Both soften the current progressive nature of the federal income tax. Both promote capital formation and economic growth. Both move toward greater simplification of the tax system. In terms of differentiation, the flat tax provides a greater degree of simplification at the expense of some loss of fairness.

Value-added and sales taxes, in contrast, also promote saving but generate a new array of problems. These range from increasing inflation to new paperwork requirements to a regressive tax structure.

Among the different approaches to fundamental tax reform currently under consideration, the Nunn-Domenici USA Tax is the most attractive because its structure provides the most favorable combination of simplification, economic incentive, and fairness.

References

Bartlett, Bruce. "A Devil We Don't Know." *Investor's Business Daily*, April 27, 1995, p. 2.

Bradford, David. *Untangling the Income Tax*. New York: Committee for Economic Development, 1986.

Bradford, David, et al. *Blueprints for Basic Tax Reform*. Washington, D.C.: U.S. Department of the Treasury, 1977.

Eisner, Robert. "The Proposed Sales and Wages Tax: Fair, Flat, or Foolish?" Paper presented to the American Enterprise Institute, Washington, D.C., January 27, 1995.

Hall, Robert, and Alvin Rabushka. *The Flat Tax*, 2d ed. Stanford: Hoover Institution Press, 1995.

Metcalf, Gilbert. "The Lifetime Incidence of State and Local Taxes." Working Paper No. 4252. Cambridge, Mass.: National Bureau of Economic Research, 1993.

Mitchell, Daniel J. *A Brief Guide to the Flat Tax*. Washington, D.C.: Heritage Foundation, 1995.

Rosen, Harvey. *Public Finance*. Homewood, Ill.: Irwin, 1991.

U.S. Advisory Commission on Intergovernmental Relations. *The Expenditure Tax*. Washington, D.C.: Government Printing Office, 1974.

U.S. Congressional Budget Office. *Effects of Adopting a Value-Added Tax*. Washington, D.C.: Government Printing Office, 1992.

Weidenbaum, Murray. *The Savings-Exempt Income Tax*. Saint Louis, Mo.: Washington University, Center for the Study of American Business, 1994.

——. *The Case for Taxing Consumption*. Saint Louis, Mo.: Washington University, Center for the Study of American Business, 1993.

5

A Hybrid Approach to the Direct Taxation of Consumption

CHARLES E. MCLURE JR. and GEORGE R. ZODROW

Introduction

Washington has recently been buzzing with proposals for a national consumption tax, most notably by Bill Archer (R.-Tex.), chairman of the House Ways and Means Committee, by Dick Armey (R.-Tex.), House majority leader, and by Senators Sam Nunn (D.-Ga.) and Pete Domenici (R.-N. Mex.).[1] Consumption taxes are more conducive to saving, investment, and economic growth than the current income tax, and they can be simpler. But consumption taxes are not all alike; they can differ greatly in their economic effects (especially their distributional effects) and their administrative features.

Indirect consumption taxes are levied on business with the expectation that they will be shifted to consumers—who pay the tax "indirectly." Such taxes, which include the familiar retail sales tax, the value-added tax (VAT), and the business transfer tax, are not discussed further here, but the appendix summarizes the salient features of these three variants.

Direct consumption taxes are levied "directly" on the consumption of individuals, commonly through the filing of tax returns. Proposals for direct consumption taxes ordinarily include wage withholding and a business tax component based on cash flow, although such features are not logically required. Although indirect consumption taxes are common around the world, there are few extant examples of generally applicable direct consumption taxes.

This chapter compares the administrative characteristics of three direct consumption tax schemes—focusing on issues of complexity and vulnerability to abuse. The appendix also compares these three schemes with the three indirect consumption taxes mentioned above. We do not discuss the well-known advantages of consumption-based direct taxation, the most prominent of which are simplicity and neutrality toward the choice between saving and consumption.[2] Nor do we discuss the thorny problems that will plague any attempt to move to a system of consumption-based direct taxation, including transition, the need to renegotiate double taxation treaties, and the treatment of gifts and bequests.[3] Rather, we take as given that there is substantial interest in a consumption-based direct tax and discuss the choice among three variants, focusing primarily on basic long-term design issues that determine how these systems would operate in practice.

The discussion that follows, focusing as it does on the administrative problems of alternative consumption-based direct tax schemes, might give the impression that these schemes are all very complicated—perhaps as complicated as the income tax—and that little simplification would be achieved by changing from the present income-based system. This is not our message. *Taxation based on income is by its nature complicated.* By comparison, *taxation based on consumption avoids the complexity inherent in income taxation.*[4]

Income taxation is inherently complex because (1) complicated timing rules (regarding, for example, depreciation allowances, capitalization of expenses, inventory accounting, and original issue discount) are needed and (2) inflation distorts the tax base, for example, by eroding the value of depreciation allowances and overstating the real value of interest payments in the absence of complicated adjustments for inflation. By comparison, being based on cash flow, taxation based on consumption automatically avoids these problems. (Of course, simplicity is not inevitable in consumption-based taxation; a potentially simple consumption-based tax can be made complex, just as the present income tax is far more complicated than it needs to be.)

Before turning to the main purpose of the chapter, it will be useful to dispose of a tangential issue—the rate structure of direct consumption taxes. Robert Hall and Alvin Rabushka (1983, 1985, 1995, and this volume) have gained considerable attention for what they call the "flat tax"—the basis for the Armey proposal. The Hall-Rabushka flat tax is a special case of the yield-exemption approach to the direct taxation of consumption described below—one in which businesses and all individuals whose tax base exceeds a threshold pay the same rate. Thus the flat tax has two distinct and separable features that distinguish it from the present progressive income tax—the base and the rate structure. This chapter concentrates on the tax base, focusing on the advantages of the hybrid system we propose, relative to both the yield-exemption tax favored by Hall, Rabushka, and Armey and a direct consumption-based tax based entirely on cash flow (also described below).

Part of the administrative simplicity of the flat tax results from the application of a single tax rate to all taxpayers (in addition to the zero rate applied to wage income below the tax threshold). In such a system there is relatively little possibility of manipulating transactions to shift the tax base from taxpayers subject to high marginal tax rates to those subject to low rates, as there is in a system with graduated rates. But this would be equally true under a flat-rate version of either of the other consumption-based direct taxes we discuss—and, indeed, it would be true of a flat-rate income tax; it has nothing to do with the base of the tax proposed by Hall and Rabushka.[5]

We believe it is unlikely that the Hall-Rabushka/Armey flat tax in its pure form will replace the income tax because it implies a substantial shift in tax burdens from high-income households to the middle class. The Tax Foundation estimates that, under the 17 percent flat tax proposed by Armey, average tax burdens would fall by 16.4 percent. (This proposal envisages enough expenditure reduction to offset the implied revenue loss.) In the income classes from $45,000 to $150,000, the tax reduction would average about 1 to 7 percent, but the reduction would be 41 percent for those with income in excess of $300,000; in the lowest income category tax liability would rise by almost 20 percent (although the average number of dollars involved would be small). Tax reductions in other income classes would not differ greatly from the average for all households. In a revenue-neutral tax reform the tax rate would be much higher than under the Armey proposal, roughly 21 percent, instead of 17 percent. With a 21 percent flat tax, middle- to upper-middle-income groups would experience substantial (11 to 23 percent) increases in liabilities, while the highest income group would experience a substantial (27 percent) tax reduction; at the bottom of the income distribution taxes would rise by more than 45 percent.[6] We posit that enacting a tax system characterized by shifts in burdens such as these is politically improbable. Thus in what follows we assume that the individual portion of any direct consumption tax would be characterized by graduated rates. Even so, most of our comments about the relative pros and cons of the consumption tax variants would be equally valid if each of the taxes were levied at a single rate.

The Three Alternatives

Because the three alternative methods of levying direct taxes on consumption differ primarily in their tax treatment of income from business and capital, we concentrate on this feature of the proposed plans. Most proposals for the direct taxation of consumption can be viewed as variants of two basic approaches, which we will call the consumed income tax (CIT) and the yield-exemption tax (YET).[7] Proposals in the CIT group tax income that is consumed, rather than saved, as well as consumption that is financed by debt. This is achieved through cash-flow treatment of saving, borrowing, lending, and net interest income at the individual level, coupled with a business-level tax that requires cash-flow treatment of both nonfinancial (real) investment and interest and debt (borrowing and lending) transactions.[8] Cash-flow taxation implies immediate deduction for all business purchases, including depreciable assets and additions to inventory.[9]

Proposals based on yield exemption also provide for cash-flow treatment of business-level nonfinancial real investment, but they ignore loans and interest at the business level; in addition, interest income and expense and all saving, borrowing, and lending transactions are ignored at the individual level. For the individual taxpayer, CIT treatment resembles a conventional individual retirement account (IRA), which allows deductions for contributions but taxes all distributions of principal or earnings thereon. By comparison, YET treatment resembles a "back-loaded" IRA (no deduction for contributions and no taxation of distributions).[10]

Each of these basic constructs has distinct advantages and disadvantages; these have been explored at length in the literature.[11] In reviewing this literature, however, we have been struck by the extent to which the relative disadvantages of the YET (and the corresponding advantages of the CIT) are concentrated in the business-level tax, while the relative disadvantages of the CIT (and the corresponding advantages of the YET) are concentrated in the individual-level tax. These observations have led us to propose a "hybrid consumption tax" (HCT), which combines the individual-level tax of the YET with the business-level tax of the CIT.[12]

Table 1 summarizes the treatment of debt transactions and interest under the three alternatives. Under the CIT, shown in column A, the receipt of principal (as proceeds of borrowing or repayment of debt) is a taxable event, and a deduction is allowed for the disbursement of principal (by lenders or borrowers when they repay debt); interest income is taxable and interest expense is deductible, as under the income tax. Under the YET, shown in column B, none of these financial transactions has any tax implications. Under our HCT approach, outlined in column C, business taxpayers would be taxed as under the CIT, but individuals would be taxed as under the YET.

Advantages of the Hybrid Approach

Although the hybrid approach creates some new problems related to the interface between the business and individual-level taxes, it is in our view

Table 1   Alternative Ways of Treating Debt and Interest
               under Three Consumption Tax Schemes

	A	B Yield- Exemption Tax (Meade R-based tax, U.S. Treasury YET, Hall- Rabushka/ Armey flat tax, Bradford X tax, McLure- Zodrow SAT)	C
	Consumed Income Tax (Meade R+F-based tax, U.S. Treasury CIT, Aaron- Galper)		Proposed Hybrid Consumption Tax
Receipt of principal (by borrowers or lenders)	Taxable	Exempt	Business: taxable Individuals: exempt
Disbursement of principal (by lenders or borrowers)	Deductible	Nondeductible	Business: deductible Individuals: nondeductible
Interest income	Taxable	Exempt	Business: taxable Individuals: exempt
Interest expense	Deductible	Nondeductible	Business: deductible Individuals: nondeductible

nevertheless superior to either the "pure" CIT or the "pure" YET from an administration/compliance point of view. This section explains our position.

THE BUSINESS-LEVEL TAX

The primary disadvantage of the treatment of borrowing and lending under the CIT approach is its complexity. Cash-flow treatment of loans (hereafter, CFTL) requires (1) that borrowers include the proceeds of borrowing and subsequently deduct interest expense and repayments of loan principal and (2) that lenders deduct the principal amounts of loans extended and subsequently include interest income and repayments of principal. The YET approach, which ignores loans for tax purposes, is far simpler. However, the complexity of the CIT approach is problematic primarily for individuals, as businesses typically would maintain comprehensive (and commonly computerized) records detailing all aspects of their borrowing and lending transactions. At the same time, applying the CIT approach at the business level avoids numerous problems—described below—that would arise if business loans were ignored for tax purposes, as under the YET. (These problems either disappear or are much less significant at the individual level.) Accordingly, in the HCT we propose cash-flow treatment of loans at the business level.

Exemption of financial intermediation. Perhaps the most important policy difficulty associated with applying the YET treatment at the firm level (thereby ignoring both interest income and interest expense) is that the interest-rate spread earned by financial institutions would be entirely exempt from tax. This is problematic both because it would be perceived to be unfair to collect no tax from a highly visible and often profitable business sector and because business tax revenues would be lost to the extent that above-normal returns were earned in the financial sector. The alternative of a separate tax on the financial sector (sometimes proposed to deal with the analogous problem under the VAT) is not particularly desirable; it would add complexity, and it would be difficult to design a separate tax that would be neutral with respect to the allocation of investment across financial and nonfinancial institutions. By comparison, the taxation of the spread earned by financial institutions occurs naturally under the CFTL prescribed by the CIT. Cash-flow treatment of financial institutions would avoid the continuous wrangling over the proper allowance for bad debts under the income tax.

Negative cash flow. Many firms experience negative cash flow (NCF) either because they are making large investments or because they are losing money. In years of large investment, deductions for expensing under a consumption-based tax would exceed deductions for economic depreciation under an income tax. However, under CFTL, this effect is offset for the debt-financed component of investment by including the proceeds of loans used to finance asset purchases in the tax. The number of firms that would be in a NCF position for tax purposes—and the aggregate amount of NCFs—would be significantly higher under the YET approach because it ignores the proceeds of loans taken out to finance real investment.

In principle, the existence of NCFs does not create major problems for a consumption-based business tax, as long as NCFs can be carried backward to previous years or carried forward with full nominal interest.[13] However, even if carryforward of NCFs with interest is allowed, selecting the appropriate interest rate will be contentious, and it seems likely that the rate chosen will be too low to reflect the true opportunity cost of funds for many if not all firms. The problem would be especially important for small new firms, with limited access to capital markets, that might not be able to survive until they recouped the tax. Moreover, given the prominent absence of interest on loss carryforwards under current law, it seems likely that NCFs would simply be carried forward without interest. In either case, serious problems would arise, although these would obviously be more troublesome if no interest were allowed on NCF carryforwards. Specifically, such treatment would give rise to artificial tax incentives for mergers, takeovers, buyouts, and otherwise uneconomical attempts to transfer NCFs among firms through the use of mechanisms such as leasing, manipulation of transfer prices, and so on. Moreover, to the extent that NCFs are less than fully adjusted and thus lose real value over time, the essential economic characteristic of a consumption-based business tax—a zero marginal effective tax rate on investment income—would be compromised and the tax system would move closer to one based on income rather than on consumption, at least for firms with NCFs. Thus, the fact that this problem is greatly mitigated with CFTL is a major advantage of the CIT approach.

Revenue consequences.   A related problem with ignoring loans for tax purposes is that government revenues would be lower during the first few years following the enactment of a YET than under the CFTL (and, of course, lower than under the income tax). Although these revenue shortfalls would be recouped in future years, the implied increase in the budget deficit might cause significant financial, economic, and political problems during the first few critical years following a consumption tax reform.

Tax avoidance.   Adoption of the YET approach would create a number of potentially serious opportunities for tax avoidance. These are described below. The treatment of interest under the YET (exemption of interest income and denial of deductions for interest expense) differs greatly from the tax treatment of other receipts (taxable) and expenses (deductible). This gives rise to a variety of potentially troublesome tax avoidance techniques involving transactions between firms subject to the YET and entities that are indifferent between interest income and other receipts and between interest expense and other expenses. Such entities include foreign firms, tax-exempt institutions (to the extent that their noninterest income would not be subject to a tax on unrelated business income), and, in some cases, individuals subject to the individual component of the YET. By comparison, these problems do not arise under CFTL, which treats all these items of income and expense symmetrically.

These avoidance techniques fall into the two general categories described below. They can be illustrated with the following examples, which assume that

Firm A is subject to a YET and that Entity B is a foreign firm subject to an income tax, a tax-exempt institution, or an individual.

In the first case, suppose that Firm A sells its output to Entity B. Firm A faces a clear incentive to sell its output at a reduced price in exchange for either (1) an above-market interest rate on a loan that it extends to B (e.g., an installment sale or other type of seller financing) or (2) a below-market interest rate on a loan from B to A. Firm A benefits from such an arrangement, because the price reduction lowers taxable receipts and either (1) the higher interest income is tax exempt or (2) the lower interest expense is not deductible in any case. At the same time, Entity B is indifferent to the manipulation of interest rates and prices. If B were a foreign firm subject to income taxation, the lower deductions for inputs purchased from A would be offset by either (1) higher interest deductions on the loan from A or (2) lower interest income on the loan to A. If B is a tax-exempt institution, none of the differences in prices has any tax consequences. Note also that the first scheme applies for consumer sales to individuals, who would be indifferent to lower sales prices coupled with higher interest rates (say, on installment sales) that were equivalent in present-value terms.

In the second general category of avoidance schemes, Firm A could agree to pay higher prices on its purchases from Entity B in exchange for either (1) a lower interest rate on a loan from B to A or (2) a higher interest rate on a loan from A to B. Under these circumstances, Firm A benefits because its deductions for inputs are higher, while the differences in interest payments have no effect on tax liability. At the same time, Entity B is indifferent to the manipulation prices and interest rates.[14] If B were a foreign firm subject to income taxation, higher sales receipts would be offset by either (1) lower interest income on the loan to A or (2) higher interest deductions on the loan from A. If B is a tax-exempt institution, the price changes would again have no tax consequences. However, these techniques would not work if B were an individual employee; the higher input prices would take the form of higher wages, which would be taxable under the individual component of the YET.

All these avoidance techniques would be difficult to prevent or even contain. Limiting them would presumably involve the use of measures such as interest-rate ceilings and floors that would eliminate much of the basic simplicity of the consumption-based approach in terms of both administration and compliance. Again, an important advantage of CFTL is that these issues do not arise.

There is, however, one major disadvantage of CFTL under the CIT approach. Under CFTL, it is necessary to distinguish deductible interest payments from nondeductible dividends paid; this issue does not arise under the YET approach because interest and dividends are not deductible. Nevertheless, on balance, the CIT approach to the taxation of business seems to be significantly superior to the YET approach.

THE INDIVIDUAL-LEVEL TAX

In contrast, we believe that the treatment applied to saving, loans, and interest under the individual-level component of the YET—simply ignoring all such transactions—is preferable to the cash-flow treatment prescribed under the individual-level component of the CIT. The rationale underlying this conclusion follows.

Simplicity. Most important, individual-level treatment under the YET is far simpler than that under the CIT—and much simpler than income tax treatment. Under the CIT's cash-flow approach, tracking all interest income, capital gains, and the return of (the principal amount of) all initial investments would pose formidable administrative problems; these would be far worse than those encountered under the income tax, which ignores principal transactions. Including the proceeds of loans in the tax base would be an unpopular and dramatic departure from current practice. Considerable amounts of additional record keeping (by many individuals who would normally keep minimal records on such transactions) would be required if repayment of debt were to be deductible. Withholding would also be more complicated under the cash-flow approach, as provisions for withholding on consumption loans and for "negative withholding" on principal and interest repayments on such loans should in principle be instituted.

Abusive transactions. Under a consumption-based tax with graduated rates, CFTL would create opportunities for abuse in the form of loans at below-market interest rates to lower-bracket children, retired parents, or relatives. Similarly, cash-flow treatment of saving and borrowing would create opportunities for tax base shifting to low-bracket family members, as transactions would be structured to attribute deductions to family members in high tax brackets and returns to those in low brackets.

Recognizing these complexities, some proponents of the cash-flow approach have recommended that individuals be allowed to ignore some minimum level of loans (e.g., $20,000) for tax purposes. Such an approach would in principle simplify compliance for many taxpayers. However, the limit would introduce new record-keeping requirements and confusion and would be difficult to enforce. It would also create a new opportunity for abuse (or at least confusion) as taxpayers might attempt (either intentionally or unwittingly) to take deductions for the repayment of principal and interest on loans incurred outside the cash-flow system. Moreover, allowing simultaneous operation of cash-flow and yield-exemption treatment of loans under the individual-level tax would create tax avoidance opportunities. For example, individuals subject to cash-flow treatment could defer tax liability by extending very short-term, end-of-year loans to individuals subject to yield-exemption treatment; indeed, tax liability could be deferred indefinitely by repeating the transactions every year.

International manipulation.   International complications would also exist under the individual cash-flow approach. The most troublesome would arise if individuals could borrow abroad without including the proceeds of the foreign loan in their tax base (either legally or illegally with little chance of detection). In this case (as above) such individuals could defer tax liability indefinitely by borrowing abroad and investing the funds domestically. Moreover, individuals who could borrow abroad outside their cash-flow accounts would find it easy to reduce their tax burden by "self-averaging"—incurring foreign debt to finance deductible domestic investments when their marginal tax rates are relatively high and making withdrawals from their cash-flow accounts to repay the foreign debt when their marginal tax rates are relatively low. Self-averaging is a standard feature of the cash-flow approach, but allowing greater access to this tax-saving device to those able to borrow abroad would be unfair. Yet it would be extremely difficult to restrict. In addition, if returns to foreign investments, including loans made abroad, were ignored (or underreported) under the CIT system, a significant avoidance opportunity would arise to the extent that deductions for saving could be allocated to the domestic cash-flow account, with the returns allocated abroad. Finally, to preclude individuals from taking deductions for saving and then avoiding tax by emigrating, transfers abroad from cash-flow accounts would have to be taxable; such treatment would also increase the complexity of the cash-flow approach.

On balance, simplicity favors ignoring saving, borrowing, and interest at the individual level, as under the YET. Although the magnitude of the problems caused by the cash-flow approach is difficult to ascertain, it would appear to be significant and would in many cases be borne by the individuals least capable of dealing with complexity.

Other issues.   A variety of other issues are relevant to the choice between the cash-flow and yield-exemption approaches at the individual level. Although several observers have argued that the cash-flow approach at the individual level is preferable because it results in larger steady-state welfare gains, this result is predicated on several questionable assumptions. First, it assumes that existing savings would be double taxed under the cash-flow approach. Second, it assumes that existing accrued gains would be untaxed under the yield-exemption approach. Neither of these seems likely to happen, for political reasons. Third, such analyses assume that the government would not offset lower private saving under the yield-exemption approach with higher public saving (deficit reduction). Although this assumption is plausible, requiring that the additional government revenues arising under the individual yield-exemption approach be directed to

increased government saving, it would not appear to pose insurmountable problems. Other transitional problems would be significant but broadly similar under
the two approaches.[15]

Income averaging also occurs more easily under the cash-flow approach.
However, given recent reductions in rate differentials, as well as the 1986 repeal
of income averaging, this difference between the two approaches would not
appear to be significant.[16] Finally, the cash-flow approach, which assesses tax on
the basis of the actual outcomes of risky investments, is often perceived to be
fairer than the yield-exemption approach, which exempts all returns, no matter
how high. However, recent research has suggested that this difference is more
apparent than real in many important cases; indeed, if the government is not able
to spread risk better than the private sector, the two approaches can be shown to
be equivalent, even in the presence of uncertain returns to investment.[17]

In summary, we believe that applying the yield-exemption method to individuals is preferable to subjecting them to cash-flow treatment. However, such
treatment of individuals is in a sense inconsistent with the application of CFTL
to firms under the hybrid consumption tax. The next section addresses the problems caused by this hybrid approach to the direct taxation of consumption.

THE BUSINESS/INDIVIDUAL TAX INTERFACE

We believe that the proposed hybrid approach is preferable to either of the
two "pure" forms of direct taxation of consumption. Nevertheless, it is clear that
the differential treatment of saving, loans, and interest across firms and individuals described above creates several possibilities for tax avoidance. These opportunities, which are also important for transactions between firms subject to CFTL
and other entities that are outside the tax system and thus not subject to such
treatment, require special rules to eliminate or greatly reduce the potential for
tax avoidance.

Loans to CFTL firms by entities outside the system. Several categories of
loans extended to firms subject to CFTL by entities outside the cash-flow system
pose problems. The most difficult issue arises for loans from foreign owners, as
well as loans from domestic individuals who are owners of taxable firms and from
tax-exempt institutions that have an equity interest in such firms. In these cases,
firms subject to CFTL face a strong tax incentive to convert nondeductible dividends into deductible interest payments, while the entity outside the cash-flow
system would generally be indifferent to this substitution. This difficult problem
is of course shared by the income tax and would presumably be attacked with
regulations designed to prevent the recharacterization of equity as debt, as well
as provisions such as "thin capitalization" rules that would limit the amount of
contributions from foreign owners that could be characterized as debt and/or

interest-rate ceilings on interest payments abroad. However, it is clear that this is one area in which the hybrid consumption tax is not simpler than the income tax alternative. (By comparison, recall that the primary advantage of ignoring loans for tax purposes at the firm level rather than adopting cash-flow treatment is that one need not distinguish between interest and dividend payments because neither is deductible.)

There would also be a tax incentive for firms subject to CFTL to overstate the interest rate on loans from entities not subject to cash-flow treatment—but only to the extent that they can compensate the firm in a way that would not be detected by the tax authorities. However, the obvious forms of compensation in the case of trading with foreigners or tax-exempt institutions—higher prices for the firm's outputs or lower prices for its inputs—would, for tax purposes, offset the effects of the higher deductions for interest expense and have similarly offsetting effects on the base of the entity outside the system. These substitutions would thus not reduce the tax liability of the firm subject to CFTL.

The primary problem in this area arises if the owner of the firm is an individual who is on the payroll because higher nontaxable interest on loans from individual owners could be substituted for lower taxable wages or salary. This avoidance technique would be attractive for individual owners. Accordingly, the proposed treatment under the HCT is that contributions of debt to a firm by its individual owners would be treated as equity contributions; that is, the proceeds of the contribution and subsequent repayments of both principal and interest would have no tax consequences. Moreover, if deemed necessary to avoid the complexity of identifying individual owners, all loans by individuals to firms subject to CFTL could be treated as equity contributions. In contrast, if this treatment were deemed to be to be too harsh, provisions for cash-flow treatment of short-term nonrenewable loans could be granted. (If deemed necessary, such admittedly harsh treatment could be applied to all loans to firms subject to CFTL by related—or even unrelated—tax-exempt institutions and/or foreign entities. Although such an approach would be more effective in limiting abuses than provisions like thin capitalization rules or interest-rate ceilings, it would heavily penalize all legitimate loans from firm owners outside the HCT system; it is thus not recommended.)

The same problem arises for financial institutions—that is, they face an incentive to pay above-market rates on their deposits if some means of compensating them without alerting the tax authorities can be identified. To curb this potential abuse, regulations would have to preclude preferential interest rates on deposits for related parties; this would be most important for employees of the financial institution, who would be willing to trade lower taxable wages for higher tax-exempt interest income.

Loans from CFTL firms to entities outside the system.   Loans extended by firms subject to CFTL to entities that are outside the tax system also pose some problems. For most nonfinancial firms, seller financing, including installment sales, is the most important category of such loans. Fortunately, seller financing poses no problems under the hybrid consumption tax, as all receipts from seller-financed sales could simply be included in the firm's cash-flow tax base. (Such treatment is economically equivalent to the technically correct approach of including the proceeds of the sale in the tax base, allowing a deduction for the amount of the loan, and then including repayments of principal and interest in the base.) There is no need to distinguish between interest and principal repayments and thus no advantage to price/interest-rate manipulations. Such treatment would extend to all forms of seller financing, including seller-financed purchases of consumer durables, such as automobiles, household appliances, furniture, and so on. Similarly, leasing would pose no problems because all lease payments would simply be included in the base of the CFT.

However, other types of loans raise two troublesome problems. First—and analogous to the case described above—firms subject to CFTL would face a strong tax incentive to make loans at below-market interest rates to entities outside the tax system, as long as the entity could compensate the firm in some way that would not be detected by the tax authorities; in the most extreme example of this strategy, the outside entity could default on the loan. Again, compensation from foreign firms and tax-exempt institutions in the form of higher prices for the output of the HCT firm or lower input prices would not reduce the HCT firm's tax liability and thus would not be an effective vehicle for tax avoidance. Rather, the primary problem area—aside from fraudulent transactions—would be loans at below-market interest rates to individuals on the firm's payroll, coupled with lower wages.

The second problem is that firms subject to CFTL could defer their tax liability by making very short-term, end-of-year loans to entities outside the system. Moreover, this process could continue indefinitely with a series of such short-term, end-of-year loans. (Loans between firms subject to CFTL are not problematic because the deduction received by the lending firm would be offset by the inclusion of the borrowing firm. Such transactions could be used to shift losses among firms. Because this would reduce the number of firms reporting losses for tax purposes and mitigate any problems associated with carrying forward losses with nominal interest, no special provisions are recommended for such loans between firms subject to CFTL.)

None of the potential ways of dealing with either or both of these two problems is particularly attractive. We recommend the draconian approach of applying income tax treatment to all loans (other than for seller financing) extended by nonfinancial firms to entities not subject to CFTL—no deduction for loans extended, no inclusion of loan principal repayments, and full inclusion of interest income. This would eliminate both problems but at the cost of adding some administrative complexity in terms of tracking two different types of loans and creating a strong tax bias against such loans, including loans to foreigners and loans to individuals that do not involve seller finance. (An exception might be allowed for the purchase of foreign debt.) For most firms, this bias would be unimportant because they typically would not extend loans other than those associated with seller financing. Moreover, to the extent that a firm subject to CFTL needed to make such loans for business purposes, it could set up a separate financial entity that would be treated as a financial institution and thus receive CFTL treatment (but could not transfer its losses to the parent firm). Alternatively, cash-flow treatment could be provided on a selective basis for loans for which a clear business purpose was demonstrated and the interest rate exceeded a rate floor.

Although such treatment is harsh, it appears to be superior to the alternatives. Treating loans by firms subject to CFTL to entities outside the tax system on a yield-exemption basis is not an attractive option because it would create all the opportunities for tax avoidance described above (in the discussion of why ignoring loans is not desirable at the firm level). A more ad hoc approach might include (1) interest-rate floors and (2) prorating the deductions for such loans across the current year and the following year, depending on the month or week in which the loan was issued, to reduce the gains to end-of-year loans. Such an approach, if applied to all nonfinancial firms, would significantly complicate compliance and administration.

Note also that the issue of the indefinite deferral of tax liability through the use of short-term loans also arises for bank deposits by firms subject to CFTL. Because it seems likely that one would want to limit the extent to which firms subject to CFTL could shift their tax liability to financial institutions, income tax treatment could also be applied to short-term deposits (e.g., 180 days or less).

Finally, note that the same problems arise for loans by financial institutions to entities outside the HCT. In this case, it is clear that income tax treatment could not be extended to such loans because they are an essential component of the business activity of the financial institution. The problem of below-market interest rates could be treated by the prohibition of preferential rates on loans to related parties, including employees. In addition, it might well prove necessary to prorate the deductions allowed for loans outside the system across the current year and the following year, depending on the month (or even the week) in which the loan was issued. Such complexity might well be required to limit tax avoidance by financial institutions and would be much less problematic than if the proposed treatment were applied to all firms subject to CFTL.

Concluding Comments

We have been early and vocal advocates of a consumption-based direct tax. Unlike most economists, we have based our advocacy of such a tax more on simplicity grounds than on economic grounds; indeed, we named the yield-exemption version we proposed in Colombia the "simplified alternative tax" to drive home the basic point that a consumption-based direct tax is a simple alternative to the conventional income tax. This fundamental fact, while not the topic of our chapter, should not be forgotten.

Further reflection has convinced us that in its pure form the yield-exemption method contains unacceptable opportunities for abuse — abuses that can be prevented by applying cash-flow treatment to the financial transactions of business firms. We believe that the hybrid consumption tax proposed in this chapter is the optimal way to avoid these problems, without accepting the complexity and other problems inherent in cash-flow treatment of individuals. But whichever of the consumption-based alternatives is chosen, it is much simpler than the present income tax.

Notes

1. See Archer (this volume), as well as the versions of the Armey and Nunn-Domenici proposals presented in Hall and Rabushka (this volume) and Weidenbaum (this volume), respectively.

2. On the economic benefits of consumption-based taxation, see Jorgenson (this volume).

3. On issues of transition, see Sarkar and Zodrow (1993) and Bradford (this volume).

4. See McLure (1988) and Zodrow and McLure (1991).

5. Indeed, because of the exemption of yield, there would actually be less opportunity for base shifting in response to graduated rates under the Hall-Rabushka scheme than under any of the other alternatives just mentioned, all of which tax the return to capital.

6. See "Armey Flat Tax Proposal" (1995). The table on page 85 has the full information contained in this document, supplemented by the authors' calculations of the effects of a 21 percent flat tax. (We do not vouch for the methodology used in the Tax Foundation estimates; we simply use them for illustrative purposes.)

7. An exception is the "S-based" tax on distributions from business to individuals proposed by the Meade Commission (Institute for Fiscal Studies 1978). It is not widely discussed and is not considered further here.

8. Because the CIT considers both real and financial transactions, the Meade Commission calls it an R+F-based tax. By comparison, the Meade Commission calls the YET an R-based tax because it taxes only real transactions. Interest on home mortgages would

Income Class (thousands of $)	AVERAGE RATE (%)		AVERAGE BURDEN ($)			CHANGE (%)	
	Now	17% Flat	Now	17% Flat	21% Flat	17% Flat	21% Flat
0–15	0.5	0.6	173	204	252	+17.9	+45.6
15–30	5.1	4.0	1,857	1,560	1,927	−16.0	+3.8
30–45	9.0	7.2	4,401	3,728	4,605	−15.3	+4.6
45–60	10.9	9.6	6,867	6,383	7,885	−7.1	+14.8
60–75	11.9	11.2	9,205	9,145	11,297	−0.7	+22.7
75–115	14.4	13.5	14,235	14,042	17,346	−1.4	+21.9
115–150	17.8	15.6	23,904	22,142	27,352	−7.4	+11.4
150–300	22.1	17.4	43,699	36,374	44,933	−16.8	+2.8
Over 300	35.3	19.8	264,226	156,331	193,115	−40.8	−26.9
AVERAGE						−16.4	

not be deductible under any of the proposals (unless the proceeds of home mortgage loans were included in the CIT tax base, which typically is not recommended).

9. Examples of CIT proposals include the cash-flow alternative described in U.S. Treasury Department (1977), the R+F-based tax proposed by the Meade Commission (Institute for Fiscal Studies 1978), and Aaron and Galper (1985).

10. The R-based tax proposed by the Meade Commission (Institute for Fiscal Studies (1978), the yield-exemption approach described by the U.S. Treasury Department (1977), the X tax proposed by David Bradford (1986), and the simplified alternative tax we have proposed (Zodrow and McLure 1991), as well as the Hall-Rabushka flat tax advocated by Armey, are YETs.

11. See McLure and Zodrow (1990) and Zodrow (1995) and references therein.

12. The Nunn-Domenici proposal, the unlimited savings allowance (USA) Tax system (1995), described in Weidenbaum (this volume), became available too late for thorough analysis. The USA scheme combines two essentially separate (and separable) consumption-based taxes: an indirect tax, the business transactions tax (BTT, described in the appendix), levied at a relatively low rate (perhaps 10 percent), and a modified CIT on individuals levied at graduated rates. While the scheme appears, for the most part, to be logically coherent, the interaction between its business and individual components is limited. Thus it differs substantially in nature from the three schemes examined here, each of which involves close coordination of the two components. Seen differently, the USA Tax is a hybrid that reverses our pairing of the treatment of business and individuals, applying the YET treatment to business and the CIT treatment to individuals. Thus it is subject to some of the problems that we are trying to avoid.

13. In principle, the tax value of NCFs could be refundable; such treatment is probably politically infeasible, despite its prevalence under the VAT. U.S. experience with "safe harbor leasing" following the Economic Recovery Tax Act of 1981 suggests that the existence of large numbers of firms with no tax liability could pose serious perception problems.

14. Opportunities to engage in such manipulation of prices and interest rates would

imply that YET would create a tax incentive for firms to engage in tied sale/loan transactions, including leases.

15. See Sarkar and Zodrow (1993).

16. It has commonly been assumed that pensions would be treated on a cash-flow basis, even under the yield-exemption approach; in that case, the differences would be even smaller. However, the attention recently devoted to "front-loaded IRAs"—essentially the YET treatment of one form of saving for retirement—suggests that this assumption may not be valid.

17. See Zodrow (forthcoming).

Appendix:
Six Consumption Tax Alternatives

Virtually all the consumption-based taxes levied in the world fall into the category of indirect taxes—taxes that are levied on business with the expectation that they will be shifted to consumers, who pay the tax "indirectly."[1] There are few extant examples of a direct consumption tax—a tax levied directly on the consumption of individuals, commonly through wage withholding and the filing of tax returns—the tax recently enacted by Croatia is the only direct consumption tax of general applicability of which we are aware.[2] Among the possible reasons for the dearth of direct consumption-based taxes in other countries, one is paramount: concern that the United States would not allow its multinational corporations to take foreign tax credits against liability for U.S. income tax for direct consumption-based taxes paid to countries in which they operate.[3]

The primary economic difference between direct and indirect taxes on consumption is the capacity of the former to allow for the circumstances of individual taxpayers—their marital status, their number of children, their aggregate consumption, and so on, which indirect taxes cannot do. It is possible to exempt a threshold level of consumption from a direct tax and to impose graduated rates on consumption above that level, thereby avoiding burdens on those with low levels of consumption and adding progressivity to the pattern of tax burdens. To avoid burdens on the poor under an indirect tax is difficult. It involves exempting food and other necessities—a blunt and inefficient tool for protecting the poor from taxation because the nonpoor also benefit from such exemptions. Thus it is commonly thought necessary to link an indirect consumption tax with reform of income maintenance policies to compensate for the burden of such taxation on the poor. It is even more difficult to achieve meaningful progressivity in indirect taxation of the nonpoor, through taxation of luxury consumption; moreover, this is an administratively cumbersome device.

INDIRECT CONSUMPTION TAXES

Retail sales tax (RST) is what most states impose, primarily on sales to households but (unfortunately) also on many purchases by business. Although relatively simple to collect and a useful benchmark for the analysis of other forms of consumption taxation, a federal RST seems unlikely. It would trespass on the fiscal turf of the states. Unless state taxes were levied as surcharges on a base defined by the federal government, administration would be needlessly complicated.

Value-added tax (VAT), the revenue workhorse in Europe (and the rest of the world, for that matter), achieves pretty much the same result as the RST but in a different and better way.[4] VAT is levied on all sales, but businesses are allowed credits for all tax paid on purchases, including capital goods; because there is ultimately no tax on business purchases, contrary to the case under the RST, only VAT on sales to households really matters. Like the RST, VAT infringes on the tax base of the states. Because the two taxes are imposed in very different ways, it would be impossible to levy RSTs as surcharges on a federal VAT. Experience in Canada confirms what many feared—that the combination of a federal VAT and state (provincial) RSTs is problematic. Because compliance and administration would be costly, especially for small business, VAT makes sense only if large amounts of revenue—say $100 billion or more—are needed. Once imposed, the VAT might become a "money machine."

Business transfer tax (BTT), sometimes called a subtraction-method VAT, also does what the RST and VAT do but in a way that resembles the income tax. Tax is levied on the difference between the sales and purchases of business (including purchases of depreciable assets but not wages and salaries). Thus the BTT uses an immediate deduction (often called "expensing" in the case of capital goods), instead of tax credits, to avoid taxation of business purchases, including capital goods. The BTT would be easier than VAT to implement. Thus, both states and business might object less to a BTT than to a VAT. That state RSTs could apparently coexist with a federal BTT make this scheme potentially attractive. Japan is the only developed country to have such a tax, which it levies at a relatively low rate.

DIRECT CONSUMPTION TAXES

The *yield-exemption tax* (YET), which we have previously proposed under the name "simplified alternative tax," modifies the BTT by allowing a business deduction for wages and levying an individual tax on wages above a given threshold.[5] (It is the capacity to "personalize" the taxation of wages that makes this a direct tax.) The tax-free amount would eliminate tax on low-income households, and applying graduated tax rates to wages above the tax-free amount would allow progressivity, if that were desired. This tax also admits the possibility of itemized deductions, similar to those in the current income tax.

The "flat tax" popularized by Robert Hall and Alvin Rabushka (1983, 1985, and 1995) and supported by Congressman Armey is a variant of the YET. The tax is said to be "flat" because there would be a single tax rate on wages in excess of the tax-free amount; the same rate would be applied to income from capital.

Debt transactions have no tax consequences under the YET. Neither businesses nor individuals pay tax on dividends, interest, and capital gains; interest expense is not deductible. The *consumed income tax* (CIT) treats financial transactions differently.[6] Proceeds of borrowing, receipt of debt repayments, and interest income are taxable; lending, repayment of debt, and interest expense are deductible. Under certain conditions the YET and the CIT are equivalent in present-value terms. The CIT could accommodate either flat or graduated rates.

The hybrid consumption tax (HCT) we have developed combines the CIT treatment of business with the YET treatment of individuals. That is, businesses pay tax on interest income and the proceeds of borrowing (unless invested) and deduct lending and interest expense. By comparison, individuals ignore all transactions in principal and interest on debt. This hybrid consumption tax is, we think, preferable to either pure form, for reasons we state in the text; it achieves the benefits of both, while avoiding most of their pitfalls.

Appendix Notes

1. This appendix is based on McLure (1995). For more detailed discussion, see McLure (1993).

2. Many income taxes contain a variety of features that are more appropriate for consumption-based taxes, and Mexico taxes small business on a cash-flow basis.

3. See McLure, Mutti, Thuronyi, and Zodrow (1990, chap. 9) for a discussion of this issue in the Colombian context. Working in Bolivia, we have recently been unable to convince the Internal Revenue Service that a business cash-flow tax (a component of direct consumption tax proposals) should be eligible for the foreign tax credit.

4. For a detailed exposition of the operation of the VAT and the BTT, see McLure (1987).

5. See McLure (1988); McLure, Mutti, Thuronyi, and Zodrow (1990); McLure and Zodrow (1990); Zodrow and McLure (1991). Bradford (1986) has also supported this type of tax. See also U.S. Treasury Department (1977).

6. See U.S. Treasury Department (1977) and Aaron and Galper (1985).

References

Aaron, Henry J., and Harvey Galper. *Assessing Tax Reform*. Washington: The Brookings Institution, 1985.

"Armey Flat Tax Proposal Would Reduce Average Taxpayer Federal Tax Burden by $1,000." *Tax Features* 39, no. 1 (December 1994–January 1995).

Bradford, David F. *Untangling the Income Tax*. Cambridge, Mass: Harvard University Press, 1986.

——. "Consumption Tax Alternatives: Implementation and Transition Issues." This volume.

Hall, Robert E., and Alvin Rabushka. *Low Tax, Simple Tax, Flat Tax*. New York: McGraw-Hill Book Co., 1983.

——. *The Flat Tax*. Stanford: Hoover Institution Press, 1985.

——. *The Flat Tax*, 2d ed. Stanford: Hoover Institution Press, 1995.

——. "The Flat Tax: A Simple Progressive Consumption Tax." This volume.

Institute for Fiscal Studies. *The Structure and Reform of Direct Taxation*. London: Allen and Unwin, 1978.

Jorgenson, Dale W. "The Economic Impact of Fundamental Tax Reform." This volume.

McLure, Charles E., Jr. *The Value Added Tax: Key to Deficit Reduction?* Washington, D.C.: American Enterprise Institute, 1987.

——. "The 1986 Act: Tax Reform's Finest Hour or Death Throes of the Income Tax?" *National Tax Journal* 41, no. 3 (September 1988): 303–15.

——. "Economic, Administrative, and Political Factors in Choosing a General Consumption Tax." *National Tax Journal* 46, no. 3 (September 1993): 345–58.

——. "A Taxpayer's Guide to Consumption Taxes." *San Jose Mercury News*, April 16, 1995.

McLure, Charles E., Jr., and George R. Zodrow. "Administrative Advantages of the Individual Tax Prepayment Approach to the Direct Taxation of Consumption." In Manfred Rose, ed., *Heidelberg Congress on Taxing Consumption*. New York: Springer Verlag, 1990, pp. 335–82.

McLure, Charles E., Jr., Jack Mutti, Victor Thuronyi, and George Zodrow. *The Taxation of Income from Business and Capital in Colombia*. Durham, N.C.: Duke University Press, 1990.

Sarkar, Shounak, and George R. Zodrow. "Transitional Issues in Moving to a Direct Consumption Tax." *National Tax Journal* 46, no. 3 (September 1993): 359–76.

U.S. Department of the Treasury. *Blueprints for Basic Tax Reform*. Washington, D.C.: Government Printing Office, 1977. Also available as Bradford, D.F., and the U.S. Treasury Tax Policy Staff. *Blueprints for Basic Tax Reform*. Arlington, Va.: Tax Analysts, 1984.

U.S. Department of the Treasury. *Tax Reform for Fairness, Simplicity, and Economic Growth*. Washington, D.C.: Government Printing Office, 1984.

"Unlimited Savings Allowance (USA) Tax System." *Tax Notes* 66, no. 11 (March 10, 1995): 1485–1575.

Weidenbaum, Murray. "The Nunn-Domenici USA Tax: Analysis and Comparisons." This volume.

Zodrow, George R. "Reflections on the Consumption Tax Option." In John G. Head, ed., *Taxation towards 2000*. Sydney: Australian Tax Foundation, 1995.

———. "Taxation, Uncertainty, and the Choice of a Consumption Tax Base." *Journal of Public Economics*, forthcoming.

Zodrow, George R., and Charles E. McLure, Jr. "Implementing Direct Consumption Taxes in Developing Countries." *Tax Law Review* 46, no. 4 (summer 1991): 405–87.

6

The Role of a Value-Added Tax in Fundamental Tax Reform

GILBERT E. METCALF

Introduction

There is currently considerable interest in shifting from an income-based to a consumption-based tax system. Most of the attention has been focused on some form of a business tax that expenses investment with either a tax on wages at the personal level (Hall-Rabushka or the Armey flat tax) or a tax on consumed income (Nunn-Domenici's USA Tax system). Another possible consumption tax that should be discussed is a value-added tax (VAT). Unlike the other consumption tax proposals, VATs are currently used in many countries. This chapter describes how a VAT might operate if implemented in the United States and discusses a number of important design issues that should be considered.[1]

The Mechanics of Value-Added Taxation

A value-added tax (VAT) taxes the value added in production through the various stages of production. Value added is simply the difference between the value of the goods (or services) sold and the value of goods (or services) purchased as intermediate inputs. There are several ways to impose such a tax. We could tax gross sales net of intermediate-good purchases at each stage of production. This forms the basis for a "subtraction method" VAT. A second method of imposing a VAT would be to tax gross sales and allow a credit for taxes paid by other firms at previous stages of production on intermediate goods. The "credit method" VAT works in this fashion.

A third method of taxing value added relies on understanding the general cash-flow equation for a firm. The following equation notes the sources and uses of cash in a firm:

$$S + K^+ = L + M + K^-$$ (1)

The equation notes that cash comes into a firm from two sources: capital inflows (K^+ includes both new equity and borrowing) and proceeds from the sale of a good or service (S). Cash is used for payments for labor (L) and intermediate goods (M). In addition, cash is used for dividend and interest payments as well as any retirement of debt and equity (K^-). At this elementary level, intermediate goods are simply any goods purchased from another company, including capital goods.[2]

From the subtraction method VAT, we know that $S - M$ is one measure of value added. But this implies that rearranging the terms in the cash-flow equation will provide an alternate measure. That is, value added (V) will equal

$$V \equiv S - M = L + (K^- - K^+).$$ (2)

In short, value added will also equal payments to labor and net capital outflows, whether they occur as dividend or interest payments or as equity and debt retirements net of new debt or equity. This approach highlights a distinction between old and new capital. *Old capital*—that is, capital already in the firm as debt or equity—is taxed either as it is retired or as income is paid to it. *New capital*, however, is excluded from the tax base and untaxed. This distinction between old and new capital is important when considering transitional concerns with consumption taxation; I return to this issue below. Equation 2 also highlights the fact that a VAT eliminates any distinction between dividends, interest payments, and share repurchases. The firm receives no deduction for cash payments out of the firm, and hence there is no bias in the tax toward debt versus equity financing.

Finally, we could impose a tax equivalent to a VAT by imposing a retail sales tax. This equivalence has often led to a VAT being termed a national sales tax. Although the economic effects of the two taxes would be the same, the design and administration of the taxes differ. A value-added tax is a tax on businesses; it is not a retail-level tax. This can most clearly be understood by noting that the business tax contained in the USA Tax system is exactly a subtraction method VAT.[3] The various methods of VAT taxation are perhaps most easily seen by considering a simple example. To produce and sell a gadget, a domestic manu-

Table 1   Gadget Production (in $)

	Foreign Producer	Domestic Manufac- turing	Wholesaler	Retailer	Total
Sales					
(domestic)	na	$1,800	$1,500	$2,000	
(foreign)	$800	na	1,500	na	
Intermediate goods	0	800	1,800	1,500	
Labor	400	800	1,100	450	
Return to capital	400	200	100	50	
Value added	800	1,000	1,200	500	$3,500
Domestic value added	800	1,000	−300	500	2,000
CREDIT METHOD VAT					
Gross VAT liability	120 [a]	270	225	300	915
(15 percent of gross sales)					
Credits	0	120	270	225	615
Net VAT liability	120	150	−45	75	300

[a] The VAT is collected on foreign production at customs when it is imported.

na = not applicable

facturer imports parts from abroad worth $800. The domestic manufacturer employs labor and produces a gadget that he sells to a wholesaler for $1,800. The wholesaler in turn sells to retailers—half in this country and half abroad. Finally, the domestic retailer sells to consumers in this country for $2,000 (see table 1).

Note that we can compute value added in a number of ways. For the domestic manufacturer, value added equals sales less the cost of intermediate goods ($1,800 − $800) or labor plus return to capital ($800 + $200). The fifth row of table 1 shows the value added at each stage of production.

The most common way of administering a VAT is to levy a tax on the total value of sales at each stage of production and allow a credit for any VAT paid on inputs in production. For purposes of claiming the credit, a firm is typically required to show proof (usually an invoice) that the VAT has been paid by its supplier. This provides a form of self-regulation in VAT enforcement because firms have an incentive to ensure that the VAT that their supplier claims to have paid has in fact been paid (see the middle part of table 1 for a 15 percent VAT).

Assume that a VAT is imposed that taxes consumption where the consumption occurs. This calls for a border tax adjustment that levies the VAT on the import of supplies for domestic production (this is discussed further below). If the VAT rate is 15 percent, $120 is collected at the border. The domestic manufacturer pays a gross VAT of $270 on sales of $1,800 and takes a credit for the $120 collected at the border for a net liability of $150. A similar story can be told at each level of production. The one difference occurs at the wholesale level, where half of sales are to foreign concerns. The wholesaler would pay a gross VAT of $450 but would receive a credit of $225 at the border for the VAT paid on the exported goods. Thus the gross VAT (before the credit for VAT paid at previous levels) would be $225. From that, the firm can credit $270 in prior VAT payments for a net obligation of -45. For design and tax evasion reasons, it would probably be best to allow a carryforward (with interest) of a negative tax liability to be applied against future taxes. The effect of the border tax adjustment is to ensure that a VAT is only collected on value added in domestically consumed goods and services.

Table 2 illustrates the kinds of information that must be kept for an invoice-style VAT. Accounting for purchases and sales at the wholesale level is illustrated, along with a sample of the tax calculation that would be done to determine tax liability. In addition to these records, there would need to be an invoice form that would document VAT payments at each stage of production.

The subtraction method VAT is subtly different from the credit method VAT. The tax base is simply gross sales less purchases of intermediate goods that have already been subject to the VAT. Unlike the credit method, there is no effort made to document the actual payments made by suppliers. Rather, it is assumed that the tax is paid at the same rate at all stages of production. If this is true, then the subtraction VAT and the credit VAT are equivalent.[4]

The Congressional Budget Office (1994) estimates that a comprehensive 5 percent VAT would raise nearly $100 billion in its first full year of operation and more than $600 billion in its first five years. For comparison, eliminating the deduction for home mortgage interest and taxing employer contributions for health insurance (but allowing an individual tax credit for premiums up to a limit) would raise slightly more than $500 billion over five years. The large revenue-raising capacity of a VAT is a major reason the tax is both alluring and frightening (depending on one's perspective).

However, the United States is unlikely to enact a comprehensive VAT, for a number of reasons. First, the administrative costs of a VAT would likely lead to certain classes of firms being exempted from taxation. Second, distributional concerns would likely lead to a VAT with multiple tax rates. One of those rates is likely to be zero—meaning that certain items on which the poor spend a high proportion of their income might not be taxed at all.

Whether a reduced rate will actually alter the distribution of tax liabilities depends on how it is applied. Consider "zero rating" at the wholesale level with a credit method VAT. Zero rating means that firms file all paperwork for a VAT and keep all necessary records. However, they apply a zero rate to their gross sales before claiming a credit for VAT paid at previous levels. In our example, the gadgets would be taxed at a zero rate and the invoice transferred to the retailer would record a zero tax payment. However, the wholesaler would still be able to

Table 2   Sample Accounting at Wholesale Level

		PURCHASES			
	Total	IMPORTS		DOMESTIC	
Vendor	*Purchases*	*Base*	*VAT*	*Base*	*VAT*
Manufacturer A	$1,150	$0	$0	$1,000	$150
Manufacturer B	920	0	0	800	120
TOTAL	2,070	0	0	1,800	270

			SALES			
	Total (including VAT)		TO REGISTERED TAXPAYERS		TO FINAL CONSUMERS	
Vendor		*Exports*	*Base*	*VAT*	*Base*	*VAT*
Firm A	$1,500	$1,500	$ 0	$ 0	$0	$0
Firm B	1,725	0	1,500	225	0	0
TOTAL	3,225	1,500	1,500	225	0	0

	TAX FORM	
	Tax Credit	*Tax Owed*
PURCHASES		
Imports	$ 0	na
Domestic	270	na
SALES		
Exports	na	na
Sales to registered taxpayers	na	$225
Sales to final consumers	na	0
TOTAL	270	225
Tax owed (credited if negative)	−45	

na = not applicable

claim the credit for VAT paid at previous stages of production and would receive a credit from the government for $270 (see the first line of table 3). Net VAT liability through the wholesaling stage would be zero. Moving to the next production stage, the retailer would not be able to take a tax credit for the $225 tax previously paid by the wholesaler. His net VAT liability increases from $75 to $300, and the total VAT liability is unchanged at $300.

In contrast, if the retailer may zero rate sales, there will be a change in VAT collections (line 2 of table 3). The retailer applies a zero rate to gross sales for a gross VAT liability of zero. It then takes a credit of $225 for previous VAT pay-

Table 3   Net VAT Liability with a Modified Tax Base:
               Credit Method VAT (in $)

	Foreign Producer	Domestic Manufac- turer	Wholesaler	Retailer	Total
Zero-rating wholesaler	$120	$150	$−270	$300	$300
Zero-rating retailing	120	150	−45	−225	0
Exempting retailing	120	150	−45	0	225
Exempting wholesaler	120	150	0	300	570

ments and receives credit from the tax authorities. Total net VAT liability is zero—gadget sales are untaxed. These are general results. Zero rating intermediate production has no effect on tax collections with a credit method VAT. However, zero rating at the final stage of production will eliminate the tax liability.

Administrative concerns with the record keeping associated with a VAT raise the possibility of exempting certain sectors of the economy from the tax. VAT exemption simply means that some stage of production is not part of the tax system. The exemption releases firms from the responsibility for collecting the VAT or filing any paperwork on sales and purchases. Small businesses are the most likely candidates for exemption.

Although exempting small businesses would reduce their paperwork, it could also increase the tax liability on the products they sell. If retailers are exempt, they do not file a tax and incur no VAT liability. However, they also receive no rebate of taxes paid at previous stages of production. Thus, in our example, the net VAT liability if retailers are exempt is $225 (line 3 of table 3). Note that the exemption at the retail level is *not* the same as zero rating. It reduces but does not eliminate the tax liability. However, if the wholesaler is exempt, the outcome is different (line 4). Now, the wholesaler incurs no VAT liability but is unable to take a credit for VAT payments made at previous stages of production. The retailer is also unable to take a credit for those VAT payments as there is no invoice documenting those payments. The result is that exempting the wholesaler (and so breaking the chain of payments and invoices) actually *increases* the total VAT liability. This happens because we have double taxed the value added by the importer and the manufacturer, the second time at the retail stage when gross rather than net value added was taxed.[5]

The examples above employ the European credit method—so-called because most of the European countries use this method to administer the tax. Devices like exemptions and zero rating are more complicated if a subtraction-type VAT is employed. A subtraction VAT looks like a corporate income tax, with the important difference that investment is expensed and labor and interest costs are not allowed as deductions. Value added is simply the difference between the value of a firm's sales and its purchases (both capital and intermediate goods). Our example in table 1 recorded sales on a tax-exclusive basis. The cost of intermediate goods for the wholesaler would actually be $2,070 if the tax is passed forward (see table 2). For the subtraction VAT, the wholesaler would compute the tax exclusive of the value of its purchases by assuming that a VAT liability was included in the cost of its materials. Thus the firm would net out the tax by dividing the cost of materials by one plus the tax rate. In our example, material costs of $2,070 would be divided by 1.15 to obtain the tax-exclusive cost of $1,800.

Misconceptions about a VAT

Introducing a value-added tax in the United States would likely have significant impacts on the economy. Before turning to more substantive impacts, I focus in this section on clearing up a few misconceptions about a VAT.

One typical concern is that a VAT would be inflationary. This view confuses a one-time price increase with a continual increase in prices. Whether prices rise or not depends on whether the tax is passed forward or passed back in the form of lower factor payments. Which happens will depend in part on the response of the Federal Reserve Board. An accommodating monetary policy would allow consumer prices to increase by the amount of the tax, whereas a tight policy would force factor payments to fall. Note that, in either case, real factor payments would fall. The distributional impact of a VAT would depend on monetary policy, in part because of the existence of unindexed transfers. I return to this point below.

A VAT can be levied on an "origin" or a "destination" basis. A second fallacy about a destination-basis VAT is that it will improve the trade balance. A destination VAT would tax consumption based on the location of consumption. Exports would be excluded from the tax base, and imports would be taxed. An origin VAT, in contrast, would tax consumption based on the origin of production. Exports would be subject to the VAT, and imports would be zero rated (or in some other fashion excluded from the tax base). The treatment of exports and imports (border tax adjustments) leads some to argue that destination VATs "favor" exports and that origin VATs "discourage" exports. As President Clinton put it when discussing a destination-style VAT in a *Fortune* (1993) interview: "The VAT is the only internationally recognized, legal way to favor your exports and to impose a burden on imports. All our competitors do it." In fact, a VAT that taxes imports and rebates the tax on exports would have no impact at all on the trade balance. Consider the decision of a domestic consumer to purchase an automobile. Introducing a VAT will not alter the relative prices of domestic and imported cars. Both will go up by a percentage amount equal to the VAT rate (assuming the tax is passed forward), in the case of the domestic car because of the imposition of the VAT throughout the production process and in the case of the import because of the border tax adjustment (plus any value added after entry into the United States). Similarly, the relative price of exported goods to foreign goods in other countries will be unaffected by the imposition of the VAT because exports are not subject to the VAT under the border adjustment.

Of course, a border adjustment is not necessary to maintain neutrality between domestically produced and foreign-produced goods, so long as prices or the exchange rate are flexible. This result is well known to trade theorists and can be motivated by thinking about importable and exportable goods separately. Consider a VAT under the origin principle. For exportable goods, the producer price for domestically consumed goods or exported goods is unchanged because the VAT is paid regardless of the destination of the good. But the consumer price of the exported good cannot rise (otherwise foreigners would substitute foreign-produced goods for the exported good). The tax is passed back to domestic producers. For importable goods, arbitrage in a competitive market requires that the domestic consumer price of a good equal the foreign price. But the imported good is not subject to the VAT. Thus the origin-style VAT is once again passed back to domestic producers. Relative consumer prices for the importable versus exportable goods are unchanged under the origin principle, and relative domestic producer prices for both goods are also unchanged; that is, both fall by the amount of the tax.

A final misconception is that a VAT will generate tax revenue from the underground economy. A simple example suffices to demonstrate that this is incorrect. Consider a plumber moonlighting on the weekend and being paid cash for his services. Currently he pays no tax on this income. Now impose a VAT. Assume either that prices are unaffected by the tax (backward shifting) or that prices fully rise by the amount of the tax (forward shifting). If the former occurs, the plumber is clearly unaffected. He charges the same price for his services and pays no more for any of his purchases. If prices rise, in contrast, it would appear that the plumber faces a loss of real income. However, with the price of a legal plumber (i.e., a plumber that pays the VAT) rising, the moonlighting plumber can raise his prices by the full amount of the tax. In either case, the relative price of legal to illegal plumbing is unaffected and the moonlighter bears no VAT burden.

Savings, Labor Supply, and a VAT

A VAT differs from the current income tax system by taxing consumption, whether in the present or in the future, at the same rate. By contrast, the present U.S. income tax taxes savers twice: once when they earn the income and again when they receive interest on their savings. A VAT eliminates the intertemporal consumption distortion that arises from taxing savings, which is one of the great appeals of any consumption tax. By raising the after-tax return to savings, a VAT will also increase the amount of savings, if the savings elasticity with respect to the interest rate is positive. The VAT's potential impact on savings appeals to the many economists who feel that savings rates in the United States are too low. Unfortunately, it is not clear that the savings elasticity with respect to the interest rate is positive. For example, Hausman and Poterba (1987) summarize research during the 1980s and conclude that this elasticity is probably close to zero. Whether implementing a VAT would increase savings rates is an open question. Note, however, that the compensated elasticity is the relevant elasticity for a reform that is revenue neutral. Shifting to a VAT in a revenue-neutral fashion should generate a savings response through the substitution effect. Simulation results presented by Kotlikoff (1995) in this volume suggest the effect on savings rates could be dramatic.

A VAT is equivalent to a tax on wages, which is to say that leisure is untaxed by a VAT. The issue of a VAT's impact on the labor supply is often overlooked. As Heckman (1993, 118) notes in a survey of research on labor supply, changes in net wages can have strong effects "at the extensive margin—at the margin of entry and exit—where the elasticities are definitely not zero." On this margin, a VAT could have substantial effects on the labor supply. However, Heckman also notes that the direct effect on hours worked of a change in the real wage is probably small.

Whether a VAT would affect labor supply likely depends on its impact through cross-price elasticities. As an example, assume that housing services and leisure are substitutes (as suggested by Triest 1992). In a world with no existing taxes, implementing a VAT that zero rated housing would affect the labor supply through two channels. First, the VAT would drive down the real wage, leading to a reduction in the labor supply (to the extent that the uncompensated labor supply elasticity with respect to the wage is positive). Second, zero rating housing would induce a substitution away from leisure toward more housing consumption. Thus the net effect on the labor supply would be ambiguous. In fact, with a zero labor supply elasticity, the VAT cum zero rating for housing would increase the labor supply. Whether the effect on the labor supply through cross-price elasticities is important is an empirical matter. Perhaps a more important channel through which a VAT could affect labor supply is in the treatment of work-related expenses. If a VAT is applied to work clothing, child care, domestic help, and other work-related expenses, there would be a considerable disincentive for work, especially for secondary earners in a household.

Except for its possible effect on labor supply, a VAT is remarkably free of distortions. This has been one of its main virtues among its proponents. McLure (1987, 28) put it this way: "The economic effects of introducing a value-added tax are, for the most part, not very interesting. . . . That the economic effects of the VAT are rather bland—we might call it a vanilla tax—is one of its chief advantages."[6] Of course, this presumes that there will not be exempted or zero-rated sectors. But if other countries are a guide, goods and services like housing, medical services, banking and insurance, and food are likely to be exempt from VAT or taxed at lower rates.

Housing is particularly interesting because there is a simple solution to the problem of exempting existing housing from the VAT (as is done in most countries). Exempting existing housing creates a consumption distortion between the purchase of new and existing housing. A better policy would be to subject all housing to the VAT once.[7] For new housing, this would occur at the time of construction; for existing housing, it would occur at the first transfer of the property after the tax was passed. In practical terms, an attachment to the deed of a house after that time could certify that the house is now "VAT free." This does raise the knotty transitional problem that we are taxing old capital. Let me return to this problem below. But suffice it to say here that this approach would mean that existing housing is treated the same as other forms of old capital.

Distributional Impact of a VAT

One traditional complaint about a broad-based VAT has been that it would be regressive. Pechman's (1985) work on the U.S. tax system is typically cited on this point. He finds that the system of excise taxes used in the United States is highly regressive.[8] However, there are problems with using the present patchwork of federal, state, and local excise taxes to draw conclusions about a VAT. A broad-based VAT would tax all (or most) goods and services at the same rate. But as Fullerton and Rogers (1993a, table 3-6) point out, excise tax rates in 1984 varied widely among goods, from a low of zero (on shelter and financial services) to a high of more than 70 percent (on alcohol and tobacco).

Moreover, Pechman's (1985) analysis was based on an annual measure of economic well-being. Recent tax incidence research has focused on the lifetime burden of taxation. Shifting from an annual to a lifetime perspective is particularly important for consumption taxation (for example, see Caspersen and Metcalf 1994). In an annual framework, the regressivity of a broad-based VAT depends on the extent to which savings rates rise with income. Because the rich consume a lower proportion of their income than the poor, a consumption tax will take a lower share of their income; that is, it appears regressive. Now consider the lifetime perspective. In the absence of bequests, lifetime income will equal the present discounted stream of consumption. From this view, a proportional broad-based consumption tax would exact the same fraction of lifetime income from everyone and the tax appears proportional rather than regressive.[9]

There are two especially important caveats to the conclusion that a broad-based VAT is not regressive: one involving nontaxed consumption (like leisure), the other involving nontaxed bequests. The labor supply effects of a VAT were discussed earlier. Whether incorporating the endogenous labor supply makes a VAT regressive over the lifetime depends on whether lifetime leisure is a luxury good with respect to lifetime income. If the income elasticity of leisure exceeds one, then the taxable consumption to lifetime potential income (income in the absence of any leisure) will fall with income and the tax will be regressive. However, the income elasticity of leisure is not likely to exceed one.[10] As a result, the fact that leisure is not taxed benefits the poor and middle class more than the rich. In this way, not taxing leisure adds progressivity to a VAT.

It has long been argued that excluding bequests from the base of a broad-based consumption tax makes the tax more regressive (Menchik and David 1982). A similar argument can be made about bequests as was made about leisure: Whether their exclusion from the tax base makes the tax more regressive depends on whether or not bequests are a luxury good.

However, the issue of bequests is complicated by the fact that although they would not be explicitly taxed under a VAT, they may be implicitly taxed— depending on one's view of the bequest motive. One motivation for bequests follows from the bequest giver deriving utility from the gift (Blinder 1974). Presumably, the utility derives from the consumption that the recipient of the bequest obtains from the gift rather than the monetary amount. Because the recipient is subject to the VAT when he or she consumes the bequest, the giver of a bequest has his or her utility reduced by the imposition of a VAT. In other words, the bequest is implicitly taxed.

Moreover, including the bequest in the base of the tax would create a distortion against bequests. A VAT that did not include bequests would apply equally to the consumption of both parents and children and thus create no distortion. Including bequests under a VAT would mean that they were taxed twice: once as a bequest and again when consumed by the recipients.

An alternative perspective views bequests as a payment for services elicited from one's children, as in the strategic bequest model of Bernheim, Shleiffer, and Summers (1985). To the extent these services provided by children are untaxed personal services (visits, phone calls, favors), a VAT that did not tax bequests in effect allows parents to purchase certain services tax free from their children and thus could distort behavior.[11] Understanding the motive for bequests is important for determining how the presence of bequests affects the incidence of a VAT.

Let me raise two additional distributional issues concerning a VAT. First, political pressure will likely lead to extensive zero or reduced ratings on certain products to increase the progressivity of a VAT. For administrative reasons, a better approach would be to maintain a single rate and give a lump sum payment to poor families to offset a portion of their VAT liability. Alternatively, the earned-income tax credit could be increased, thereby targeting the payment toward the working poor. One concern with a cash payment to households is the possibility of fraud. Clearly some mechanism (perhaps based on Social Security numbers) would be necessary to prevent individuals receiving multiple cash payments. Second, the incidence of the VAT will depend in part on how the Federal Reserve Board reacts and how Congress treats unindexed transfer payments like Aid to Families with Dependent Children. If the Fed accommodates a one-time price increase from imposing a value-added tax, prices will rise and part of the burden will fall on those whose income is not indexed against inflation, like the very poor. Alternatively, as Browning (1985) has pointed out, if real benefits from transfer programs are kept constant, the burden of the VAT will fall on workers (along with owners of old capital), rather than consumers as a group.

Another way to view the progressivity issue is to ask what tax a VAT would replace. The above discussion is in reality an exercise in absolute tax incidence. Fullerton and Rogers (1993b) consider the lifetime incidence of substituting a flat consumption tax for a number of existing taxes. Their work suggests that replacing personal income taxes with a flat consumption tax would be regressive. A number of points are relevant here. First their distributional tables reflect the steady-state incidence and ignore transitional burdens associated with the reform. To the extent that a shift to consumption taxation incorporates a wealth levy, any regressivity would be mitigated. Let me return to this in the next section. Second, Fullerton and Rogers's results illustrate the importance of designing a progressive consumption tax. As noted above, there are ways to add some progressivity to a VAT (zero rating, lump sum family payments, and so on). However, these are rather limited instruments. For purposes of constructing a progressive consumption tax, a VAT may be inferior to a progressive-rate consumed income tax or a progressive tax prepayment system (e.g., Bradford's X tax).

Transitional Concerns

One of the most vexing issues in implementing a VAT is the treatment of old capital in the transition. In practice, this translates into a concern about a VAT's impact on the elderly during the transition. As noted earlier, a VAT is effectively a tax on wage income and old capital. Auerbach, Kotlikoff, and Skinner (1983) point out that the tax on old capital is a lump sum tax that mitigates efficiency losses for the VAT as compared, say, with the wage tax alone. Herein lies an important policy issue that has not been raised in the current debate over a shift to consumption taxation. Many of the current proposals explicitly eliminate most of the wealth levy on grounds of fairness. There are a number of reasons to object to this approach. Let me discuss them and relate them to the potential attractiveness of a VAT.

As is well understood in the theory of tax reform, any change in the existing tax system involves redistributions both across classes of taxpayers and between taxpayers and the government. Although any redistribution resulting from tax reform is inherently unfair, one should ask whether one should single out a subset of redistributions to address while ignoring others (see, for example, Graetz 1979). Also, one should ask whether it is appropriate to single out *any* of the redistributions but rather view redistributions as a risk that taxpayers should protect themselves against through diversification (see Kaplow 1992 for a development of this argument). In light of Auerbach and Kotlikoff's findings of large intergenerational transfers to the current elderly, one must ask whether an explicit effort to undo a windfall tax on the wealthy elderly (among others) is fair.

Moreover, eliminating the lump sum tax on old capital reduces much of the attraction of the consumption tax. At the crudest level of abstraction, the debate between income and consumption taxation on efficiency grounds is a debate between a broad tax base (all income) with intertemporal consumption (i.e., savings) distortions and a narrower tax base (consumption) with higher rates but no savings distortion. We cannot determine a priori which is the more efficient system. Many economists have analyzed the question of efficiency and concluded that a consumption tax would reduce deadweight loss. However, as Auerbach and Kotlikoff (1987) have shown, the gain in efficiency comes in the main from the ability to lump sum tax existing wealth. This lump sum tax allows tax rates to be lower than they would be in the absence of the tax. Indeed, removing the lump sum tax makes the resulting consumption tax system less efficient than the existing income tax system. On efficiency grounds alone, we should resist the temptation to eliminate the tax on existing wealth.

We should also resist the temptation on equity grounds. Eliminating the tax throws away a highly progressive element of the tax reform that can offset a regressive shift away from income taxation. Again, note that the existing system can be viewed (in the most simplistic fashion) as a two-tiered system in which we tax returns to capital and returns to labor at different rates. To the extent that there is a double tax on dividends and capital gains through the corporate and personal income tax, this simply translates to a higher tax rate on returns to capital. If capital income is predominantly received by wealthier people, then the double taxation is simply a form of progressive taxation.[12] A consumption tax now taxes all income once. Such a reform is inherently regressive. The wealth tax levy offsets some if not all of that regressivity.

Even if we decide that it is inappropriate (either politically or philosophically) to tax existing wealth, we should be careful not to engage in reforms that provide a lump sum subsidy to existing wealth. Consider the treatment of dividends and capital gains under any of the flat tax proposals. The owners of old capital made investments under the presumption that any dividends and capital gains would be taxed at the personal level. Shifting to a flat tax relieves them of any personal tax liability on anticipated profits. The forgiveness of future taxes is a form of a lump sum subsidy to existing capital.[13] Is this a policy choice that we should be making?

A value-added tax is not immune from problems with the transition. For example, consider the stock of unused depreciation deductions. Those deductions would be lost in the shift to a VAT just as they would be in the shift to either a flat tax or a consumed income tax such as the USA Tax system. Just as there is pressure to maintain the deductions on old investments in the current proposals, there would be pressure to maintain them under a VAT.

If it is decided that these arguments are correct and that any reform should include the lump sum tax on existing wealth, then an important question is how to go about it. It may be that a VAT can play an important role in an incremental approach to shifting from income to consumption taxation. Consider a staged process of implementing a VAT at a low level and using the proceeds to reduce corporate income tax rates. A gradual increase in VAT rates could be used to slowly phase out the income tax. If done in sufficiently small increments, the pressure to provide transitional relief is greatly reduced. The attraction of a VAT is that it can serve as a transitional tax. At some point in the future, we can then make the final jump either to a flat tax (such as Bradford's X tax or Hall-Rabushka) or to a consumed income tax (such as the USA Tax system). Using a VAT as a transitional tax would be in keeping with the tax systems in other developed countries. Goods and services taxes in most developed countries constitute less than a quarter of the tax collections (see table 4). In those countries a VAT replaced turnover taxes; here the VAT could be used to reduce rates in the income tax.

Administrative and Compliance Costs

The General Accounting Office (GAO) (1993) recently estimated that the total costs of administering a fully implemented, broad-based VAT in 1995 would be $1.8 billion a year. In addition, there would be one-time transition costs of about $800 million. Substantial savings can be achieved by exempting small businesses. Exempting firms with annual gross receipts of less than $25,000 would reduce the number of returns needing to be filed by about one-half; raising the exemption to $100,000 would reduce returns filed by nearly two-thirds. Ad-

Table 4   VATs in Other Countries (in %)

Country	VAT Rate	GOODS AND SERVICES TAXES AS FRACTION OF	
		GDP	Taxes
Belgium	19.5%	7.2%	16.0%
Canada	7	5.3	14.1
Denmark	15	9.9	20.6
France	18.6	7.9	17.8
Germany	15	6.4	16.4
Greece	18	9.9	25.9
Italy	19	5.7	14.3
Japan	3	1.4	4.4
Luxembourg	15	7.2	14.9
Netherlands	18.5	7.3	15.6
New Zealand	12.5	8.6	23.8
Norway	22	8.2	17.4
Portugal	16	6.8	19.0
Spain	15	5.5	15.9
Switzerland	6.5	3.0	9.7
Turkey	12	6.5	22.2
United Kingdom	17.5	6.7	18.5

SOURCE: *Price Waterhouse Guide to Doing Business in [various countries]*. Also Eurostat (1993). Rates are as of January 1, 1993. Revenue figures are for 1991 and are from OECD *Revenue Statistics.*

ministrative costs in this latter case would fall by one-third. According to the GAO report, in 1987 business taxpayers under the $25,000 threshold accounted for 0.7 percent of gross receipts. Business taxpayers under a $100,000 threshold accounted for only 2.6 percent of gross receipts. Thus, they project little fall in tax collections from exempting small firms.

As noted above, exempting small firms would affect effective tax rates depending on whether the small firms are at the end of the production chain or in the middle. One possible outcome of exempting these firms would be to discriminate against small intermediate production firms and favor small final producers. The adverse effects of exemption could be eliminated by making registration optional for small firms. Those with significant expenditures on VAT-taxed inputs would be inclined to register to take advantage of the credit in a credit invoice VAT system. Of course, this reduces some of the administrative savings that arose from allowing the exemption in the first place. The figures cited above assume voluntary registration.

A VAT with multiple rates or other complexities would drive up the administrative costs of the tax. The GAO (1993) estimates that audit costs would rise between $400 and $700 million and taxpayer services about $140 million with a more complex tax. Transition costs would also increase.

In addition to administrative costs for the government, taxpayers will incur compliance costs as well. Based on the experience in the United Kingdom, the Congressional Budget Office (1992) estimates private compliance costs between $4 and $7 billion in 1988 for a VAT that exempted businesses with gross receipts less than $25,000. This compares to an estimated compliance cost of $21 to $33 billion (in 1988 dollars) for federal and state income taxes (Slemrod and Sorum 1984).

Offsetting these higher costs are the administration and compliance costs that are avoided by implementing a VAT rather than raising existing tax rates. Higher marginal tax rates for existing taxes are likely to increase tax avoidance and evasion activities, thereby requiring increases in monitoring, administration, and compliance costs for existing taxes. Whether a new VAT is preferable from the point of view of administrative and compliance costs to increasing revenues from existing taxes is not clear a priori.

Conclusion

There are many good reasons to consider switching from income to consumption taxation. Although not emphasized in the current debate, one of the most appealing reasons is that we fundamentally cannot measure income (Bradford [1986] has thoroughly developed this argument). Among other problems, our efforts to measure income lead to a complex tax structure and, I believe, contribute to the popular perception that we have a progressive income tax system in name only. Moreover, the movement to bring tax rates on the returns to capital down to the same levels as rates on wage income may increase investment and contribute to productivity and hence wage growth.

One advantage of using a VAT to contribute in the transition to consumption taxation is that we can benefit from the experience of a large number of countries in the world that employ this tax. Although it is tempting to conclude that a defect-free VAT cannot be implemented based on the experience in other countries, one should balance that observation against the fact that a defect-free consumption tax of any form is unlikely to be implemented. Given limitations placed on tax designers by the political process, how does a VAT stand relative to other consumption taxes? I think it has great potential if employed in an incremental fashion to avoid the sorts of regressive transfers that are likely with other existing consumption tax proposals.

Notes

1. Some sections of this paper draw from Metcalf (1995).

2. Allowing full deduction for purchase of capital is a property of a consumption-type VAT. Alternatively, an income-type VAT would allow a depreciation deduction only. VATs are generally of the consumption type.

3. The Hall-Rabushka and the Armey flat taxes are also subtraction method VATs except that the taxation of payments to workers is shifted over to the personal tax.

4. Some adjustment must be made for the VAT included in the cost of materials. For example, if M is the cost of materials, then $M^* = M/(1 + t)$ should be the value of materials included in the subtraction method VAT where t is the effective tax rate.

5. Note the incentive for vertical integration. Exemptions typically occur to reduce administrative burdens on small producers. There is an incentive for production carried out by small exempt firms to be done by a larger taxable firm and thereby avoid breaking the tax chain.

6. Of course, optimal tax theory does not imply that uniform commodity taxation is optimal.

7. In effect, this policy would tax the consumption stream of housing services on a tax prepayment basis.

8. Pechman's work, as well as others' work on consumption tax incidence, assumes competitive markets and forward passing of the tax. Recent work by Besley and Rosen (1994) challenges the assumption of competitive markets and finds evidence of overshifting for a number of commodities.

9. The argument that a broad-based consumption tax is proportional over the lifetime applies equally to a broad-based sales tax. This argument is developed further in Metcalf (1994).

10. Defining leisure is a bit problematic (do we include sleep?), but as an approximation, mean leisure is probably at least as large as mean labor supply. If equal, then the income elasticity of leisure equals (in absolute value) the income elasticity of labor supply; if leisure exceeds labor supply, the elasticity is smaller than the elasticity of labor supply.

11. It is not clear a priori whether the untaxed services would increase or decrease if a VAT were implemented. Because the services are untaxed, there would be a rightward shift of the demand curve for services. From the children's point of view, a VAT is analogous to a wage tax and the supply curve for services would shift left if the supply elasticity is positive.

12. Of course, it is not obvious that returns to capital are taxed more heavily than wage income. Realization-based capital gains taxation along with a 28 percent ceiling on the capital gains tax rate both serve to reduce the effective tax rate below the statutory top marginal tax rate.

13. This problem exists for a consumed income tax also. Old savings can now be reinvested and earn the before-tax rate of return. But the decision to save had been made with the assumption that savings would receive the after-tax rate of return.

References

Auerbach, A. and L. Kotlikoff. *Dynamic Fiscal Policy*. Cambridge, Eng.: Cambridge University Press, 1987.

Auerbach, A., L. Kotlikoff, and J. Skinner. "The Efficiency Gains from Dynamic Tax Reform." *International Economic Review* 24(1983): 81–100.

Bernheim, B.D., A. Shleiffer, and L. Summers. "The Strategic Bequest Motive." *Journal of Political Economy* 93(1985): 1045–76.

Besley, T., and H. Rosen. "Sales Taxes and Prices: An Empirical Analysis." Department of Economics, Princeton University, 1994.

Blinder, A. *Toward an Economic Theory of Income Distribution*. Cambridge Mass.: MIT Press, 1974.

Bradford, D. *Untangling the Income Tax*. Cambridge Mass.: Harvard University Press, 1986.

Browning, E. "Tax Incidence, Indirect Taxes, and Transfers." *National Tax Journal* 38(1985): 525–33.

Caspersen, E., and G. Metcalf. "Is a Value Added Tax Regressive?" *National Tax Journal* 47(1994): 731–46.

"Clinton Speaks on the Economy." *Fortune*, August 23, 1993, pp. 58–62.

Fullerton, D., and D. Rogers. *Who Bears the Lifetime Tax Burden?* Washington, D.C.: Brookings Institution, 1993a.

———. "The Lifetime Incidence of a Consumption Tax." American Enterprise Institute Conference Paper, December 16–17, 1993b.

Graetz, M. "Implementing a Progressive Consumption Tax." *Harvard Law Review* 92(1979): 1575–1661.

Hall, R., and A. Rabushka. *Low Tax, Simple Tax, Flat Tax*. New York: McGraw-Hill, 1983.

Hausman, J., and J. Poterba. "Household Behavior and the Tax Reform Act of 1986." *Journal of Economic Perspectives* 1(summer 1987): 101–20.

Heckman, J. "What Has Been Learned about Labor Supply in the Past Twenty Years?" *American Economic Review* 83(May 1993): 116–21.

Kaplow, L. "Government Relief for Risk Associated with Government Action." *Scandinavian Journal of Economics* 94(1992): 525–41.

Kotlikoff, L. "Saving and Consumption Taxation: The Federal Retail Sales Tax Example." This volume.

McLure, C. *The Value-Added Tax: Key to Deficit Reduction?* Washington, D.C.: American Enterprise Institute, 1987.

Menchik, P., and M. David. "The Incidence of a Lifetime Consumption Tax." *National Tax Journal* 35(1982): 189–203.

Metcalf, G. "The Lifetime Incidence of State and Local Taxes: Measuring Changes during the 1980s." In *Tax Progressivity and Income Inequality*, ed. J. Slemrod. New York: Cambridge University Press, 1994.

——. "Value-Added Taxation: A Tax Whose Time Has Come?" *Journal of Economic Perspectives* 9, no. 1 (1995): 121–40.

Pechman, J. *Who Paid the Taxes: 1966–85?* Washington, D.C.: Brookings Institution, 1985.

Slemrod, J., and N. Sorum. "The Compliance Cost of the U.S. Individual Income Tax System." *National Tax Journal* 37(1984): 461–74.

Triest, R. "The Effect of Income Taxation on Labor Supply When Deductions Are Endogenous." *Review of Economics and Statistics* 74(1992): 91–99.

U.S. Congressional Budget Office. *Effects of Adopting a Value Added Tax*. Washington, D.C.: U.S. Government Printing Office, 1992.

——. *Reducing the Deficit: Spending and Revenue Options*. Washington, D.C.: U.S. Government Printing Office, 1994.

U.S. General Accounting Office. *Value Added Tax: Administrative Costs Vary with Complexity and Number of Businesses*. Washington, D.C.: U.S. General Accounting Office, May 1993.

7

The Economic and Civil Liberties Case for a National Sales Tax

STEPHEN MOORE

In recent months a political consensus has begun to emerge that the current income tax system is in need of radical surgery. There are two points of general bipartisan agreement on the defects of the U.S. tax code. First, the U.S. tax system reduces economic growth through punitive tax rates on savings and investment. Second, the needless complexity of the tax code imposes large costs on U.S. businesses and workers.

But there is also a third source of large-scale public dissatisfaction with the income tax that has so far escaped much of the policy debate over tax reform in Washington. That defect is the tremendous and growing intrusiveness of the income tax system. Increasing numbers of Americans object not just to the level of taxation but to the invasive and intimidating manner in which taxes are collected today.

Several tax reform proposals have been introduced in Congress to repair the income tax. These include most promonently the Dick Armey flat tax plan and the Domenici-Nunn consumed income tax. A third proposal that is gaining political momentum is the national sales tax as a complete replacement of the income tax. House Ways and Means Committee chairman Bill Archer will soon introduce a national sales tax bill, as will Reps. Dan Schaefer and Billy Tauzin. Archer says that he wants to "pull up the income tax system by its very roots."

This chapter examines these three leading proposals in the context of the three defects of the income tax: (1) it reduces economic growth, (2) it is too complex, and (3) it is too intrusive. The chapter also adds a fourth important criterion for assessing these tax plans: tax visibility. In the context of these four criteria, the Domenici-Nunn proposal is good; the Armey flat tax is better; the Archer plan is best. This chapter will first enumerate the major defects of the current tax system; second, explain why the Archer plan is superior; and finally outline the features of a well-constructed national sales tax.

The Economic Deficiencies of the Income Tax

Today the typical American household pays more than $16,000 in federal taxes.[1] This constitutes roughly 40 percent of family household income and is roughly twice in inflation-adjusted dollars the level of taxes imposed in the 1960s.[2] Taxes clearly impose a heavy burden on U.S. workers and businesses.

Although most attention seems focused on the issue of the burden of taxes, U.S. workers and businesses are increasingly disadvantaged by the economically *destructive way that the federal government imposes taxes.* One problem with the current tax code is the disincentive effects of high marginal tax rates.

The highest marginal income tax rate at the federal level today is 42 percent. When state taxes are included in the calculation, many individuals face a more than 50 percent marginal tax rate. Studies show that these lofty income tax rates apply in large part to small business owners.[3] Paradoxically, punitive tax rates are designed to soak the rich, but lower tax rates generally lead to higher tax contributions by the wealthy. For example, after the Kennedy tax cuts in 1963, which lowered the top income tax rate from 90 to 70 percent, reported taxable income by the richest Americans rose by 40 percent.[4] Similarly, after Ronald Reagan cut income tax rates in the 1980s, the share of income taxes paid by the wealthiest 1 percent of Americans went from 18 percent in 1981 to 25 percent in 1990.[5] But since the 1990 tax rate increases, the share of taxes paid by the rich has fallen slightly. The federal government is estimated by the Joint Economic Committee of Congress to have lost about $50 billion in tax revenues from 1987 through 1991 because the federal government raised the capital gains tax rate from 20 to 28 percent.[6]

The working elderly are particularly victimized by our punitive income tax rate structure. Senior citizens in the workforce face high marginal income tax rates, special earnings penalties, and just-enacted higher taxes on Social Security benefits. The National Center for Policy Analysis calculates that some working elderly face marginal tax rates of up to 80 percent.[7]

Even middle-income workers face high marginal tax rates today. Most middle-income earners are in a 28 percent federal tax bracket, a 15 percent payroll tax bracket, and a 5 percent state/local income tax bracket. This means that the tax collector snatches 48 cents of every additional dollar a middle-income worker earns today.

These high marginal tax rates reduce economic output and national savings. A study by economist Robert Genetski shows that high marginal tax rates are inversely related to productivity growth.[8] Productivity and thus wages tend to rise when marginal income tax rates are low, but productivity falls or grows more slowly when marginal income tax rates are high—as they are today.

High tax rates discourage capital formation. The United States imposes some of the highest tax rates on capital of any developed nation. For example, the federal government's 28 percent long-term capital gains tax rate is unindexed for inflation. This is among the highest in the world; it compares with a 20 percent rate in Germany, a 16 percent rate in France, and a 0 percent rate in Japan.[9]

The 1993 tax increase was especially inimical to capital investment in the United States. The National Center for Policy Analysis concludes that, because of the new Clinton income taxes, the new marginal tax rate on capital in the United States will be 58.5 percent. Investment is expected to decline by a staggering $1.8 trillion below what it would otherwise be between 1994 and 1998.

The income tax system also retards long-term economic growth by double taxing savings and investment via capital gains, corporate income, and other such taxes on capital formation. The result has been an alarming reduction in the American savings rate. The U.S savings rate is now about one-third what it was in the 1950s. Today the savings rate in the United States is one-half that of Europe and one-third that of Japan. A survey of twelve developed countries recently placed the United States last in savings.[10] This is a prescription for very slow long-run economic growth.

Economists have attempted to estimate the lost output that results from the growth disincentives in our current tax code. Harvard economist Dale Jorgenson suggests that the efficiency loss could be more than $200 billion per year.[11] In other words, Jorgenson finds that with a more economically efficient tax system, the federal government could collect roughly the same amount of tax revenues and raise economic output by about $2,000 per household.

Complexity of the Tax Code

The income tax also imposes costs on the economy through its unnecessary complexity. It is worth noting that the original 1913 income tax was a two-page form, with a two-page instruction sheet and just fifteen pages of tax law. The top tax rate was 6 percent (with some legislators complaining that it would soon reach the unthinkable level of 10 percent). Less than 1 percent of Americans even needed to fill out an income tax return.[12]

Today, virtually all workers must file a tax return. There are now more than nine thousand pages of tax law. Despite past efforts at tax simplification, most Americans do not view the tax code as simple or easy. About two-thirds of the tax returns using professional tax preparers in 1992 were filed by Americans with incomes below $50,000. *Money* magazine discovered in 1991 that 70 percent of the members of Congress on the two major tax-writing committees—House Ways and Means and Senate Finance—used professional tax preparers to figure out their taxes.[13] All told, Americans spend about $30 billion a year for the services of tax accountants and lawyers.[14]

A 1992 study by political scientist James L. Payne estimated that Americans spend roughly 5.4 billion man-hours computing their taxes.[15] This is more man-hours than used to build every car, van, truck, and airplane manufactured in the United States. It is more than the total number of hours worked in a year by every resident of the state of Indiana. The deadweight economic loss is estimated by Payne to be well over $200 billion.

These figures do not consider the complications added to the tax code by the Clinton tax bill enacted into law in 1993. The Clinton tax hike not only raised marginal tax rates but set in motion an unraveling of the Tax Reform Act (TRA) of 1986, which had been a small step in making taxes less complicated.

Clearly, the well-intended 1986 TRA to simplify the code has failed. Judged on simplicity grounds, the U.S. tax system receives failing grades.

Intrusiveness

The intrusiveness of the income tax is not a subject widely studied by economists. The reason is clear: intrusiveness is more a civil liberties issue than an economic issue. But for economists to reject the significance of the growing civil liberties complaints about the Internal Revenue Service is to ignore perhaps the major issue that is driving the populist clamor for tax reform.[16] It is possible that any plan that fails to address the issue of the overly intrusive nature of the income tax will fail politically.

The Internal Revenue Service now has 115,000 auditors and agents. To put the size of this police force in perspective, the IRS has roughly the same number of employees as all other federal regulatory agencies. That is, the IRS has more enforcement personnel than the Environmental Protection Agency, the Bureau of Alcohol, Tobacco, and Firearms, the Occupational Safety and Health Administration, the Food and Drug Administration, and the Drug Enforcement Administration combined. Today, without a search warrant, the IRS has the right to search the property and financial documents of U.S. citizens. Without a trial, the IRS has the right to seize property from Americans—and it does so routinely.

Last year, Congress added five thousand IRS agents even as it was forced to acknowledge that hundreds of auditors were illegally scouring the returns of U.S. citizens.

With the IRS, privacy rights are relegated to secondary status behind compliance enforcement. Fred Goldberg, former commissioner of the IRS during the Bush administration, recently wrote that "the IRS has become a symbol of the most intrusive, oppressive, and nondemocratic institution in our democratic society."

This chapter is not meant to prove the case that the IRS is overly intrusive. That case has been made in several exhaustive studies and books in recent years.[17] The Cato Institute recently published a study entitled "Why You Can't Trust the IRS," which lays out the civil liberties case against the IRS in a concise fashion.

Assessing the Leading Reform Proposals

To these three defects of the current income tax system a fourth must be added: visibility. A sound tax system is one that is highly visible to the taxpaying public. Hidden taxes are undesirable because they disguise the true cost of government to the voters.

There are now three major tax overhaul bills before Congress. The first is the Nunn-Domenici plan. Simply stated, the Nunn-Domenici proposal would transform the income tax code into a "consumed income tax." The consumed income tax works very much like the current progressive income tax system, but it allows the tax filer to deduct all savings from taxes. On the business side, the Nunn-Domenici plan would replace the corporate income tax with a value-added tax, or VAT. This would allow businesses to deduct all capital investment from taxation.

How does Nunn-Domenici fare on our four criteria for judging tax proposals? By ending double taxation of savings by individuals and investment by businesses, Nunn-Domenici is a substantial improvement on economic efficiency grounds over the current tax system. However, because Nunn-Domenici retains the progressive rate structure of the current code, it leaves unsolved the problem of high marginal tax rates on consumption. Because the purpose of earning income is to consume it eventually, high tax rates on consumption will discourage work and investment.

On each of the last three reform criteria Nunn-Domenici rates poorly. It does not simplify the tax code. It does not make it less intrusive. Finally, Nunn-Domenici may actually make taxes less visible to the voter. The value-added tax is an invisible tax. In Europe the evidence is persuasive that the VAT has been an engine of government growth.[18] Although the switch to a consumed income tax on the personal income tax side would be an improvement, on the business side a VAT is no improvement over the current corporate income tax.

The Dick Armey flat tax proposal is modeled after the Hall-Rabushka plan first developed more than ten years ago.[19] It would eliminate all deductions, credits, and loopholes; end the withholding tax; end the double taxation of savings; and institute a 20 percent flat-rate tax. All income would be taxed once and only once at the 20 percent rate. The real selling point of the Armey plan is the postcard return. Americans currently spend about twenty hours figuring out their taxes each year. Under the Armey plan this would be reduced to twenty minutes.

How does the Armey plan fare on our four criteria? Like Nunn-Domenici, it ends the double taxation of savings and investment. It scores better than Nunn-Domenici on this measure because the low marginal tax rates in the Armey plan also promote work.

The postcard feature of the Armey plan makes it much simpler than the curent system. It passes the simplicity test with flying colors.

Because the flat tax is still an income tax, however, it does not make our tax system less intrusive. The IRS would still need to investigate the private pecuniary financial transactions of all Americans. Indeed, if withholding taxes were abolished (an idea I support), the IRS's enforcement budget would probably have to be increased substantially to ensure compliance.

The Armey tax would make taxes more visible than the current system — especially because it would end withholding. The Armey plan would require the taxpayer to write a check each month to the IRS. On the other hand, the Armey plan retains the corporate income tax, which is one of the more invisible taxes.

The final plan to examine is the national sales tax proposal. This is the only plan that fixes every one of the defects of the current income tax system. Here is how:

1. Because the sales tax exempts all savings and investment, the double taxation problem would be eliminated. Because the sales tax is a single flat rate, the disincentive effects from high marginal rates would be eliminated.

2. The sales tax eliminates the income tax entirely. Compliance costs would be substantially reduced.

3. The sales tax would virtually eliminate the Internal Revenue Service. The sales tax is the only plan that solves the invasive nature of the current system.

4. A sales tax would be paid by consumers every time they purchased a good or service at the cash register. The tax would appear on the receipt. Hence, the sales tax is one of the most visible taxes.

Table 1   Rating the Leading Tax Reform Proposals

	Economic Impact	Simplicity	Privacy	Visibility
Current system	Poor	Poor	Poor	Poor
Nunn-Domenici	Good	Poor	Poor	Very poor
Flat tax	Excellent	Excellent	Poor	Good
Sales tax	Excellent	Excellent	Good	Excellent

Table 1 summarizes how each of the three major tax reform proposals fares on each of the four criteria discussed above. The current system fails on each of the criteria; the sales tax is the only plan that succeeds on each criteria.

Economic Impact of a National Sales Tax

In 1993 the Cato Institute commissioned a study by economist Laurence Kotlikoff of Boston University to examine the economic impact of replacing federal income taxes with a national sales tax.[20] The sales would apply to all consumption purchases—including services. Only real estate and securities would be exempted. The purpose of the Kotlikoff study was to determine (a) What would be the impact of the sales tax on economic variables such as savings, wages, and output? and (b) What is the necessary sales tax rate to completely replace on a revenue-neutral basis the federal personal income, corporate income, and estate taxes?

Kotlikoff discovered that to completely replace federal income taxes would require an initial sales tax rate of 17.4 percent. After five years the rate could be reduced to 15.4 percent, and after ten years the rate could be lowered to 13.9 percent. The reason the rate can be lowered is that the study finds a positive economic feedback from the tax change. Specifically, the Kotlikoff study finds that, after ten years, a national sales tax would

1. More than double the national savings rate.
2. Increase the capital stock by 8 percent above the level attained under the current tax system.
3. Raise income and output by 6 percent more than would be achieved under the current tax system. That would increase national output by almost $400 billion per year.
4. Lift the real wage rate by 3 percent.

5. Reduce interest rates by 8 percent.

Kotlikoff concludes the study by issuing the following endorsement for a sales tax: "A shift to a national sales tax has the potential for dramatically improving the incentives to save. The distortion to save is so great under our current system of income taxation, that it appears we could switch to consumption taxation. . . . and end up with much higher rates of saving and capital accumulation and a higher level of per capita income."

The Features of a National Sales Tax

A national sales tax has the virtue of being simple, nonintrusive, visible, flat, and economically efficient. But there are potential political problems with a national sales tax as well. One of these is that a sales tax is said to be regressive. Another is that a sales tax of more than 15 percent is said to encourage large-scale evasion. And a third potential problem is that the sales tax may not be a replacement but rather an *add-on* to the current income tax.

First, the regressivity issue can be easily overcome. If we were to provide a rebate on a generous portion of the tax that every American pays, then the regressivity disappears. I advocate that every individual receive a rebate on the tax paid on the first $5,000 of purchases he makes during the year. This would mean that a family of four would pay no tax on its first $20,000 of purchases each year. There are various ways of providing this rebate. Assuming that the sales tax were set at 18 percent, a family of four would be entitled to a rebate of $3,600 ($20,000 × 18 percent) for the year. The government could send a quarterly rebate check of $900 to every family of four, a $450 check to every family of two, and so on.

Another possibility would be to provide every family with an annual "smart card" that would have a sales tax credit based on family size. A married couple with no kids would receive a $10,000 credit on its card. Each time the couple made a purchase, the smart card would deduct that amount until the card's $10,000 credit was used up. After the first $10,000 worth of purchases, the family would begin to pay the sales tax. Regardless of how the rebate is offered, the main point is that a sales tax need not be regressive.

What about the problem of evasion without a massive federal revenue collection police force? First, one virtue of the national sales tax is that forty-five states already have a sales tax. Hence, states could be made responsible for collecting the tax and most of the IRS could be dismantled. A small IRS enforcement force should be retained for the purpose of ensuring that states were collecting the tax. A national sales tax of 18 percent, when added to the existing states' sales taxes, would bring the total sales tax to between 20 and 25 percent. (Over time, as the economy expanded from this tax change, the rate could be lowered by 4 or 5 percentage points.)

Critics are right when they argue that a sales tax this high would encourage evasion. But evasion is already a large-scale problem with the income tax. An estimated $150 billion of income tax goes uncollected each year—according to the IRS's own calculations. Moreover, states report that their sales taxes are generally easier to collect than their income taxes.

Moreover, the sales tax may not stay at 18 percent for long. According to the Kotlikoff study, when accounting for the dynamic economic feedback effects of the sales tax, after about ten years of a consumption tax, the sales tax rate could be lowered by 2 to 3 percentage points because of higher wages and output. Hence, the rate would then be closer to 15 percent. More important, because of the high visibility of the sales tax, I believe there would be a positive public choice dynamic to this tax system. Americans would begin to demand less government because taxpayers could receive an immediate dividend from reductions in spending—via a reduction in the sales tax rate. Politicians could ask the voters: Which would you rather have, a Department of Energy or a 1 percentage point reduction in the national sales tax?

Finally, there is the very real concern voiced by many policy analysts that America will end up with *both* a sales tax and an income tax. This has been the experience with the consumption VATs in Europe. For this reason, some critics argue that the sales tax is only acceptable if the 16th Amendment to the Constitution authorizing a federal income tax were repealed. That would certainly be desirable but is not necessary. First, a condition of approval for the sales tax would be the outright repeal of all federal income taxes. To prevent the income tax from returning, a supermajority requirement to raise taxes would be ample protection against efforts to reintroduce the income tax.

Conclusion

Broad-based tax reform seems almost a political certainty over the next two years. The debate is being driven by concerns about the failure of the current tax system with respect to economic growth, simplicity, and intrusiveness. This chapter argues that only the national sales tax redresses each of these problems.

For tax reform to succeed, the reform proposal needs to be economically sensible and politically salable to the public. Economists and business lobbyists must recognize that tax reform will be driven not so much by the tax code's economic failings as by its civil liberties failings. The political appeal of the Armey flat tax is the postcard. The political appeal of the national sales tax is that it would no longer be the government's business how much money a person makes.

The populist appeal of the flat tax or the sales tax is clearly what is energizing the politics of the tax reform debate. The fix on the capital formation side is likely to occur only in the context of a plan that the public views as simpler and fairer than the current system.[21] For this reason, I believe that many of the reform ideas now in the mix will soon fall out of the picture and that the national debate will begin to revolve around just two proposals: the flat tax and the national sales tax. My preference is the sales tax, but either of these would be a vast improvement over the current system.

Notes

1. "Government: American's Number 1 Growth Industry," Institute for Policy Innovation, Lewisville, Tex., 1995.

2. Data from Tax Foundation, Washington, D.C., 1995.

3. Gary Robbins and Aldona Robbins, "Tax Fairness: Myth and Reality," National Center for Policy Analysis, Dallas, Tex., 1991; and Gary Robbins and Aldona Robbins, "Capital, Taxes, and Growth," National Center for Policy Analysis, Dallas, Tex., 1992.

4. Lawrence Lindsey, *The Growth Experiment* (New York: Basic Books, 1990), pp. 15–27.

5. Stephen Moore, "Weighing Reaganomics," *San Diego Union*, November 10, 1991, pp. C-1, C-4; and Lindsey, *The Growth Experiment*, pp. 82–104.

6. "Capital Punishment: How High Capital Gains Tax Rates Are Harming the Economy," Joint Economic Committee, 1993.

7. Robbins and Robbins, "Capital, Taxes, and Growth," 1992.

8. Robert Genetski, *Taking the Voo Doo Out of Economics* (Chicago: Regnery, 1986).

9. American Council for Capital Formation, Washington, D.C., 1991.

10. Data compiled by Merrill Lynch, 1995.

11. Dale Jorgenson, "Constructing an Agenda for U.S. Tax Reform," testimony before the Ways and Means Committee, U.S. House of Representatives, December 18, 1991.

12. Peter Meyer, "A Short History of Form 1040," *Harpers*, April 1977, p. 22.

13. Cited in Dan Pilla, *How to Fire the IRS* (Saint Paul, Minn.: Winning Publications, 1994).

14. Ibid.

15. James L. Payne, *Costly Returns: The Burden of the U.S. Tax System* (San Francisco, Calif.: Institute for Contemporary Studies, 1991), p. 21.

16. Stephen Moore, "Ax the Tax," *National Review*, April 17, 1995, pp. 38–43.

17. David Burnham, *A Law Unto Itself: Power, Politics and the IRS* (New York: Random

House, 1990); and Charles Adams, *For Good and Evil* (Washington, D.C.: University of America Press, 1992).

18. Grover Norquist, "Why the VAT is Bad," Americans for Tax Reform, Washington, D.C., 1994.

19. For a summary of the Armey plan, see Dick Armey, "The Freedom and Fairness Restoration Act," U.S. House of Representatives, Washington, D.C., 1994.

20. Laurence J. Kotlikoff, "The Economic Impact of Replacing the Federal Income Tax with a National Sales Tax," *Policy Analysis* (Cato Institute), April 15, 1993.

21. "Take Fairness Head-On," *Wall Street Journal*, April 14, 1995, editorial page.

PART THREE

EVALUATING TAX REFORM PROPOSALS

8

Consumption Taxes: Some Fundamental Transition Issues

DAVID F. BRADFORD

Introduction

Motivated by a desire to simplify compliance and improve incentives, there is currently interest once again in restructuring the U.S. tax system. Most of the proposed reforms would move toward a system based on consumption, rather than income. In this chapter I use *uniform* (single rate) consumption and income taxes to highlight certain central problems of transition and implementation that confront the reforms.

We may distinguish three consumption-oriented reform plans currently under discussion:

This is a revised version of a paper prepared for the Hoover Institution Conference on Frontiers of Tax Reform, Washington, D.C., May 11, 1995. While preparing this revision, I enjoyed the hospitality of the Economic Policy Research Unit at the Copenhagen Business School, where I especially benefited from discussions with Peter Birch Sorensen and Niels Frederiksen. I would also like to acknowledge, in particular, helpful exchanges of ideas with Louis Kaplow. Thanks, in addition, to Alan Auerbach, Michael Boskin, Dale Jorgenson, Laurence Kotlikoff, Stephen Moore, Rudolph Penner, Harvey Rosen, Robert Scarborough, Dan Shaviro, Joel Slemrod, Eric Toder, Murray Weidenbaum, and George Zodrow for very helpful comments. Finally, I would like to express my appreciation for the support of the John M. Olin Foundation and Princeton University's Woodrow Wilson School and Center for Economic Policy Studies for my research on transition and implementation issues. None of these organizations or individuals should be implicated in conclusions expressed herein.

- A retail sales tax, or a value-added tax
- A flat tax
- The unlimited savings allowance (USA) Tax

As far as I know, there has not yet been an actual legislative proposal for a federal sales tax, but Representative Bill Archer, chairman of the Ways and Means Committee of the House of Representatives, and Senator Richard Lugar have been notable supporters. There have been a number of value-added tax proposals, including a highly detailed plan introduced by Representative Samuel Gibbons. Representative Richard Armey is a particularly well-known advocate of a flat tax, although several others have advanced similar proposals. All of these are modeled on the flat tax developed by Robert Hall and Alvin Rabushka (1983, 1995), which I take as representative of the breed. The USA Tax, developed by Senators Pete Domenici and Sam Nunn, was introduced by them in April 1995.[1]

All three approaches would bring about a shift of the U.S. tax system to a consumption base. In terms of implementation, they have certain features in common. The first approach, a retail sales tax, is a proportional tax paid by businesses. The second and third, the flat tax and the USA Tax, both consist of integrated systems. Each uses a proportional tax paid by businesses, more or less similar to a value-added tax, and a personal-level tax, along the lines of the existing individual income tax. In the case of the flat tax, the individual tax is imposed only on a person's compensation, such as wages and salary, which is deducted from the base of the business tax. The individual-level tax in the USA system is an example of what has come to be called a "consumed income" tax. That is to say, it is based on something like the present taxable income with a deduction for net saving (and inclusion of net dissaving). In the USA system, there is no deduction from the business tax base for payments to individuals (although there is a coordinated set of credits for payroll taxes).

All three systems are conceived of as replacements for the federal income tax, both corporate and individual. In addition, the USA Tax integrates the Social Security taxes through a system of credits.

It would be a considerable task just to describe these three alternatives, let alone to develop in any detail the problems of transition to each of them. Instead, I have set myself the goal of identifying and highlighting certain generic problems of transition that they confront. For this purpose, I study the problem of making a transition from a *uniform* income tax to a *uniform* consumption tax in order to

- Explain how the problem of taxing "old savings" or "old capital" manifests itself in the shift from an income to a consumption base
- Indicate the trade-offs that must be confronted in dealing with this phenomenon

- Show how price-level changes that may or may not accompany a transition affect the distribution of gains and losses
- Sketch out how a transition might affect interest rates and asset prices (including owner-occupied housing)
- Explore the case in equity for protecting the tax-free recovery of old savings
- Emphasize the incentive problems that arise if savers and investors anticipate a change in the tax rate in a consumption-based system (a transition from a zero to some positive rate on introduction is a particularly important instance)

In focusing on this "pure" case, I give short shrift to many important questions. Thus I do not discuss the treatment in transition of unrealized capital gains, business assets with basis less than market value, undistributed corporate earnings and profits, accumulated tax-deferred pension claims, unused tax credits, or tax-exempt bonds. I have also decided, in the interest of simplicity, to take up the case of a closed economy, putting to one side the treatment of imports and exports, transfer pricing, and international capital flows. All these matters are important, but the issues they raise are in addition to the ones addressed here.

Furthermore, in examining issues of transition, I do not go into the question of how to measure the degree of progressivity of the tax system or how much progressivity there should be. As a proportional tax, a retail sales tax, thought of in isolation from other tax and transfer changes that might be introduced at the same time, would be less progressive than the existing income tax. The flat tax, as usually specified, would be progressive. On a "static" basis, depending on the details of rate and exemptions (and assuming the continuation of the earned-income credit), it would probably impose lower burdens on poor and well-to-do families and somewhat higher burdens on the middle of the distribution. Its advocates would, however, claim that the positive economic effects of adopting such a system would lead to after-tax gains throughout the income distribution. At the tax rates included in the legislative draft, on a static basis, the USA Tax is claimed to be at least as progressive as the existing system.

These characteristics relate to the reforms as ongoing systems. My focus is on what happens to whom in getting from here to there. In the process I mention some of the major arguments in favor or against various policies. These are included to put issues in context, not to advocate one position or another.

A final prefatory matter: There is by now a considerable body of literature addressing the effects of time-varying tax policy, including transitions of the sort considered here. These analyses are complementary to my undertaking, which attempts both less, in raising but leaving open the answers to questions about the quantitative effects of policy changes, and more, in addressing aspects of transition on which the models to date are largely silent. For excellent examples of the more technically detailed models, see Auerbach and Kotlikoff (1983, 1987), Howitt and Sinn (1989), Keuschnigg (1991), and, especially, Sarkar and Zodrow (1993).

The chapter is organized as follows: In the first section, I specify uniform consumption and income taxes, implemented at the level of the business firm. The second section describes the main transition issues, and the third section addresses possible ways of dealing with them. In the fourth section, I touch on some of the arguments that go to the merits of seeking to moderate transition effects. The final section contains brief concluding remarks.

Uniform Consumption and Income Taxes

UNIFORM TAXES IMPLEMENTED AT THE BUSINESS LEVEL

As I have suggested, all three of the reform models bring about a switch to a consumption base. To set up the discussion of the issues of transition to *uniform* (single rate) versions of income and consumption taxes, I start with the description of how such taxes might be administered at the level of the business firm.

Many people are familiar with the idea that a consumption tax can be administered as a tax paid by businesses. Indeed, a retail sales or value-added tax is often identified with "consumption tax." The idea that an income tax could be administered in much the same way is less familiar. In this section I first lay out a *subtraction-method value-added tax of the consumption type* as the archetype of a consumption tax. I then explain how one can implement a uniform accretion-income value-added tax and use the two models to investigate the basic transition issues.

A Value-Added Tax of the Consumption Type. The building block of a value-added tax is the business firm subject to tax. The definition of business firm is a matter for policy, but typically it would not distinguish among businesses according to legal form. In particular, there would normally be no difference between the treatment of corporations and that of other businesses, such as partnerships or proprietorships.

Under a subtraction method of implementing a value-added tax, the tax base of a firm consists of the difference between the payments received for sales of all kinds of goods and services and the purchases of goods and services from other firms. This total is subjected to tax at some fixed rate. That is it. In the ordinary case, financial transactions, such as borrowing and lending, issue and repurchase of stock, payments and receipts of dividends, and the like, do not enter the calculation of the taxable base.[2] (There are some interesting questions about how to distinguish a financial from a real transaction. For example, is the purchase of a piece of paper giving rights to use a trademark a financial or a real transaction? Financial institutions also present special problems. I neglect these issues in this chapter.)

Because what is sold by one business to another results in an increase in the tax base of the selling firm and a deduction *at the same time and in exactly the same amount* by the purchasing firm, and because both are subject to tax at the same rate, transactions between businesses give rise to no net tax liability to the government.[3] The only circumstance under which a net tax liability is created is when there is a sale by a business to "the public" or, more precisely, to a person or organization that is not a business firm subject to tax. At that point there is no deduction taken to offset the tax paid by the seller. The aggregate business tax base is thus the aggregate of sales by business to nonbusiness, which is a measure of aggregate consumption.

From this description it is evident that the subtraction-method value-added tax of the consumption type gives rise to exactly the same flow of revenues as would a tax on sales by businesses to nonbusinesses. This describes a form of retail sales tax. The two taxes would be in effect identical if the definition of sales subject to tax were the same (for example, both including, or not, sales of clothing or medical services).

A value-added tax is sometimes described as a tax levied at each successive level of production. As applied to a uniform tax of the kind I have just sketched out, this is actually a somewhat misleading characterization, inasmuch as any sale from one level of the production process that is subject to tax gives rise to an *immediate* offsetting deduction from the base of the firm at the next level of the production process. There really is no tax until the last stage of the process, the sale to the public.

The description also makes clear that, *provided the rate of tax is the same*, a value-added tax of the subtraction type is exactly equivalent to a value-added tax of the invoice-and-credit type. This is the type of tax employed in European systems. Under the invoice-and-credit method, the selling firm pays a tax on all sales, noting the amount of tax on the sales invoice. A taxable firm making a purchase is allowed a credit against tax liability of the amount shown on the invoice. A sale from one business to another thus gives rise to *simultaneous* payment of tax by the seller and equal credit taken against the tax by the buyer. There is no net tax paid to the government until the point of sale to a buyer other than a taxable firm. The invoice-and-credit method value-added tax thus gives rise to exactly the same flow of revenues to the government as does a subtraction-method value-added tax or a retail sales tax, with the *proviso*, again, that the same goods and services are subject to tax at the same rate.

A contrast is often drawn between a sales tax or a value-added tax of the invoice-and-credit type, each of which is said to be a "transactions tax," and an income tax or subtraction-method value-added tax. It is apparently thought that the former are accounted for on a transaction-by-transaction basis, whereas the latter are aggregated. In fact, to implement an income tax or a subtraction-method value-added tax, it is necessary to track individual transactions, just as it is in the other methods. An additional sale is punched into the cash register and adds to the tax base in all of these taxes. In an income tax it may be necessary to do more than simply add and subtract transactions. For example, the purchase of an asset is added to the depreciation basis of a company and then deducted over a period of years. But all these taxes are transaction based. As far as the value-added taxes are concerned, given equally effective enforcement, all economic effects, including the revenue flows, from the subtraction and invoice-and-credit methods of implementation should be the same.[4]

It is sometimes asserted that a value-added tax is the same as a tax on all the payments to factors of production, that is, wages, salaries, and profits. Whether or not this is so depends on how one defines these terms. The term *profit*, in particular, as used by accountants, although not always as used by economists, includes the normal return to the capitalist for waiting and taking risks. The return for taking risks is taxed in the same way under both income and consumption-type value-added taxes. The normal return for waiting is subjected to tax in an income-type value-added tax but not in a value-added tax of the consumption type. This is the result of the way capital purchased by firms is treated. In the value-added tax, outlays by a business for investment purposes, to add to inventory, for example, or to add to the stock of buildings or fixed equipment, are deducted immediately. If the investment is successful, it will generate future tax liabilities in excess of the tax saved by virtue of the current deduction. For an investment that is barely worth undertaking, the combination of the current tax saving and the future extra tax will have a market value of zero. (More conventionally if less precisely put, the expected net present discounted value of the combination is zero.) It is in this sense that a value-added tax of the consumption type may be said to exempt the income from capital. For what economists call an "extramarginal" investment, that is, an investment opportunity that will beat the market, the tax is positive. (More precisely, the anticipated distribution of cash flows to the government is one that would have a positive value in the capital market.)

By contrast, under an income tax, the deduction of the investment outlay is postponed. Conceptually, it is recovered as the value of the asset is depleted. This timing difference means that the cash flow to the government associated with an investment that is a barely breakeven proposition will have a positive market value.

There are various ways to express what it is that is exempt from tax in the case of the consumption-type tax. One way is as the yield on a riskless investment, typically taken to be the Treasury bill rate. A value-added tax of the consumption type allows investors to get the Treasury bill rate on riskless investments free of tax. A riskless rate of return in excess of this rate is taxed. A riskless rate of return below the market rate is, in effect, compensated with reduced tax. By contrast, under a true income tax, returns in excess of zero are taxed. To put this in quantitative perspective, the real riskless rate of return available to a tax-exempt investor has historically been less than one percent a year.[5]

The treatment of the reward to bearing risk requires some analysis. Most assets do not have a risk-free return. Even Treasury bills suffer from the risk of unpredictable inflation. The average real rate of return available to a tax-exempt investor in the stock market has historically been about 9 percent a year.[6] This higher average return is bought at the price of substantial risk. Can one also say that under a consumption-type tax, the investor obtains the reward to risk taking free of tax?

The answer is a qualified yes, but this is also the answer to the same question with regard to an income tax. This point is, I think, not widely understood, probably because we are accustomed to seeing risk and waiting intertwined.[7] Under a uniform proportional income tax, a pure bet that does not involve time is shared with the tax collector on fair terms, through the allowance for losses.[8] If there is a risk premium, a uniform tax will have positive expected revenue but will not impose a burden on the investor. The positive expected revenue is the risk premium collected by the government for assuming part of the risk, via the tax system. The same result is obtained under a consumption-type tax, except that the cash flow to the government may not be simultaneous with the outcome of risk taking, so the argument needs to take into account discounting for differences in timing. Essentially, an income tax and a consumption tax treat risk the same. Under both systems, any positive expected revenue is the market-determined reward for the risk that the government takes and is not a burden to the taxed investor.

Under either form of tax, if it is administered at the business level, the government's risk premium is extracted ahead of the cash flow to the investor. Thus, we would expect the stock market to display more risk and a higher risk premium in a system that taxes the payoff to investment at the individual level than it does in one that collects the tax at the firm level. The net effect should, however, be the same.

Like an income tax, a value-added tax of the consumption type *does* subject to tax much of what is regarded as "profit" in ordinary parlance. If a business enterprise discovers oil on its property, all the payoff is subjected to tax, as is the reward to an innovation, such as the development of a successful software product, or to "intangible property," such as the value of a trademark established through a successful advertising campaign. Through the device of the value-added tax of the consumption type, the general public becomes a proportional shareholder in all enterprises.[9] If the payoff exceeds the normal rate of return (risk adjusted), the general public shares in the good fortune. If the payoff falls short, the general public, having "invested" via the deduction for investment outlays, shares in the shortfall.

It is also often said that a value-added tax of the consumption type is equivalent to a tax on wages or a tax on labor income. Again, whether this is so depends on one's definition of the terms *wages* or *labor income*. The payoff to the oil gusher or the successful advertising campaign or the development of Microsoft DOS might not be regarded as wages or labor income in ordinary parlance, but they are subject to a value-added tax of the consumption type.

As the discussion above of the effective taxation of risk bearing suggests, in either case the tax may or may not represent a burden. We may think of the activity of an individual entrepreneur or firm as one of selection from "ideas" that arise, perhaps randomly or perhaps as a result of investment of funds and effort. The unprofitable ideas are rejected. Those that are accepted are believed to be, at least, breakeven propositions in the sense that the associated distribution of cash flows will have a market value of at least zero. Both consumption tax and income tax systems will place a burden on profitable ideas. The resulting incentive effects will depend on the details of the process by which ideas are generated.[10] To the extent that oil gushers and the like represent just the upside of investments that were expected to produce the risk-adjusted market rate of return, the positive revenue in a consumption-type system is just the market-determined reward to the to the government (i.e., other taxpayers) for taking on risk. Under a true income tax there is, in any case, a burden put on postponement of consumption, as reflected in the risk-free real interest rate; in the same sense, a disinvestment project is subsidized.

A value-added tax of the income type.   It would be possible to administer a value-added tax of the *income type* as a uniform tax on business accretion income. (Although it was not called a value-added tax, just such a scheme was worked out by the U.S. Treasury in 1992.) To do so would require substituting accretion income for cash-flow accounting by the firm. The accounting system would be more or less the familiar financial accounting system used now to track the fortunes of companies (although it would properly incorporate systematic correction for inflation). An income statement should report the change in the firm's *net worth* during the year. When a firm acquires a unit of capital equipment, it exchanges one asset (money in the bank) for another (the piece of equipment). If the investment is a wise one and expected in the capital market, there is no change in the value of the firm. Thus, such outlays are capitalized for purposes of income accounting, which means they are not deducted currently. By contrast, over time a typical piece of equipment declines in value. It is necessary to account for this value change in the income statement, even though it does not correspond to any current cash flow. The accountants, then, take depreciation charges against current income. Similarly, for goods acquired to add to inventory, the outlay does not reflect any change in net worth. The accountants, therefore, employ methods to keep track of when inventory is actually incorporated into goods and services sold by the firm. Their cost is "recovered" in the deduction for the cost of goods sold. Note that there is an inevitable arbitrariness in associating some past outlays with current receivables, which is why, for example, accountants distinguish operating costs from overhead. This is one of many problems in pinning down accounting concepts for income purposes that do not arise in the cash-flow accounting system appropriate for taxing on the basis of consumption.

The essential difference between accrual income accounting and cash-flow accounting is a matter of timing. A tax based on the *income* of a firm would be based on the difference between amounts receivable from sales and a measure of the firm's costs that included the appropriate recovery of past outlays on equipment, inventories, and the like. If the sale is to another business, the purchasing business has a deduction in its income calculation that will generally be *less* than the inclusion for the selling firm. This is because the purchaser will have to capitalize some of the outlay, to be recovered in its income calculations in the future.

There is a sense in which a true income tax, by contrast with a subtraction-method value-added tax, *would* effect a tax at each stage of production. The point is most easily understood if we think about each "stage of production" as if it were carried out by a separate firm. (Strictly speaking, the flow of revenue to the government from a true income tax should not depend on the timing of transactions at all. The income calculation would be based on accruing gains and losses, which are theoretically independent of the timing of transactions.) The aggregate amount subject to tax would roughly equal the difference between the value of the goods and services sold and the *discounted value* of the future deductions by purchasing firms in the form of depreciation allowances and other forms of cost recovery. The aggregate of the taxable incomes of all the firms would equal the sum of the sales to the public and the net increase in the stock of capitalized past outlays in the hands of the firms. We have identified the former as aggregate consumption, and the latter (which could be negative) is a measure of the increase in aggregate net worth, or *saving*.[11] (The tax calculation of a vertically integrated company, combining several stages of production, should theoretically lead to the same result.)[12]

There are several reasons for going through this exercise. The first is simply to emphasize the role of timing. The distinction between an income tax and a consumption tax is essentially a matter of timing—the time value of money. (In both systems there is recovery of the costs of production, but it comes earlier under a consumption tax.) A second reason is to demonstrate that one could use an indirect tax to implement a *uniform* income tax, just as one is accustomed to thinking one can use such a system to impose a uniform consumption tax.[13] A third reason is to call attention to the important differences in accounting. Income accounting is much more difficult to do well than cash-flow accounting, and the difficulty is responsible for much complexity in the present income tax. (This is a major theme of Bradford 1986.) A fourth reason is to draw attention to the logic behind the fact that under an income tax at any given time a company has a stock of past outlays that may be thought of as an accumulation of tax-prepaid claims on consumption in the future. These claims, represented by basis in the company's assets, belong to the company's owners. This assumes great significance in any transition from an income- to a consumption-based tax system.

Owner-occupied housing under consumption and income taxes.   The income tax in the United States exempts the yield from investment in household capital, by which I mean durables such automobiles, boats, washing machines, electronic equipment, and the like. Quantitatively the most important example is owner-occupied housing (including second homes). To capture such capital in an income tax would involve treating the household as in the business of selling to itself the services of these investments. Because the income tax does not attempt to do this, it puts such forms of investment at an advantage, relative to ordinary business capital.

One of the features of consumption-based taxes that makes them appeal to economists is that they could, in a simple way, tax household capital on an even plane with business capital. (See, for example, Jorgenson 1995.) This result would obtain not by setting up the household as a business under a value-added tax of the subtraction type but by leaving these implicit businesses out of the set of firms subject to tax. The advantage for these implicit firms is that they are not subject to tax on their implicit sales (for example, the sale of housing services by owner occupiers to themselves). The disadvantage is that they are not eligible to deduct (in the case of the invoice-and-credit approach, obtain credit for the taxes paid on) their purchases. With a taxable business, the general public shares in the investment and payoffs in proportion to the tax rate. In making investment decisions, the taxable firm considers its share. For a tax-exempt household "business," the general public does not share in the investment or the return. The investment decision is based on the full cost and the full return. The breakeven requirement will be the same for a taxable and a tax-exempt business.

If the sale of housing is treated like all other sales under a subtraction-method value-added tax, it will remove the tax advantage that owner-occupied housing enjoys under the income tax.[14] A question of some interest is what this change will imply for the value of existing houses. I take up this question below.

ALLOCATING CONSUMPTION OR
INCOME BASES TO INDIVIDUALS

Deducting wages from a subtraction-method value-added tax. Little would be changed if the subtraction-method value-added tax were amended to permit companies to deduct the amounts paid out to employees, provided the payments to workers were subject to tax at the same rate. The same cash flows to the government would result, and we would predict the economic effects to be identical. More generally, the payments to workers might be subject to tax at a different rate or according to a graduated rate schedule. If the schedule consists of an exempt amount plus a single rate for amounts above the exempt amount (the same single rate as applies to firms), this produces the flat tax.

Deducting wages and interest from a value-added tax of the income type. Similarly, little would be changed if companies were allowed to deduct interest paid to creditors, as well as amounts paid out to employees, under the value-added tax of the income type, again provided the rate of tax applicable to these income recipients were the same as the business-level tax. Apart from graduated rates, this is a rough approximation of the way the combination of corporate and individual income taxes works. Actually, *caricature* might be the better word. As long as the same rate applies to the deduction by the firm and inclusion in taxable income of the bondholder, the combination has no real significance. It is not identical to measuring the accretion income of bondholders, nor does it bring with it all of the complexity that such measurement implies, such as distinguishing between interest payments and accruing interest income. It is a simple reassignment, from the company to the bondholders, of the responsibility for given tax payments.

We would expect bondholders to require compensation for taking over the obligation to pay the taxes; thus the stated interest rate will be different when interest is deductible than when it is not. When there is no tax at the bondholder level, the bondholder receives an after-tax interest rate; with the other treatment of interest, the stated rate will be the before-tax rate.

I introduce the possibility of deducting interest and taxing it at the bondholder level because the commitment to make interest payments according to a fixed contract creates an important transition problem that is taken up below.

Transition Issues

One of the critical characteristics of any tax system is its pattern of incidence, particularly its degree of progressivity. The general subject of distributional analysis is beyond the scope of this chapter. There is, however, typically a cross-cutting set of incidence issues with which we are concerned here raised by any major change in policy. One way to come to grips with issues of transition is to suppose that we have been operating for a long time with a value-added tax of the income type and contemplate switching to a value-added tax of the consumption type. The analysis can, in turn, be broken down into the effect of introducing the value-added tax of the consumption type and the effect of eliminating the income tax. To start with, I focus on the cases with no allocation of cash flow or income payments to individuals.

INTRODUCING A VALUE-ADDED TAX
OF THE CONSUMPTION TYPE

I find a concrete example helpful in sorting out transition issues. My preferred example is of a retail store whose owners have purchased, on the day before the value-added tax is introduced, a stock of canned goods for $10,000. They sell the goods the day after the value-added tax is introduced. To focus on the key issues, assume that they have no other transactions. In calculating the business's value-added tax liability, the proceeds from the sale of the canned goods are on the inclusion side of the ledger. But because there was no outlay for the goods sold during the period (the inventory purchase was in the previous period), there is no offsetting deduction. The effect is a one-time tax, at the value-added tax rate, on the stock of inventory at the time of transition.

This little story captures the essence of the way imposition of a consumption-type tax, with no special transition rules, would impose a one-time tax on the stock of wealth in the economy, so-called old capital or old savings. In the example, the extra tax on the stock of inventory was imposed immediately because the goods were sold to the public on day one of the new system. In actuality, the tax payments that effect the one-time tax would take place over time, for example, over the lifetime of a piece of fixed equipment. But the discounted present value of the extra tax imposed is the same as if the assets were sold immediately to the public (provided the tax rate is constant).

Most people who have an ownership interest in a business have it indirectly, via stock in corporations. Even the ownership of stock may be indirect. For example, it may be via a claim on a defined-contribution pension plan, the assets of which are held in the form of stock. The imposition of a value-added tax of the consumption type would be predicted to generate a fall in the market value of stock commensurate with the extra one-time tax liability. I use the term *commensurate* because one critical aspect of the path of adjustment—the impact of the policy change on the general level of prices—will have a large effect on the transition incidence.

Price-level changes. It is conventional wisdom that, on its introduction, companies will "pass forward" a value-added tax in the form of higher prices. It is important to recognize that whether or not this occurs (a) is not a matter that is settled by well-developed theory and (b) does not affect the one-time wealth tax in the aggregate, although it may affect its distribution. In a competitive economy a value-added tax of the consumption type must be extracted from the difference between the value of goods sold by companies and what they pay to noncompany suppliers, which we may here take to be workers. That much is clear. Whether, however, a newly introduced tax leads to an increase in the prices of things sold or a decrease in the wages of workers is not well determined. It will depend on the institutions of wage and price setting and on monetary policy. It is commonly believed, however, that introducing a value-added tax of the consumption type will bring with it a monetary policy adjustment that would result in a one-time increase in the price level (not a change in the *rate* of inflation) and no change in payments to workers in *nominal* terms (so that, before taking into account any offsetting reduction in income taxation, nominal wages are unchanged, but *real* wages of workers decline by the amount of the tax). By contrast, it is generally thought that introducing a tax levied on the earnings of workers will lead to a decrease in their take-home pay and no change in the prices charged by companies. The real result for workers is the same.

If there *is* a change in the price level, and if this change in price level has not been anticipated and therefore built into transactions expressed in dollar terms (for example, through an adjustment in interest rates), then introducing the value-added tax of the consumption type will bring about a redistribution of wealth from lenders to borrowers, through a decline of the real value of the dollar.

Leverage and the wealth tax effect. That the matter is of some importance, and that policy makers might want to encourage such an "accommodating" monetary policy, is suggested by considering the situation of the business owners who have financed the acquisition of business assets by issuing debt with fixed nominal terms. In my earlier example, suppose the store's owners have borrowed the $10,000 to buy the inventory of canned goods, expecting to sell the goods the next day for a little more than $10,000 and repay the loan. (Interest on the loan is not important in this very short-term transaction.) If, in the meantime, the value-added tax has been introduced, *and* there is no change in the price level, the owners of the inventory will suffer a loss equal to the tax rate times $10,000 even though they have no net wealth at all. The lender who holds the $10,000 note, who does have some wealth, will experience no loss.

By contrast, if the price level increases by the amount of the tax, the owners of the inventory will suffer no loss; they will have $10,000 left after tax with which to repay the loan. Instead, the transition loss will be borne by the lender via the erosion of the purchasing power of the $10,000. (There would be, in addition, the usual distributional effects of inflation on fixed-income recipients, for example, or on holders of currency. See Browning 1978.)

Translating this story to the stock market, we would expect the transition loss to be spread equally across the debt and equity claims to companies if the transition brings with it an unexpected one-time increase in the price level. Equities would keep their market value but lose in real value a proportion equal to the tax rate, and the same would be true of nominally denominated assets and liabilities. At the other polar case of no adjustment in the price level (*polar case* is a somewhat misleading term here; anything could happen), nominally denominated assets and liabilities would keep their real value and the entire loss, of the tax rate times the sum of debt and equity value, would be borne by equity holders. For a company for which equity constitutes a fraction e of the value of the company's assets, the implied percentage decline in value of the shares would be t/e, where t is the value-added tax rate. For a sufficiently leveraged firm ($e < t$), the transition incidence would imply bankruptcy! (Howitt and Sinn 1989). (Note that, if everyone holds the market portfolio of all financial instruments, the effect of price level change is neutralized.)

A tax on the elderly?.   An important question is who are the owners of assets who would bear the cost of transition to a consumption-type tax (barring special provisions to mitigate the effect)? As has just been emphasized, the impact of the transition will depend both on the extent to which it is accompanied by price level changes *and* on the composition of people's portfolios (especially the division between nominal and real assets and liabilities). It is generally assumed that the impact will be roughly proportional to wealth (that is, either wealth owners have similar portfolios or there is an unanticipated price-level adjustment). Apart from knowing that the distribution of wealth ownership is highly skewed, with a large fraction of wealth owned by a relatively small fraction of the population, we also know that, owing to life-cycle factors in the process of accumulation, wealth is also correlated with age. This means that the policy regarding transition to a consumption-type tax should be thought about in the framework of intergenerational distribution. Many commentators (in particular, Kotlikoff [1992] and Auerbach, Gokhale, and Kotlikoff [1993]) have noted the tendency of fiscal policy in the United States over the past thirty years to shift the net burden of financing the government away from older and toward younger and future generations. To the extent this tendency describes fundamental political factors, it would suggest we should expect to see any transition to a consumption-type tax accompanied by rules that would protect the interests of older generations. To the extent there is a movement toward readjusting the fiscal balance (arguably, the proper economic interpretation of deficit reduction), we might expect to see a transition to a consumption-type tax taken as an opportunity to lighten the projected burdens of young and future generations.

The effect on the analysis of taxing wages at the level of the worker. If we modify the example to permit companies a deduction for wages, there will be a change in the locus of tax payments—the bulk of tax collections will be from workers, rather than businesses—but, from a formal point of view, none of the issues discussed above will be affected. I use the word *formal* advisedly because it is commonly believed that workers are likely to resist changes in their before-tax wages. If before-tax wages are fixed and wages are not allowed as a deduction, then the price level must increase to accommodate the tax.

If wages are allowed as a deduction (and taxed at the worker level), holding constant the level of wages before tax means a reduction in wages after tax. In that case, there would be no adjustment in the price level necessary to establish equilibrium in the relationship between prices and wages.

ELIMINATING A VALUE-ADDED TAX OF THE INCOME TYPE

Our idealized tax reform involves introduction of a consumption-type tax and elimination of an income-type tax, represented in the present analysis by a value-added tax of the income type. Under a value-added tax of the income type, the yield on business investment is taxed, at the value-added tax rate, at the business level. In the pure case, there is no tax at the individual level. Interest (along with other forms of reward to owners of capital) is "pretaxed" at the company level. (This is the scheme outlined in the U.S. Treasury's Comprehensive Business Income Tax Plan [1992].) In an equilibrium with a value-added tax of the income type, the interest rate on financial assets would equal the *after-tax* rate of return on investment. This is in contrast to the result when interest is deducted by business borrowers and taxed in the hands of the individual. In that case, the interest rate tends to equality with the before-tax rate of return on business investment.

Under a value-added tax of the consumption type, changes in the tax rate (for example, from zero to a positive rate at the time of introduction of the tax) produce changes in the value of a company, along the lines just discussed. By contrast, under an income-type tax, with proper accounting rules, changes in the rate of tax do not produce changes in the market value of assets. (The qualification "with proper accounting rules" is important. Technically, what is required is that the basis of assets be equal to their market value. With accelerated depreciation, for example, the basis will be less than market value. In that case, a decline in the income tax rate produces an increase in a company's value because of the reduction in the tax liability that will come due when the difference between the asset's basis and its market value is realized in future transactions.)

Consequently, the transition issues raised by a switch from a pure value-added tax of the income type to a pure value-added tax of the consumption type are the same as those involved in introducing value-added tax from a situation with no tax.

THE EFFECT OF A REGIME SHIFT ON INTEREST RATES
AND ASSET PRICES

Thus far I have focused on transition effects apart from impacts on relative prices. Among the most important of the latter is the interest rate and its correlative, asset prices. Changes of policy of the magnitude under consideration here might be expected to produce significant changes in these. Unfortunately, asset price effects are hard to predict, yet they may constitute an important part of the transition story. Because my objective is to lay out issues, not necessarily to resolve them, I sketch out here the implications of what might be taken to be the polar possibilities. At one extreme is the "infinite elasticity of demand for capital" assumption that the opportunities to invest at the going rate of return are unlimited within the relevant range. Such an assumption would be reasonable for a small economy open to the world capital market. This possibility is modeled as a fixed before-tax rate of return on investment. At the other extreme is the "infinite elasticity of supply of capital" assumption that the amount of wealth people are willing to hold at the going rate of return to savers is unlimited within the relevant range. This assumption can be justified on the basis of very long life-cycle or dynastic purposes of saving (Summers 1981). It is modeled as a fixed after-tax rate of return to savers.

An additional behavioral or technological feature of importance is the cost of adjustment. Here the question can be thought of as whether owners of existing capital have a temporary advantage over potential competitors for investment opportunities when interest rates fall. In this case, the incumbents can earn supernormal profits during an adjustment period during which new assets are constructed. If new assets can be put in place instantaneously, with no extra cost, the price of existing assets will equal their replacement cost, regardless of interest-rate changes. If, as is certainly the case to some degree, expanding the capital stock quickly brings with it extra costs, owners of existing assets will reap a capital gain upon a change that leads to a higher level of the capital stock.

The opposite effect applies to owners of assets for which adjustment requires a fall in the stock. This might be the case for assets that are favored by the existing tax law. Under a true, uniform income tax, all assets are treated alike. We would then expect a shift to a new regime to call for expansion or contraction of all asset stocks. But under the actual income tax, some assets are more lightly taxed than others, and a shift to a uniform consumption-type tax that might call forth an expansion of regular business investment might involve contraction in the stocks of formerly tax-favored assets. Adjustment cost in this case refers to the time required to work off an excess in the supply of an asset type, relative to that justified by the costs of reproduction. The practical case of such an asset of most importance is owner-occupied housing, which I discuss further below.[15]

In view of the influence of such assumptions on the results, the analysis here can only indicate the nature of transition problems and does not substitute for quantitative modeling.

Interest Rates. If adjustment costs were zero, eliminating a uniform business tax on accretion income would not change business asset prices, except insofar as they reflected any transition wealth tax. The policy change could, however, lead to a change in the rate of interest received by savers. At the one pole is an unchanged rate of return on investment before tax. Because the tax being eliminated was paid at the business level, competition would drive up the rate of interest by the amount of the former tax. The interest rate net of tax would therefore rise by the amount of the former income tax rate, providing wealth owners with a higher yield. At the other pole is an unchanged rate of interest net of tax, the case of an "infinitely elastic" supply of capital. In this case the market rate of interest would be unchanged, but expansion of the capital stock would drive down the rate of return on investment by the amount of the former tax. Wealth holders would see no change in the yield on their holdings. If interest were taxed at the level of the recipient, rather than at the level of the paying firm, the outcomes would be the same, but because the market rate of interest would then be a before-tax rate, the description would need to be revised accordingly.

Concentrating on the case of no change in the before-tax yield on investment, we see that the higher rate of return works to compensate wealth holders for the loss imposed on the transition to a consumption-type tax. Whether a particular wealth holder gains or loses depends critically on the planned timing of consumption. For people who are planning to draw down their wealth in the near future, even a very large increase in the rate of return will not compensate for the one-time loss. For people who are planning to defer consumption for a long time, the one-time wealth loss will be more than made up by the increased yield.[16]

The analysis of these polar cases establishes several points:

- In general, imposition of a consumption-type tax will cause a one-time loss to owners of certain assets. The loss will be spread over all wealth owners to the extent the transition is accompanied by an unanticipated increase in the price level.

- Substitution of a consumption-type tax for an income-type tax may bring with it a higher after-tax yield to holders of wealth.

- A higher yield is a compensating factor for a transition wealth loss, but the offset depends on the consumption plans of the holders. Those planning a long postponement will gain. Those planning near-term consumption will lose. If there is no increase in the yield on wealth, there is no compensating offset to the loss of wealth on transition.

- There is thus a considerable range of outcomes possible, depending in particular on the response of the rate of return on saving to the change in policy and on the distribution of preferences in the wealth-holding population. Empirical research will be required to draw more specific conclusions.

Owner-occupied housing. A person in the business of renting housing would face the same one-time asset tax effect of a transition to a consumption tax as would one in any other business. So would a person in the business of building houses for sale who has a stock of houses in inventory. By sharp contrast, real assets in the hands of households, including consumer durables and inventories of goods, as well as houses for personal use, are not subject to the one-time tax. The builder's houses in inventory and the owner-occupier's house would compete in the same market and would therefore sell for the same price. But the builder would have to pay tax on the ultimate sale of the houses, whereas the owner-occupier would not.

There is a second possible impact of reform that might affect the price of houses. Under the existing income tax, investment in owner-occupied housing is favored, relative to ordinary business investment. Under a consumption tax, the two forms of investment would be treated equivalently. If that means the required rate of return on owner-occupied housing increases, a downward adjustment in the stock of housing may be called forth. In connection with the discussion of business capital above, the case of no adjustment costs was highlighted. In that case, the stock of business capital is assumed to adjust so that all forms of investment have the same yield at the margin (the going interest rate). The corresponding assumption for owner-occupied housing would lead to the same result: the value of the stock of housing would not be affected by any change in the interest rate brought about by the shift in tax regime.

To illustrate the effect of positive adjustment costs, suppose the stock of housing in the income tax era is adjusted to yield the after-tax risk-free interest rate of 1.5 percent when the market risk-free interest rate, before tax, is 2 percent. Owner-occupied housing will attract investment until its yield, which is exempt from tax, is 1.5 percent. The regime shift produces a decline in the market interest rate to, say, 1.75 percent as a result of an expansion of saving and capital accumulation. To get to a yield of 1.75 percent on the margin in housing investment requires a downward adjustment in the stock of housing. We might expect such a downward adjustment to take time, which is to say to involve adjustment costs. In this case the regime shift would have a depressing effect on housing prices and result in losses to owners of housing capital.

THE EFFECT ON THE ANALYSIS OF TAXING WAGES AND INTEREST AT THE INDIVIDUAL LEVEL

A simplified version of a shift to consumption-type tax from something like the present tax system would involve a change from an income-type tax with a deduction at the level of the firm for interest payments and wage payments (and taxation, at the same rate, at the level of wage and interest recipients) to a consumption-type tax at the business level with no deduction for interest (or taxation of interest received) and possibly no deduction for wages (and in that case, no taxation of wages received). I have argued that the equilibrium results obtained should not depend on the level (payer or recipient) at which interest or wages is taxed. The alternative tax treatments will be reflected in compensating differences in the terms of the transactions between payers and recipients. There is, however, a potential transition problem posed by contracts entered into in one tax regime that are to be carried out in the other.

Starting with a system that taxes interest and wage payments at the level of the individual implies the existence of commitments, fixed for some period of time, that will incorporate the expectations of the parties about the tax treatment of the payments. Consider first the case in which the shift to a consumption-type tax is *not* accompanied by a change in the general price level. Then, during the period covered by the contractual commitment, the interest recipient or wage recipient under a contract made before the change will gain and the payer will lose. The gains and losses will be simply the amount of the tax.

Alternatively, if there is a one-time price-level change in connection with the introduction of the consumption-type tax, the purchasing power of the recipient who no longer pays tax will be the same as before the change. The transition problem is thus linked to the price-level determination.

It may be reasonable to single out interest commitments in this regard as being fixed for a longer term than is likely in other contracts and, perhaps, as being less amenable to renegotiation. (In a sense, most employment contracts are in a continual process of renegotiation.) But the difference is one of degree.

Moderating Transition Incidence Effects

At the business level two points at which special transition rules would seem likely are the basis in assets and liabilities and the commitments to interest with a presumption of deductibility established before the shift in regimes. The more generous the allowances, the less the potential loss from transition, at a cost in terms of the revenue that must be made up in a higher tax rate in the new system.

PROVIDING FOR BASIS IN BUSINESS ASSETS

For the simple case of substitution, overnight, of a uniform subtraction-method value-added tax of the consumption type for a uniform income tax, a "cold turkey" transition would effect a one-time tax on the holders of real assets, perhaps reallocated to the holders of wealth more generally, via price-level effects.[17] Eliminating any one-time tax on existing real assets would require allowing immediate deduction of the company's basis. As far as the past investment decision is concerned, this would have the effect of putting it on the income tax system up to the time of the switch and on the consumption tax system from then on. We can describe it as a policy of fully protecting old capital.[18]

It is often said that protecting old capital in this way would unacceptably increase the government's budget deficit. Dealing with the deficit consequences is, however, a matter of structuring the rules to achieve the desired cash flow. Thus, a policy economically equivalent to permitting immediate write-off of existing basis would be to permit write-off over a period of time, as long as desired, provided there were an allowance of interest earnings on the as yet undeducted basis. The effect would be to provide taxpayers with the same discounted value of tax savings as an immediate deduction but with a very different cash flow to the government.

The revenue effect of taxing or not taxing existing stocks of assets is, however, not a matter of detail. In their modeling of such transitions, for example, Auerbach and Kotlikoff (1987) conclude that a switch from an income tax to a consumption tax, while fully protecting old capital (a policy they refer to as a wage tax), might well generate an effective reduction in national welfare, whereas a switch that provided no protection to old savings would generate large gains in every case. This is because the lump sum character of the one-time tax on wealth (in their analysis, they treat the change as unanticipated) allows a lower tax rate, thereby enhancing future efficiency.

Such particular conclusions are a function of the specifics of the modeling of the economy and the policies. (For example, Auerbach and Kotlikoff do not incorporate the smoothing of revenues that might be accomplished by delaying the recovery of basis along the lines discussed above.) The generic point is, however, unavoidable, and it is a centrally important element of policy choice. A one-time tax on old savings can generate a great deal of revenue, and if it is really unanticipated, it can do so with no efficiency cost at all, just the distributional consequences discussed above. I return below to both the efficiency and the distributional questions.

As an alternative to fully protecting old capital, permitting businesses to continue to take as deductions against the value-added tax of the consumption type the depreciation allowances to which they would have been entitled under the income tax might seem a reasonable policy. It would appear to fulfill the expectations of businesses that had made investments with certain expectations about the tax treatment of the transactions. As the discussion thus far should make clear, however, this is not the same as fully protecting existing assets from the one-time tax that would result from a simple switch to consumption tax rules. The pattern of incidence is also somewhat curious: Owners of assets with short remaining lives would be closest to fully protected, whereas those owning assets with long remaining depreciable lives, such as recently constructed buildings, would come closest to incurring the full one-time tax. It is not clear such a pattern of incidence has anything to offer in terms of either efficiency or equity.

PROVIDING FOR PREEXISTING COMMITMENTS TO PAY INTEREST

As I have suggested, the commitment to pay interest would seem particularly prominent among the various preexisting commitments that might attract special transitional treatment. I have also suggested that adjustments for preexisting commitments will occur automatically if there is a one-time price-level change. In the alternative case of no change in the price level, it would appear feasible in the framework of *uniform* systems to adopt a grandfathering approach: With regard to those commitments that predate the transition to the new system, retain the old tax rules. The deduction by one taxpayer and inclusion by another taxpayer at the same rate of tax has no allocational significance, but if the applicable tax rate is the same in the income and the consumption tax systems, both borrowers and lenders will be unaffected by the change in rules. This observation applies to deduction by mortgage borrowers of interest on preexisting contracts, just as it does to businesses.

The neat symmetry and simplicity of this transition rule would be considerably complicated by the presence of multiple rates of tax (for example, both taxable and tax-exempt entities) in the preexisting system or in the new system. In some way preserving preexisting expectations with regard to interest payments and receipts may, however, provide a way to moderate an effect of shifting to a new system that has no obvious policy merit. (That effect imposes an unexpected burden on borrowers and provides an unexpected windfall on lenders by virtue of the change in treatment of payments labeled interest.)

The issue of the treatment of prechange commitments to pay and receive interest needs to be distinguished from the issue of the impact of the change in the rate of interest as a relative price. If the after-tax interest rate increases as a consequence of the regime shift, net creditors will gain and net debtors will lose. This phenomenon is taken up in the next section.

Should Old Capital Be Taxed?

EFFICIENCY ARGUMENTS: TRANSITION INCENTIVES

Thus far I have concentrated on the incidence effects of a switch between a uniform income tax and a uniform consumption tax. There are two important incentive-related aspects of the transition.

First, as has been discussed, the one-time wealth tax potentially provides the revenue to permit a relatively low tax in the new system. One can, I think, make too much of this. It is true that a lump sum tax has no distorting effect on behavior (i.e., causes no efficiency loss). Imposing a lump sum tax would provide revenue to reduce taxes that do distort behavior, such as taxes on earnings from work or saving. As demonstrated by Auerbach and Kotlikoff (1987 and, especially, 1983), the gains from lower tax rates could actually permit everyone, including those on whom the one-time wealth tax is imposed, to gain from the transition. To establish whether these conditions are fulfilled in fact, and whether a particular transition plan would effect such a general gain, would require more-detailed empirical analyses than have been carried out to date.

To be a lump sum tax, the tax on wealth must be unanticipated. Otherwise people will take steps to avoid the tax by consuming more rapidly, saving and investing less. This is the second important efficiency aspect of transition. An anticipated introduction of a consumption tax, or an anticipated *increase in its rate*, for which no compensating transition rule is provided, will discourage saving and investing, encourage current consumption. Assets held at the time of an increase in rate suffer a one-time percentage tax equal to the change in consumption tax rate. There is an incentive to convert assets to consumption before the rate change. An investment project will result in a deduction today at the lower rate, but its future payoff will be taxed at the higher rate. There is an incentive to postpone investment projects. It is easy to see that these incentive effects could be very strong.

Concern about incentive effects of this sort lead policy makers to establish an "effective date" on the day of first serious consideration of programs, such as an investment tax credit, designed to encourage investment. It is recognized that an anticipation that investment will be more favorably treated in the future than in the present will lead to a postponement, typically the very opposite of the desired effect.

POLITICAL ECONOMY ARGUMENTS: TIME CONSISTENCY

There is a certain contradiction in the idea that imposition of a consumption-type tax is unexpected, and therefore is effectively a lump sum tax, with no disincentive effects, whereas an increase in the *rate* of a consumption tax may be anticipated, discouraging investment. The logic is "We'll only do this just this once." The *potential* that a government *may* introduce a consumption-type tax without compensating transition rules presumably has disincentive effects as soon as it is felt to be operative (as perhaps in the present time). In any case, once a consumption-type tax is in place, the consequences of anticipated changes need to be taken into account.

There are basically two directions to take toward dealing with this problem on a more systematic basis. The first is to design into the systems mechanisms that limit the variability in tax rates. An example would be enacting special majority rules for tax-rate increases. Another example is the self-averaging feature of the Cash Flow Tax described in the U.S. Treasury's *Blueprints for Basic Tax Reform* (U.S. Treasury 1977, also Bradford et al. 1984). In briefest sketch, the *Blueprints* Cash Flow Tax would operate wholly at the level of the individual (rather than the firm), producing a consumption-type base by allowing deduction of net deposits to "qualified accounts" and otherwise leaving interest and similar flows out of the tax base. The resulting base would be taxed at graduated rates. In such a system it would be in the individual taxpayer's interest to "self-average" to maintain a constant tax rate over time.[19] Self-averaging is generally thought of as a way to deal with variations in the individual's tax base due to life-cycle or other sources of changing economic circumstances. But self-averaging could also deal with anticipated changes in legislation, leading taxpayers to engineer a current tax increase for themselves in anticipation of an upward shift in the tax-rate schedule to be brought about through legislation or a tax decrease in anticipation of a downward shift in the tax-rate schedule. In the process, adverse incentive effects on investment would be eliminated.

The second approach is to establish a principle or mechanism to assure that changes in rates will be accompanied by measures to reduce or eliminate the effective wealth levies, for example, by grandfathering provisions. (Another example of such a device is the common practice in the legislative process, when investment incentives are likely to be affected by rule changes, of announcing an effective date after which transactions will come under the new rules if enacted.) It seems easier to imagine grandfathering rules to protect taxpayers from having their wealth taken by a rate increase than ones that would extract the wealth gain from a tax-rate cut. A practical instance of such a gain was effected by the Tax Reform Act of 1986, which resulted in substantial reductions in the taxes on pension benefits that had been deducted earlier at higher marginal rates.

There is thus an interaction between a general practice of protecting investors from the sort of wealth tax that we have been discussing and the degree to which tax-rate changes need to be inhibited.

EQUITY ARGUMENTS

Early and late consumers.   There are two main strands of equity arguments in connection with the transition to a consumption-type tax.[20] The first one focuses on the fact that, under a consumption-type tax, owners of wealth will obtain their normal yield free of further tax. This applies to wealth accumulated after the transition and is an aspect of the argument in favor of the consumption approach. But for those who accumulated their wealth before the transition, goes the argument, the new rules may effect an unexpected, if not undeserved, gain.

As discussed above, any one-time tax on wealth in the transition is, to greater or lesser degree, compensated if the rate of return to owners of wealth increases in the process (a likely, although not necessary, outcome). For a wealth owner who plans to consume immediately after the change in regimes, an increase in the rate of return is of no value. There is no compensating gain. For one who plans to postpone consumption for a long time (for example, by passing wealth along to heirs), the gain in rate of return may more than compensate for a one-time tax.

If it were desired as a matter of policy to achieve rough neutrality in the transition, that is, generate neither gainers nor losers, it would be necessary to develop a way of discriminating among wealth owners according to their likely consumption horizons. If the distinction is based on behavior (that is, on when people actually consume), giving greater effective protection from the wealth tax on transition to those who consume (dissave) earlier, a price will be paid in the form of both equity and efficiency consequences at variance with the philosophical underpinnings of consumption taxation. Any attempt to discriminate with any precision among people according to the timing of their planned consumption is likely to introduce such incentives precisely because of the need to refer to people's behavior to determine their preferences.[21]

Consistent application of consumption tax philosophy.   Many people advocate a shift away from income and toward consumption taxation on grounds of efficiency. In particular, they seek the neutrality of a consumption tax (at least a uniform consumption tax) with respect to the decision to save. I have elsewhere (1986) suggested that a principal argument in favor of a consumption approach is, rather, one of equity. In brief, if two people are otherwise similarly situated but differ in their preferences as to the timing of consumption, a consumption tax will impose the same burdens on them but an income tax will discriminate in favor of the one who prefers to consume earlier. The same argument that suggests it would be unfair to discriminate between people according to their preferences for clothes of different color would imply it would be unfair to discriminate on the basis of differences in preferences for the timing of consumption.

A sketch of the way this line of argument might be carried over to policy toward transition goes as follows. Consider the two people who are similarly situated except that one prefers to postpone consumption more than the other. By the transition date, the late consumer has a larger stock of savings than the early consumer and will have paid more in taxes. After the transition, the two will pay the same amount of tax *except* for any wealth tax effect of the transition itself, which will work to the relative disadvantage of the late consumer. The argument for neutrality of treatment according to preferences about the timing of consumption would seem to imply at least protecting the wealth in the transition. Viewed from the perspective of the lifetime treatment at the hands of the tax system, fully protecting wealth in transition leaves the discrimination against the late consumer to the extent of the duration of the income tax regime.

Concluding Remarks

There seem to be two main attitudes toward transition in connection with major tax reform. One approach is to minimize it in the interest of moving ahead to achieve the reformer's objective. The other is to become intimidated with the problems of transition so that they form a roadblock to change. Major tax changes have taken place (good examples in the United States include the tax reforms in 1981 and 1986) that have presumably had significant transition effects but have somehow been carried out anyway. I hope the analysis presented in this chapter will assist policy makers both to put in perspective problems of transition to consumption-based taxes and to address those that are important.

Notes

1. For useful discussions of current proposals see U.S. Congress, Joint Committee on Taxation (1995) and Arthur Andersen (1995). A detailed description of the USA Tax, prepared by Alliance USA, was published as a special supplement by *Tax Notes*, March 10, 1995. The actual legislative proposal was reproduced as a special supplement by the Bureau of National Affairs, April 26, 1995.

2. In the helpful terminology of the Meade Committee Report (Institute for Fiscal Studies, 1978), this is an R-based ("real" transactions, as opposed to "financial") tax.

3. Throughout, the assumption is made that deductions (and credits) can be used. This would apply if losses (and net credits) were carried forward with interest, for example, or were refundable.

4. It is sometimes argued that the invoice-and-credit method is more easily enforced

because the buyer can be required to show the tax paid by the seller, but it would seem equally easy to trace the purchases deducted by the buyer to the tax returns of the sellers in a subtraction-method system. In contrast to the case of an income tax, there should be an inclusion on a selling business's tax return for every deduction by the buyer.

5. Under the U.S. income tax, *nominal* interest payments are included in the base of the recipient and deducted by the payer. Nominal interest rates include compensation for anticipated inflation and so generally exceed real interest rates. (For a discussion of the consequences, taking into account the presence of multiple marginal tax rates, see Bradford (1981).) One important effect of a shift to a consumption-type tax would be automatic indexing for inflation.

6. For details on historical rates of return, see R. G. Ibbotsen Associates (1995).

7. For a related discussion, see Gordon (1985).

8. This statement applies to a tax based on accruing income, so losses and gains are reflected immediately in the tax due. The way the deductibility of losses balances the taxation of gains was emphasized in a famous treatment by Domar and Musgrave (1944) of the effect of taxation on risk taking. Apart from problems relating to inflation, U.S. business income taxation is reasonably close to an accrual basis, although there are many exceptions. In the individual income tax, however, a "realization-based" approach complicates the story considerably. For a discussion of the complex effects of current realization-based income tax rules on incentives for risk taking, see Scarborough (1993).

9. The general public's claim is on a share of the assets of the company, which it has helped finance through the tax deduction. The general public does not share in the reallocation of the claim through debt finance.

10. For elaboration of this point, see Kaplow (1994).

11. There are substantial problems in implementing even a uniform tax on a *real* (inflation corrected) market-value basis. For a discussion, see Bradford (1986). For a discussion of similar issues that arise in national income accounting, see Bradford (1991).

12. Thanks to Joel Slemrod for clarifying this point.

13. The distinction between "direct" taxes (such as income, including corporate profits, wealth, and property taxes) and "indirect" taxes (such as sales and value-added taxes) is a matter of custom and is not based on any fundamental economic difference.

14. It is an open question whether an actual consumption-type system would treat housing consistently with other forms of consumption.

15. Auerbach (1989) studies the dependence of the effects of investment incentives on the cost of adjustment. See also the discussion and references in Sarkar and Zodrow (1993).

16. For further discussion of the trade-off, see Bradford et al. (1984, 180–84).

17. Hall and Rabushka (1995) advocate this form of transition to the flat tax.

18. Although I do not develop the point here, it might be noted that a similar line of argument leads to the conclusion that to protect old savings from the one-time tax on transition to a consumed income tax at the personal level would involve allowing immediate recovery of basis.

19. Taking into account risk leads to an interesting modification of this story.

20. I have particularly benefited from discussions with Louis Kaplow on the subject of this section. Some of his ideas about transitions in general are set out in Kaplow (1986) and about transition to a consumption-type tax in Kaplow (1995).

21. This point is emphasized by Kaplow (1995) in his analysis of the USA Tax. The USA Tax proposal incorporates a system for individuals to recover the basis in their wealth at the time of transition, but the recovery is postponed until such time as the taxpayer becomes a net dissaver.

References

Alliance USA. "USA Tax System." *Tax Notes*, special supplement 76, no. 11 (March 10, 1995).

Arthur Andersen, Office of Federal Tax Services. "Tax Reform 1995: Looking at Two Options." Arthur Andersen & Co., South Carolina, May 1995.

Auerbach, Alan J. "Tax Reform and Adjustment Costs: The Impact on Investment and Market Value." *International Economic Review*, 1989, pp. 939–62.

Auerbach, Alan J., Jagadeesh Gokhale, and Laurence J. Kotlikoff. "Generational Accounting: A Meaningful Way to Evaluate Fiscal Policy." *Journal of Economic Perspectives* 7 (1993).

Auerbach, Alan J., and Laurence J. Kotlikoff. "National Savings, Economic Welfare, and the Structure of Taxation." In Martin Feldstein, ed., *Behavioral Simulation Methods in Tax Policy Analysis*. Chicago: University of Chicago Press, 1983.

———. *Dynamic Fiscal Policy*. New York: Cambridge University Press, 1987.

Bradford, David F. "Issues in the Design of Savings and Investment Incentives." In Charles R. Hulten, ed., *Depreciation, Inflation and the Taxation of Income from Capital*. Washington, D.C.: The Urban Institute, 1981, pp. 13–47.

———. *Untangling the Income Tax*. Cambridge, Mass.: Harvard University Press, 1986.

———. "On the Incidence of Consumption Taxes." In Charls E. Walker and Mark A. Bloomfield, eds., *The Consumption Tax: A Better Alternative*. Cambridge, Mass.: Ballinger, 1987, pp. 243–61.

———. "What Are Consumption Taxes and Who Bears Them?" *Tax Notes*, April 18, 1988.

———. "Market Value *versus* Financial Accounting Measures of National Saving." In B. Douglas Bernheim and John B. Shoven, eds., *National Saving and Economic Performance*. Chicago: University of Chicago Press, 1991, pp. 15–44.

Bradford, David F., and the U.S. Treasury Tax Policy Staff. *Blueprints for Basic Tax Reform*, 2d ed., rev. Arlington, Va.: Tax Analysts, 1984.

Browning, Edgar K. "The Burden of Taxation." *Journal of Political Economy* 86 (August 1978): 649–71.

Bureau of National Affairs. "USA Tax Act of 1995," special supplement, Report No. 80, April 26, 1995.

Domar, Evsey D., and Richard Musgrave. "Proportional Income Taxation and Risk Bearing." *Quarterly Journal of Economics* 55 (1944): 382–482.

Gordon, Roger H. "Taxation of Corporate Capital Income: Tax Revenues versus Tax Distortions." *Quarterly Journal of Economics* 100 (February 1985): 1–27.

Hall, Robert E., and Alvin Rabushka. *Low Tax, Simple Tax, Flat Tax*. New York: McGraw-Hill, 1983.

———. *The Flat Tax*, 2d ed. Stanford: Hoover Institution Press, 1995.

Howitt, Peter, and Hans-Werner Sinn. "Gradual Reforms of Capital Income Taxation." *American Economic Review* 79 (1989): 106–24.

Institute for Fiscal Studies. *The Structure and Reform of Direct Taxation: The Report of a Committee Chaired by Professor J. E. Meade*. London: George Allen & Unwin, 1978.

Jorgenson, Dale W. "The Economic Impact of Fundamental Tax Reform." This volume.

Kaplow, Louis. "An Economic Analysis of Legal Transitions." *Harvard Law Review*, January 1986.

———. "Taxation and Risk Taking: A General Equilibrium Perspective." *National Tax Journal* 47, no. 4 (December 1994): 789–98.

———. "Recovery of Pre-Transition Basis under an Individual Consumption Tax: The USA Tax System." *Tax Notes*, August 28, 1995.

Keuschnigg, Christian. "The Transition to a Cash Flow Income Tax." *Swiss Journal of Economics and Statistics* 127, no. 2 (1991): 113–40.

Kotlikoff, Laurence J. *Generational Accounting: Knowing Who Pays, and When, for What We Spend*. New York: Free Press, 1992.

R. G. Ibbotsen Associates. *Stocks, Bonds, Bills and Inflation: 1995 Yearbook*. Chicago: R. G. Ibbotsen Associates, 1995.

Sarkar, Shounak, and George R. Zodrow. "Transitional Issues in Moving to a Direct Consumption Tax." *National Tax Journal* 46, no. 3 (September 1993): 359–76.

Scarborough, Robert H. "Risk, Diversification and the Design of Loss Limitations under a Realization-Based Income Tax." *Tax Law Review* 48, no. 3 (1993): 677–717.

Summers, Lawrence H. "Capital Taxation and Accumulation in a Life Cycle Growth Model." *American Economic Review* 71 (September 1981): 533–44.

U.S. Congress, Joint Committee on Taxation. *Discussion of Issues Relating to "Flat" Tax Rate Proposals* (JCS-7-95). Washington, D.C.: U.S. Government Printing Office, 1995.

U.S. Treasury Department. *Blueprints for Basic Tax Reform*. Washington, D.C.: U.S. Government Printing Office, January 1977.

———. *Report on Integration of Individual and Corporate Tax Systems: Taxing Business Income Once*. Washington, D.C.: U.S. Government Printing Office, January 1992.

9

Providing Appropriate Information on Tax Reform

KENNETH J. KIES

A real focus of attention in 1995 for the Joint Committee on Taxation, of which I am chief of staff, has been the whole estimating issue. The economists on the joint committee have helped educate me on a lot of the key issues we are going to have to grapple with in assessing major tax reform and tax restructuring proposals. That process started very quickly when the Joint House and Senate Budget Committees held a hearing on January 10, 1995, to focus on the whole issue of the estimating process with a good deal of the focus being on the macroeconomic issues. This sensitive issue in the academic community, on the Hill, and even in the tax practitioner community is the extent to which the Joint Committee on Taxation, in evaluating any revenue proposal, whether it be a major restructuring proposal or just individual proposals, like capital gains cuts and things of that nature, should take into account the macroeconomic effect. I might say that in our testifying I think we laid out the basic view of the joint committee, not only of the staff but of the members (five on the House side and five on the Senate side) and that our objective is to deliver the most accurate and reliable information, however that is prepared. And that is the underlying objective of the Joint Committee on Taxation.

In our testimony we said that, although we agree that if we were able to take into account macroeconomic effects, it would improve the value of the estimates, assuming we could take them into account in a reasonable manner, there are at least four major hurdles that needed to be overcome to be able to do that on a regular basis.

The first is developing a reliable model that would be able to predict macroeconomic consequences in an acceptable way. The second is that we currently do not apply macroeconomic analysis to the spending side, and some members of Congress will argue that spending programs have macroeconomic benefits. They will point to things like education and other proposals and assert that if you are going to apply macroeconomic analysis to the revenue side, you should also apply it on the spending side.

A third obstacle (which I do not view as the most formidable) is the statutory budget provisions that we operate under. It is the view of the Congressional Budget Office (and a view we tend to share) that the statutory budget act provisions will have to be somewhat modified if we are to take into account macroeconomic effects. The fourth hurdle (which I do view as significant) is the lack of consensus from time to time within the economic community about what effect certain major proposals may have on the economy, particularly long-term macroeconomic considerations. An example is the proposal for a neutral cost recovery system (NCRS). Our revenue analysis for the first five years on NCRS is that the provision will increase revenues by $16.7 billion, but by the ten-year horizon, which is the horizon that the Senate will have to use to consider this provision, it would lose revenues of $88 billion. That analysis is shared by some; some think that it is too optimistic and that the revenue loss could even be greater; and others believe that our analysis is too pessimistic. In fact two economists, formerly with the Treasury Department, have suggested that the proposal, if enacted, in the first five years would increase capital savings in the United States, increase capital investment by $8.9 trillion, and increase tax revenues by some $500 billion. Such varying views within the economic community put us in a very difficult spot because, for budget act purposes, members of Congress need to have a number that they score against the overall budget to determine whether or not it violates various caps or objectives that they have established either through a budget resolution or through other budget legislation.

Let me now turn to restructuring and talk about the types of information that the joint committee provides to members in this process and some of the difficulties that we see as this process unfolds. The first is information about our current tax system. Members want to know things like what is the current distribution of income tax? an area where there is a fair amount of misunderstanding. Senator Packwood, in looking at his flat income tax, has requested a number of pieces of information about the distribution of the current tax system. This raises the issue of distributing the corporate income tax. Putting aside the corporate income tax piece, let me bring your attention to some of the important statistics about our current income tax system because there is a popular view, at least outside the beltway, that the current income tax system is unfair and that rich people do not pay enough, which is one of the reasons there is a significant amount of momentum for restructuring the tax system.

The actual statistics indicate a far different picture. The taxpayers in the bottom 40 percent bracket pay 4.9 percent of the combined income tax and Social Security taxes, assuming all Social Security taxes are paid by the employee. The top 1 percent pays 18.6 percent. The top 10 percent pays about 48.6 percent. So when you consider our current system of Social Security/ Medicare taxes, all the employment taxes plus the income tax, it is a fairly progressive picture. The corporate income tax, which is an area of controversy, is not distributed in those statistics that I just gave you. We are in the process of looking at how the corporate income tax should be distributed relative to these overall restructuring proposals. Many of them propose a complete repeal of the corporate income tax and replacing it with some other tax system that may have a point of collection relating to individuals or business, but they all raise the basic question of how the current corporate income tax should be distributed and then how to compare the current system with a new system that would replace the corporate income tax.

One of the difficulties I have is the varying views among the economics community about who pays the corporate income tax. During a vacation to Florida I read a book that Greg Ballantine edited on who pays the corporate income tax. In reading Ballantine's book I concluded that the disagreement concerns whether we are talking short term or long term. But as I looked through the book, not one economist was willing to define what the difference between short term and long term was. And as best I could tell, short term was anywhere between three and fifty years and long term was anywhere between four and two hundred and fifty years. Perhaps I take too simplistic a view of this whole distributional issue, but I view our role as providing decision-making information to members of Congress. And in that regard, I think it is critical that what the members of Congress are getting is as close to reality as possible, given that we are talking about complicated concepts.

As an example I will use the approach that we have taken on the capital gains reductions. This has produced some controversy because prior administrations changed back and forth, either variously preparing capital gains reduction analysis by including induced realizations as part of the overall revenue analysis or distributing those induced realizations in showing what the effect is by various income classes. The current administration, and some past administrations, does not take into account induced realizations in reflecting the effect of a capital gains cut.

The committee's view is that, in presenting information to members of Congress, we should do it on a taxes-paid basis because that is what most members of Congress think they are looking at when they get one of our distribution tables on something like capital gains, no matter how much we footnote it. My view is that, at least on something like a capital gains cut, what the members of Congress are looking for, or what they believe they are looking at, is the effect on the taxes that are paid by individual taxpayers depending on whether or not there is a reduction. That goes to the issue of whether we are trying to give them something that is academically pure or something that comes closer to their commonsense understanding. Clearly, there is no right answer here, but there are clearly differing views.

On the overall corporate income tax issue, the source of the controversy is who pays the corporate income tax—whether it's paid by owners of equity, whether you include equity held by qualified pension plans, whether you include equity that is held only by defined contribution plans versus defined benefit plans, and then to what extent you assume that a corporate tax increase might be borne either short term or long term by workers, consumers, and other potential targets. Although I am not sure we will have an answer soon, we have to come up with something because most of the restructuring proposals are looking at complete substitutions of the corporate income tax.

We are also getting a lot of requests from members for information on who benefits from various tax deductions. Members want to know how many people benefit from the mortgage interest deduction and what the distribution is of the mortgage interest deductions that are claimed. That is one of the more sensitive points in the current system, and the same thing could be said of the charitable deduction and other simple deductions. State and local taxes are the other high-visibility deduction provision that members want to know about, including the profile of taxpayers that are currently using that provision.

In terms of information about proposals, and our role in examining them, the number-one thing that all members want to know is whether a specific proposal produces the same amount of revenue. I think this is because there is a general consensus that, among all of the various restructuring proposals, whatever proposal is ultimately approved by Congress should be revenue neutral against the current tax system.

The second major area that members want information about is behavioral response. Thus they want to know what effect a value-added tax system or a consumption-based income tax system would have on savings. As you may know, the Armey flat tax proposal has an unlimited 401(k) component that would allow employees to put away as much in the form of savings as they desired, so members want to know what to expect in terms of increased savings rates. Although we are not prepared to make that sort of macroeconomic projection about savings rates, to do the revenue analysis we need some idea of how much additional utilization of super 401(k) plans would occur under an Armey-type proposal.

Under a Nunn-Domenici-type proposal we must project the extent to which the super individual retirement account proposal would be used as a savings vehicle. Another area we are asked to look at is whether or not these proposals will achieve the stated objectives that a particular member of Congress may have. House Ways and Means Committee chairman Bill Archer has identified five major objectives in his proposals: border adjustability, additional savings, compliance, hitting the underground economy, and simplicity. To respond on an issue such as the underground economy, we have to analyze how large the underground economy is today, the extent to which Chairman Archer's proposal would get at it, and what kind of compliance problems we would have with a replacement system. Another area of inquiry, and it tends to be the last one that comes up, is transition, the surface of which has only been scratched in terms of complexity, if we are going to move to a completely different type of system than the one we have today.

Another role of the joint committee is the technical drafting process. Many of the proposals, as currently articulated, are somewhat conceptual in form. When one actually starts to draft a statute is when a lot of the issues come to the surface. A good example of that is the whole pension area. In looking at Congressman Armey's flat tax proposal, a whole variety of pension issues that no one had thought about before started to surface. Even in the complete income tax replacement systems, like the value-added tax, there are a whole variety of issues about the role of the Employee Retirement Income Security Act in a post-income tax system: To what extent will employers still have a role as the sponsors of qualified plans, even if they are not income tax based, and to what extent will the various rules governing fiduciary obligations, investment requirements, and so on still apply in the qualified pension plan if there is no longer a particular income tax incentive associated with either depositing money in, or taking money out of, such a plan?

Another extremely complex area is the whole business of financial intermediaries. Another is foreign issues, particularly in those systems that retain an element of the income tax. The treaty network comes into play when you talk about replacing our income tax system. We have tax treaties with, I believe, some eighty countries around the world, all of which are based on, in some cases very specific, components of the Internal Revenue Code, many of which would be replaced. That would raise the issue of how to renegotiate our tax treaty network, not a simple task given the personnel and complexities of some of the various treaty partners.

Finally (although not an end to this list, which tends to be endless), the whole pass-through entity area presents a lot of complexities, including how to index the basis of capital gains. Much has been written about the complexities of applying an indexing system to a capital gains proposal; the problems one has to address in the pass-through entity area when we talk about complete replacement systems multiply that many fold.

Those are some of the issues that we are beginning to review. We are working with members on both the House and Senate side, Democrat and Republican, and also interacting with a lot of people on the outside. I see that process continuing through this year into next year and perhaps even beyond that.

Q&A

Q: Going briefly over this matter of capital gains estimation and the controversy that it created, it was embarrassing for all agencies that both the Treasury and the joint committee switched their treatment of this issue in a way that seemed to accord with the political purposes of their masters. As far as I can tell that is not the case, though I thought it was quite damaging, unfortunately, to the professionals. Did you consider putting out the analysis in two forms, and then letting the members of congress figure it out? It doesn't seem that complicated.

A: Actually you don't realize what a softball you jsut threw me because (and I swear I did not set this up), the Joint Committee on Taxation did not change its method under the current control of the Congress. That change was made last summer, before the change in control. In the case of the administration, I guess the change occurred under the new administration. We did consider putting it out in two forms.

And to come back to the point I made, it is my view that most members of Congress, when they look at this information, think that they are looking at, in the case of something like capital gains, taxes paid. They do not understand why a provision that has a revenue effect of −$31.5 billion has a distributional chart that shows an impact of, say, $55 billion. When you start to try and explain that, you've lost them. If you put out two different charts, it only compounds their confusion level. We were criticized for putting out year-by-year charts, but I thought in the case of capital gains, because the first-year effect of a capital gains proposal, owing to a higher level of induced realization, does not reflect the kind of effect you would see in the fifth year, we should put out year-by-year tables and then allow members to observe how the provision actually changes over time. We were criticized because people said that we were trying to put so much out there nobody would understand it. How do you win that battle? At that point it's impossible.

My view was twofold: (a) if we put it out both ways, it would only further confuse members because most members of Congress think they are looking at taxes paid and (b) our distribution charts are meant as a decision-making tool for members of Congress, not as something academically pure.

Q: I think that you have set up an interesting standard for what the joint committee should do, what members of Congress expect, and what they can make their decisions based on. What I don't understand is, based on those criteria, how could you not distribute the corporate tax? Why do a big study after the red book was published? What am I supposed to say when I write a piece about the flat tax and Dick Armey calls me up and says I missed the point because a lot of the burden shifts from the personal tax to the business tax, the business side? I say,

"Well, that is not the way the joint committee tables look," and he says, "We're working on that."

A: Well, you could just say, "I'm sorry." Let me make a couple of observations. The first is that when we are talking about a complete substitute for the corporate tax, which is about $110 billion a year, let us remember that the individual tax is about $600 billion and all the employment taxes are around $500 billion, which comes out to about $1.1 to $1.2 trillion. Thus, the corporate income tax piece, $110 billion, is not statistically that significant relative to the entire package. So the amount of attention being focused on distributing the corporate income tax may overstate its importance in terms of being able to analyze the proposals.

Having said that, the difficulty we face in deciding what to do about the corporate income tax is that, depending on which member of Congress you talk to, there are different views about who pays the corporate income tax. And although the prevailing view within the economic community is that it is paid by equity, that is not a view that was held ten years ago. (And if my observation of what has been written in the economic community is right, it may not be the view held ten years from now.) Thus I'm not sure that we should make a single call that all members of Congress are going to have to live with in making their decisions. Like my own current view, which differs from what I told the earlier questioner, perhaps we should do it two or three different ways and get the members to realize that we have made certain assumptions (they don't tend to read footnotes) and chosen a couple of different alternatives but that they must understand that we are not sure what the right answer is. The problem with distribution charts is that most people would like to think that they have all the answers to what a major change in our tax system will do. It's not that simple.

Q: I have two related questions. First, I believe it can be very misleading to report changes in taxes paid but ignore changes in transfers received. What can be done about that? Second, the distribution tables tend to be a snapshot of income, whereas most economists would look at average, or permanent, income, at least over a few years, if not the entire life cycle. What can be done to extend the analysis to a multiyear income-averaging framework?

A: The answer to that question is easy, we merge with the Congressional Budget Office (CBO). That's a serious answer in the sense that the joint committee's role is to look at the tax piece (and I think you have correctly identified one of the fragilities of the congressional system) where CBO generally looks at spending, whereas economists, and I think correctly so, view them as related. In the case of the earned-income tax credit, which is sort of the exception to the rule, although it is actually a spending program, 90 percent of it is refundable, so it's also a direct payment, which we show as a negative tax. For example, if there are changes in

Social Security taxes, we don't ever reflect any change in the Social Security benefit side. That is one area where the estimating process and the interaction between CBO and the joint committee can improve things.

The other area that I view as equally important is this generational issue of looking at tax proposals and realizing that people have different consumption and savings patterns throughout their lives. Yet our tax analysis (and again this is one of the problems with distributional analysis), looks at people on an expanded income class at a snapshot in time. So people, for example, earning $10,000 and under show up as low income, but they may be students. To me, that is a serious problem with the whole distributional picture.

Q: My last question is related to the generational issue, which is endemic to budgeting in general, but because most things are done on a cash rather than an accrual basis, it is not just an accrual of future liabilities in funded pension plans or things of that sort. Many of the proposals under analysis would change the timing of taxes. For example, many of the proposals had IRA-type expansions and so on. Those are basically tax deferred, not tax free. And as I understand it, the existing system just takes the amount collected under those things, minus the amount that is forgone, and we don't carry a column anywhere in our books saying "deferred taxes owed the government."

We have a big national debt, we have $4 trillion or $5 trillion worth of pensions, and, by my estimate, we have over a trillion dollars of deferred taxes due the government, and we never come close to, even in the aggregate, getting that information out and offsetting it against the official debt, let alone evaluating individual programs emphasizing the tax deferral. Is there a way to deal with tax deferral and these accrual issues?

A: Well, I think it's certainly a legitimate issue to raise. Whether there's a way to deal with it that is both understandable and defensible is a much tougher question. We have to step back and realize that the primary reason we do revenue estimates is because the federal budget is on a cash-flow basis, that is the way it functions. And I'm not sure that that's necessarily a bad general rule. Think about your own personal lives. Most people think about "how much money will I make this year, and how much am I going to spend? I hope I don't end up with a negative." Even when Congress operates on that simple basis, it doesn't do it very well.

So if we were going to take it to a more complex approach (and I must say, it doesn't really operate that simply even today; there are deferral mechanisms that do exist in the system), I get nervous, given our current success with balancing the budget, about putting aside the current process, which may succeed. But I also get nervous about trying to move to a modified accrual system when we haven't handled the cash-flow system very well. That doesn't mean that we shouldn't pay more attention to the difference between permanent exclusions versus timing issues and realize that in doing policy analysis and making judgments that there is a difference. I think that's a way to start into that process. One of the things I expect Chairman Archer and Vice Chairman Packwood of the joint committee to do in the next week or so is to announce some improvements in the way we do estimating that are intended to be a little more innovative in that direction. I think you are going to see that we are listening to what people have been saying about the estimating process and trying to respond to it.

Q: You've mentioned a couple of times that members of Congress don't read the footnotes; have you thought about using 14-point bold type? or precautionary notes where, for example, you mention points of disagreement in Congress. There are lots of things the members are not in disagreement about. For example, if someone is increasing the estate tax, as they did recently, why not include a precautionary statement to the effect that "by the way there is something called estate planning that has an effect on the income tax and that isn't taken into consideration in this table"? or "by the way, if you're going to raise marginal tax rates on secondary earners to 36 or 40 percent, you will probably have fewer two-earner families, which will mean that these revenue estimates are not as accurate as they may be." I realize they want point estimates; I wouldn't ask you to change the macroeconomic assumptions, but these aren't macroeconomic questions, they are just where we know static revenue estimates are not plausible, they can't possibly be right.

A: Let me just respond by saying that I think both the examples you used may be wrong; we actually do take those into account. We do not do static revenue estimates. For example, the 1993 estimates that were done on the 1993 increases in income tax rates assumed a 7 percent decline in taxable income; that would be a response. There is disagreement from Marty Feldstein and others about whether the 7 percent reduction accurately predicted what would be the behavioral response, but part of that was an analysis of two-earner couples. I don't disagree with the general proposition of your comment, which is that we should be working to refine our behavioral analysis. I think in the case of the estate tax changes, if we don't take into account observable changes on the income tax side, we should be.

10

Saving and Consumption Taxation: The Federal Retail Sales Tax Example

LAURENCE J. KOTLIKOFF

Introduction

After almost a decade of being forgotten, consumption taxation is once again a hot topic, as evidenced by the national sales tax, flat tax, and personal consumption tax proposals now being advanced by members of Congress. Renewed focus on the consumption tax as a means of reducing consumption and raising saving is not surprising. Our country continues to save at a critically low rate and, correspondingly, consume at an extremely high rate. In the 1990s, our nation's net national saving rate has averaged just 2.7 percent a year—less than one-third the rate observed in the 1950s and 1960s.[1] Our saving rate is not only low by historical standards, it's also low by international standards. We now routinely save at about one-third the rate of Japan and one-half the rate of Germany.

In saving so little, we are providing meager amounts of additional funds to businesses for financing their investment. And, indeed, the secular decline in the rate of U.S national saving has been associated with a secular decline in the rate of U.S. domestic investment.[2] Because U.S. domestic investment equals the increase in our country's capital stock—its residential structures, plant, and equip-

This paper draws heavily on my paper "The Economic Impact of Replacing Federal Income Taxes with a Sales Tax," which was financed and released by the Cato Institute in December 1992. The overlapping material is reproduced here with the permission of the Cato Institute. I thank the Cato Institute as well as the Hoover Institution for research support.

ment—slower growth in domestic investment means slower growth in capital per unit of labor. This means slower growth in labor productivity, which, in turn, means slower growth in real wages.

This study considers the impact on U.S. saving, investment, and growth of the total elimination of personal and corporate income taxes in favor of a consumption tax, specifically a uniform national sales tax. Although the study takes the retail sales tax as its example, its results carry over to other forms of consumption taxation. Indeed, they carry over directly to other forms of proportional consumption taxation and, with some differences, to forms of progressive consumption taxation.

I begin this chapter by examining the dimensions and causes of the U.S. saving crisis. I then discuss the choice of the tax base, indicating that consumption taxation provides greater incentives to save than does income taxation. Next I turn to a brief description of recent tax policy, stressing our failure to clearly decide what it is we want to tax. This indecision has produced a series of major flip-flops with respect to tax policy, leaving us straddled with a hybrid tax system—part income tax and part consumption tax—which provides considerable latitude to use the provisions of one tax base to save taxes with respect to the other.

Economists refer to this as tax arbitrage. Tax arbitrage has permitted millions of Americans to reduce their taxes and, as a result, spend more on consumption. The additional consumption financed by tax arbitrage is one of several reasons the United States has spent the past decade saving and investing at rates unbecoming a developed country. The shift to a national sales tax would eliminate this form of tax arbitrage. In addition, as this section of the chapter points out, the shift to a national sales tax would eliminate a number of significant tax distortions prevailing under our current system of income taxation.

Finally, I get to the main purpose of this chapter, which is to illustrate the potential saving, investment, and growth effects of switching to consumption taxation by considering the enactment of a national sales tax. My tool here is a computer simulation model, namely, the Auerbach-Kotlikoff Dynamic Life-Cycle Simulation Model. This model is highly stylized; nonetheless, it captures a great deal of the complex processes that would be touched off by switching to a national sales tax.

The Decline in U.S. Saving

In 1950, the U.S. rate of net national saving was 12.3 percent. In 1994, it was only 3.5 percent. The difference in these saving rates is illustrative of a dramatic long-term decline in U.S saving. The U.S saving rate averaged 9.1

Table 1   Saving and Spending Rates

Period	Net National Saving Rate $(Y-C-G)/Y$	Government Spending Rate G/Y	Household Consumption Rate C/Y	Household Saving Rate $(Y-G-C)/$ $(Y-G)$
1950–59	.091	.210	.699	.115
1960–69	.091	.221	.688	.117
1970–79	.085	.214	.701	.108
1980–89	.047	.213	.740	.059
1990–94	.027	.207	.766	.031

percent a year in the 1950s and 1960s, 8.5 percent in the 1970s, 4.7 percent in the 1980s, and just 2.7 percent in the first five years of the 1990s.

The decline in U.S saving has been associated with an equally dramatic decline in U.S. domestic investment. Since 1990, net domestic investment as a share of net national product has averaged 3.6 percent a year, compared with 8.2 percent in the 1950s, 7.9 percent in the 1960s and 1970s, and 6.1 percent in the 1980s. The low rate of domestic investment has limited growth in labor productivity and, consequently, growth in real wages. Since 1980, labor productivity has grown at less than half the rate observed between 1950 and 1979, and total real compensation (wages plus fringe benefits) an hour has grown at only one-eighth its previously observed rate.

Table 1 reports average values of the net national saving rate for the 1950s, 1960s, 1970s, and 1980s as well as the first five years of the 1990s. The net national saving rate is defined at $(Y-C-G)/Y$, where Y refers to net national product, C to household consumption, and G to government spending (purchases of goods and services). The table also reports rates of government and household consumption out of output, G/Y and C/Y. In addition, the table reports my preferred measure of private-sector saving, which I call the *household saving rate*. It's defined as $(Y-G)/(Y-G)$, that is, the share saved of the output left over to the household sector after the government has consumed (i.e., the share of $Y-G$ that is not consumed by the public).

As table 1 indicates, government spending is not responsible for reducing the rate of national saving. Indeed, the rate of government spending, G/Y, has declined since the 1970s. Furthermore, government spending in the 1990s has averaged just 21.0 percent of output—as low a rate as any observed in the five periods. The rate of household consumption spending, in contrast, rose from 69.9 percent of output in the 1950s to 76.6 percent in the early 1990s. This increased rate of household consumption was associated with a decline in the household saving rate from 11.5 percent in the 1950s to 3.2 percent in the 1990s.

Table 2   The Growth of Household and Medical Consumption

Period	Rate of Household Consumption C/Y	Rate of Medical Consumption M/Y
1950–59	.699	.039
1960–69	.688	.052
1970–79	.701	.072
1980–89	.740	.101
1990–93	.765	.128

Table 2 considers the role of health-care spending in the growth of household spending. It shows that medical expenditures have increased from 3.9 percent of net national product (NNP) in the 1950s to 12.8 percent in the 1990s. In the 1950s health-care spending represented less than 6 percent of household consumption. So far, in the 1990s, it has represented almost 17 percent. The increase in the rate of medical spending was associated with only a modest reduction in the rate of nonmedical spending. In the 1950s, nonmedical consumption averaged 66.0 percent of NNP. In the 1990s, it averaged 63.7 percent. Thus, although the rate of medical consumption rose by 8.9 percentage points between the 1950s and 1990s, the rate of nonmedical consumption fell by only 2.3 percentage points.

WHOSE CONSUMPTION HAS RISEN?

If the driving force behind the decline in U.S. saving is an increase in the rate of household consumption, it's natural to ask whose consumption within the household sector has risen so rapidly? The answer is the elderly's. Tables 3 and 4 document this fact.[3] They show a remarkable increase in the relative consumption of the elderly over four periods for which Consumer Expenditure Survey data are available. This increase is more pronounced if medical care is included in the measure of consumption, but the increase in the relative consumption of nonmedical goods and services is also striking. According to tables, seventy-year-olds in 1960–61 consumed about 71 percent of the amount consumed by thirty-year olds in 1960–61, whereas their consumption now exceeds that of thirty-year-olds by 18 percent. In the case of nonmedical consumption, seventy-year-olds consumed about 56 percent of the amount consumed by thirty-year-olds in 1960–61, compared with 85 percent now. The increase in relative consumption of the elderly based on other age pairings is equally dramatic.

The striking increase in the relative consumption of the elderly has coin-

Table 3   Consumption of the Elderly Relative to the Young

Comparison	1960–61	1972–73	1984–86	1987–90
Age 60/age 20	1.17	1.37	1.58	1.59
Age 70/age 20	0.97	1.21	1.56	1.64
Age 80/age 20	0.89	1.16	1.61	1.60
Age 60/age 30	0.86	0.93	1.09	1.15
Age 70/age 30	0.71	0.82	1.07	1.18
Age 80/age 30	0.65	0.79	1.11	1.16
Age 60/age 40	0.77	0.83	0.87	0.91
Age 70/age 40	0.64	0.73	0.86	0.94
Age 80/age 40	0.58	0.70	0.89	0.92

SOURCE: Gokhale, Kotlikoff, and Sabelhaus (1995).

Table 4   Nonmedical Consumption of the Elderly Relative to the Young

Comparison	1960–61	1972–73	1984–86	1987–90
Age 60/age 20	1.11	1.28	1.43	1.42
Age 70/age 20	0.86	1.04	1.22	1.28
Age 80/age 20	0.75	0.91	1.16	1.11
Age 60/age 30	0.81	0.86	0.97	1.02
Age 70/age 30	0.63	0.70	0.83	0.91
Age 80/age 30	0.55	0.61	0.78	0.80
Age 60/age 40	0.73	0.78	0.77	0.80
Age 70/age 40	0.57	0.63	0.66	0.72
Age 80/age 40	0.49	0.55	0.62	0.63

SOURCE: Gokhale, Kotlikoff, and Sabelhaus (1995).

cided with an equally remarkable increase in their relative resources. The term *resources* refers to a generation's net worth plus the present values of its future labor income, pension income, and Social Security, Medicare, and other transfer payments less the present value of its future taxes. Table 5 presents ratios of average resources of sixty-, seventy-, and eighty-year-olds to those of twenty-, thirty-, and forty-year-olds. In 1960–61, the average resources of seventy-year-olds were only 72 percent as large as those of thirty-year-olds. In 1987–90, they were 15 percent larger than those of thirty-year-olds. The resources of other older cohorts have also grown significantly relative to those of younger cohorts over the past three decades. In addition to the elderly consuming more because they've been handed more resources, the older members of the elderly have also been

Table 5   Resources of the Elderly Relative to the Young

Comparison	1960–61	1972–73	1984–86	1987–90
Age 60/age 20	1.10	1.41	1.72	1.81
Age 70/age 20	0.85	1.14	1.49	1.58
Age 80/age 20	0.63	0.71	0.76	0.83
Age 60/age 30	0.92	1.07	1.26	1.31
Age 70/age 30	0.72	0.86	1.09	1.15
Age 80/age 30	0.53	0.54	0.56	0.60
Age 60/age 40	0.82	0.95	1.05	1.10
Age 70/age 40	0.64	0.77	0.91	0.96
Age 80/age 40	0.47	0.48	0.47	0.51

SOURCE: Gokhale, Kotlikoff, and Sabelhaus (1995).

consuming more of each dollar of resources. Indeed, the consumption propensities of the old old have more than doubled since 1960.

EXPLAINING THE DECLINE IN U.S. SAVING

As documented in Gokhale, Kotlikoff, and Sabelhaus (1995), the decline in United States saving can be traced to two factors: (1) the redistribution of resources toward older generations, with high propensities to consume, from younger ones (including those not yet born), with low or zero propensities to consume, and (2) increases among the older old in their propensities to consume privately purchased as well as government-provided goods and services.

Much of the redistribution to the elderly reflects the growth in Social Security, Medicare, and Medicaid benefits. The increase in the elderly's consumption propensities may also reflect government policy, namely, that government transfers to the elderly come in the form of annuities. In providing these annuities, which are, of course, indexed for inflation, the government has, in effect, told the elderly they needn't worry as much about overconsuming and running out of income. In addition, the medical care annuities that the government provides through Medicare and Medicaid come in the form of in-kind consumption of medical goods and services that the elderly cannot help but consume.

IMPLICATIONS OF THE CAUSE OF THE U.S. SAVING DECLINE TO THINKING ABOUT CONSUMPTION TAXATION

The fact that government's past and ongoing intergenerational redistribution appears to be the chief culprit for the decline in U.S. saving is worth bearing in mind in considering switching from income to consumption taxation. As described below, such a switch would offset somewhat this process of taking from the young and unborn and giving to the old. It would do so by placing a somewhat higher tax burden on the initial elderly and a somewhat lower tax burden on younger and future generations. In switching tax structures and thus redistributing from the elderly with high propensities to consume to the young and unborn with low or zero propensities to consume, the government can engineer a reduction in aggregate consumption and a concomitant increase in national saving. Such redistributional, or "income," effects are the key reason that consumption taxation increases national saving.

The Choice of Tax Base and Its Impact on Saving

To understand the different tax bases available to the government and how their taxation affects saving decisions, let's start by considering a government that wants to tax all of output at a fixed rate τ. To do so it can levy a tax at rate τ on output as it is sold by firms to the private sector. Alternatively, it can levy a tax at rate τ on the factors of production—labor and capital—as they receive the proceeds from the sale of output in the form of wage income and capital income. A third possibility is to tax income recipients when they use their income to purchase consumption goods or to acquire assets (i.e., when they save). Because what is saved is invested (i.e., saving equals investment), our hypothetical government can also tax income by taxing consumption plus investment.

A little algebra helps clarify the equivalency of these four different ways of taxing output. If we let Y stand for aggregate output or income, Yl for aggregate labor income, Yk for aggregate capital income, C for aggregate consumption (including government consumption), S for aggregate saving, and I for aggregate investment, we have the following identities: $Y = Yl + Yk = C + S = C + I$. Thus taxing output Y at a flat rate, say τ, is equivalent to taxing both Yl and Yk at the rate τ, and both, in turn, are equivalent to taxing C plus S or C plus I at the rate τ.

But there is no requirement that governments tax all output either directly, by taxing it when it is produced and sold, or indirectly, by taxing it when it is received as income or when it is used to purchase consumption or acquire assets (finance investment). Governments can, instead, choose to tax only a component of income. For example, they can choose to tax labor income but not capital income. Or they can choose to tax only one use of income, say consumption, but not investment.

If a government chooses to tax consumption, it can do so directly, by taxing the purchase of consumption goods, or indirectly, either by (1) taxing income when it is received by individuals in the form of wage income and capital income but allowing a deduction (or subtraction) for the saving these individuals do or (2) taxing wage income at the personal level, taxing capital income at the business level (before it is paid out), but allowing a deduction at the business level for investment. The equivalence of these ways of taxing consumption can be seen from our simple identity: consumption C equals income Y minus investment S, but it also equals YI plus the difference between Yk and I.

In the United States we have attempted to tax consumption indirectly both by (1) allowing deductions from personal income taxes for certain forms of saving and (2) allowing full deductions from business profits taxes for certain forms of business investment. Ignoring gasoline and other federal excise taxes, the federal government has never attempted to tax consumption directly through a uniform national sales tax.

Given that governments can tax consumption directly or indirectly and that they can do so with either progressive or proportional tax rates, why would they want to tax only output that is consumed and exempt from taxation output that is saved (invested)? The answer is that a consumption tax provides more incentive to save (invest) than does an income tax. As our identity $Y = C + S$ indicates, taxing output can be viewed as taxing saving as well as consumption. Now economists view saving, not as an end in itself but as a means to finance future consumption. So by taxing consumption and saving, an income tax effectively taxes future consumption twice, once when households save funds for future consumption and once when they engage in that future consumption. Because current consumption is taxed only once (ignoring past taxes on saving because bygones are bygones), in deciding between consuming more now and saving for future consumption, an income tax provides an incentive, at any point in time, to consume more now and save less for the future.

In addition to providing better savings incentives, moving from an income to a consumption tax produces, as previously mentioned, an intergenerational redistribution away from older generations toward younger and future generations that also lowers aggregate consumption and raises national saving. The reason this intergenerational redistribution occurs is that older generations pay a larger share of consumption taxes than they do of income taxes.

Economists refer to the changes in economic behavior, such as saving, that arise from a change in one's resource position as income effects. They refer to changes in economic behavior due to changes in incentives, holding resources constant, as substitution effects. The above discussion indicates that the substitution and income effects of moving from income to consumption taxation would reinforce one another. Both would work in favor of lowering aggregate consumption and raising national saving.

The Legacy of Tax Flip-Flops —
a Hybrid U.S. Tax Structure

Over the past dozen years, we Americans have had a great penchant for reforming our tax system. We did so in 1981, 1982, 1984, 1986, 1990, 1993, and we may well do so again in 1995 or 1996. We seemingly cannot decide for once and for all whether our taxes are too high or too low, too progressive or too regressive, or too replete with loopholes or too devoid of incentives. In addition, we can't seem to make up our minds who it is—business or individuals—or what it is—income or consumption—that we want to tax. Nor can we decide whether to tax all components of a given tax base, such as income from dividends and income from capital gains, at the same rate?

The products of this indecision are fourfold. First, in reforming every couple of years the previous tax "reform," we aren't giving any one set of tax incentives enough time to produce its intended result. Second, the prospect that a given tax incentive will be eliminated in the near future limits the effectiveness of that incentive. Third, in continually changing taxes, we destabilize the overall economy or, at least, important sectors of the economy. Fourth, we've enacted partial, rather than full, reforms, with the result that we've arguably ended up with a worse tax system than the one with which we started.

In 1981 we attemped to move the tax structure toward consumption taxation, not by taxing consumption directly but by taxing income less investment, which, as indicated above, equals consumption. Our method of trying to tax the difference between income and investment involved increasing the tax deductibility of business investment. But in trying to provide these deductions, via the Accelerated Cost Recovery System (ACRS), we went overboard. The result was a system that provided, in many cases, deductions that were too large and, consequently, too expensive in terms of lost revenues. As a result, we scaled back this legislation with the Tax Equity and Fiscal Responsibility Act of 1982 and the Deficit Reduction Act of 1984. Then, in 1986, we completely reversed course by passing the Tax Reform Act. This new law reduced tax deductions for business investment to levels that were less generous than those available before the enactment of ACRS. For certain industries, such as real estate, this seesaw pattern of investment incentives led to overexpansion in the early 1980s followed by a crash in the late 1980s.

In addition to destabilizing specific industries as well as the economy, tax legislation in the 1980s has left us with a hybrid federal personal tax structure, with some features appropriate to an income tax and some appropriate to a consumption tax. The prime example here is our treatment of tax-favored saving accounts, including individual retirement accounts (IRAs), Keogh accounts,

401(k) plans, and employer-provided pension plans. In permitting funds placed in these accounts to be deducted from personal income taxes, these accounts afford consumption tax treatment (the taxation of $Y - S$) to this form of saving.

The problem is that to truly tax output less saving (i.e., consumption), the government must permit the deductibility from income only of net saving (gross saving minus gross borrowing), not simply gross saving. But to ensure that households only deduct net saving, the government must require households to add to their taxable income any additional borrowing the household does, be that borrowing in the form of a home mortgage, a car loan, or an outstanding credit card balance. This, the federal government has failed to do.

In failing to include gross borrowing in the income tax base, the government has invited all taxpaying Americans to engage in tax arbitrage in which they borrow funds, place them in their tax-favored saving accounts, and, thereby, lower their taxes The taxes saved through this arbitrage permit Americans to consume more—precisely the result that the tax-favored saving accounts were supposed to discourage. Although the federal government has, in recent years, restricted somewhat the ability of Americans to arbitrage the personal income tax, considerable scope for tax arbitrage remains. The arbitrage opportunities afforded by tax-favored saving accounts are contributing to our national saving crisis. This point notwithstanding, our politicians are currently debating expanding these accounts as well as relaxing restrictions on withdrawals from the accounts for purposes of spending on housing, medical care, and education—all of which are forms of consumption.

In addition to its arbitrage opportunities, the current tax system contains a number of distortions that also could be eliminated by switching to consumption taxation. One of these distortions is the differential tax treatment of corporate and noncorporate business that distorts businesses' ownership and control decisions. A second is the differential tax treatment of capital gains and dividends that distorts firms' decisions about retaining earnings and that locks investors in from selling shares of stock that have accrued capital gains. A third is the implicit subsidy to home ownership, automobiles, and other durable goods that arises from our failure to tax, under the income tax, the rental income we implicitly earn from the services on these durables.[4] A fourth is the subsidization of current relative to future consumption (the tax on saving) associated with the taxation of capital income. A fifth is the differential tax treatment of investment in equipment, structures, and inventories. A sixth is the distortion in corporate financial structure due to the deductibility of interest payments but the nondeductibility of dividends. And a seventh is the subsidization of health insurance premiums and other fringe benefits that are currently exempt from income taxation but would be treated like wage compensation under most consumption tax proposals.

The distortion of labor supply incentives associated with income taxation would also be eliminated by the proposed tax shift. But a consumption tax would distort this margin of choice as well, so one needs to compare the efficiency gains from eliminating the income tax's distortion of labor supply with the efficiency loss from adding the consumption tax's distortion of labor supply. There is good reason, however, to expect the tax shift to result in a net reduction in the distortion of labor supply. The reason is that consumption taxation will extract a larger share of its revenues from older generations, many of whom are retired. As a result, the total tax that needs to be collected form working generations is smaller under a consumption tax than it is under the income tax.

The National Retail Sales Tax— an Example of Consumption Taxation

The national sales tax considered here would be paid by all consumers when they purchase goods and services from retail establishments. Sales of all goods and services would be taxed at the same rate. In eliminating all income taxation in the United States, the proposal would eliminate taxation of all capital income, including capital gains. In the short run the tax rate of the proposed national sales tax would be roughly 23 percent, 17 percentage points of which would be required to replace federal personal and corporate income taxation and the remaining 6 percentage points of which would be required to replace state and local income taxation. Over time, as the sales tax stimulated economic growth, the national sales tax rate would, according to the predictions of this study, fall to 17 percent.

A full switch to a national sales tax would represent a radical departure from current fiscal arrangements. But nothing short of radical change may ever transform the tangle of tax provisions that is the income tax code into a clear and simple system of taxation. Because of its clarity and simplicity, a national sales tax might be the one tax that would have enough staying power to put an end to our politicians' constant, and costly, tinkering with taxes. In choosing a national sales tax we also would finally be making a choice between taxing consumption or income and picking the tax base, namely, consumption, that is most conducive to saving, investment, increased labor supply, and output growth.

Switching to a national sales tax would also improve the efficiency of the economy by eliminating the previously mentioned economic distortions arising under our current tax structure. Of course, a national sales tax would introduce distortions of its own, but the net impact of replacing federal income taxes with a national sales tax would, it appears, be a significant overall reduction in the misallocation of economic resources.

ARGUMENTS AGAINST A RETAIL SALES TAX

There are two main arguments against a proportional national sales tax. The first is that it would reduce the progressivity of the tax system. The second is that an immediate switch from the existing tax system to a national sales tax would lead to the shifting of tax burdens toward older generations who pay a larger share of consumption taxes than they do of income taxes.

The first concern—the lack of progressivity of a proportional national sales tax—has been overstated because progressivity has been measured in terms of annual, rather than lifetime, income. In any case, a national sales tax could be made progressive by combining it with a refundable tax credit. Each household would file a form requesting the tax credit and receive a check from the IRS equal to the amount of the credit for which the household qualifies. The value of the tax credit could be fixed per household, independent of the household's income, or it could be graduated (made to decline with the household's income). In addition, the value of the household credit might depend on the number of children and other dependents of the household.

In principle, the same degree of progressivity characterizing our current income tax system could be achieved with a national sales tax cum graduated refundable tax credit. In addition, if the credit were set sufficiently high, it could eliminate the need for, and stigma of, our welfare system. An alternative way of making the national sales tax progressive is to exempt from taxation those goods and services on which the poor spend a larger fraction of their income than do the rich. Examples of such commodities are food and housing.

Another way to institute a progressive retail sales tax is to adopt my proposed electronic consumption tax (the ECT). Actually, the ECT falls between a retail sales tax and a personal consumption tax. Like a retail sales tax, it taxes consumption directly. But like a personal consumption tax, it taxes consumption at progressive rates. Under the ECT, households would be required to run their consumption tax cards (ECT cards) through an electronic reader in making their consumption purchases. The amount of the purchase would be recorded by the household's bank. Running the ECT card through the reader will be required regardless of whether the houehold pays for its purchases with cash, with its ATM card, or with its credit card. Each month the total amount of households' consumption purchases (*but not the composition of these purchases*) would be reported to the government, and estimated taxes would be withheld, on a progressive basis, based on the amount reported. Tax withholding would be made electronically either as payroll deductions or as deductions from the household's checking account, so there would be no need for households to file any tax forms. At the end of the year, the government would calculate, on a progressive basis, each household's annual consumption and its annual consumption tax. Households that overpaid taxes during the year would receive an electronic refund, and those that underpaid would experience an electronic withdrawal. Consequently, there would be no filing of tax returns.

The second concern associated with switching tax regimes, namely, the shifting of greater tax burdens onto the current elderly, could be addressed by directly compensating the elderly (e.g., raising their Social Security benefits). Rather than consider in detail all of the arguments for and against a national sales tax, our main goal here is to illustrate the potential advantages of consumption taxation by considering the saving, investment, labor supply, and output growth implications of a switch to a national sales tax.

The Auerbach-Kotlikoff Dynamic Life-Cycle Simulation Model

The Auerbach-Kotlikoff model (henceforth, the AK model) can provide some sense of the potential saving, investment, and growth effects of shifting to a national sales tax.[5] The AK model calculates the time path of all economic variables in its economy over a 150-year period. The model has fifty-five overlapping generations. Each adult agent in the model lives for fifty-five years (from age twenty to age seventy-five).

There are three sectors in the model: households, firms, and the government. Households (adult agents) make decisions concerning how much to work and how much to save based on the after-tax wages and after-tax rates of return they can earn in the present and the future on their labor supply and saving, respectively. The work decision involves not only deciding how much to work in those years that one is working but also when to retire. The AK model's particular form of consumption and leisure preferences that agents use in making their labor supply and saving decisions were chosen in light of evidence on actual labor supply and saving behavior.

As agents age in the model, they experience a realistic profile of increases in wages. This age-wage profile is separate from the general level of wages, the time path of which is determined in solving the model. Fiscal policies affect households by altering their after-tax wages, their after-tax rates of return, and, in the case of consumption taxes, their after-tax prices of goods and services. The model is equipped to deal with income taxes, wage taxes, capital income taxes, and consumption taxes. It is also able to handle progressive as well as proportional tax rates.

All agents are assumed to have the same preferences, so differences in behavior across agents arise solely from differences in economic opportunities. Because all agents within an age cohort are assumed to be identical, differences in economic opportunities are present only across cohorts. In this study, the model's population growth rate is set at a constant 1 percent rate, with the population of each new cohort being 1 percent larger than that of the previous cohort.

The AK model's production sector is characterized by perfectly competitive firms that hire labor and capital to maximize their profits. The production relationships that underlie firms' hiring decisions and production of output are based on empirical findings for the United States. The government sector consists of a Treasury that collects resources from the private sector to finance government consumption and an unfunded, "pay-as-you-go" Social Security system that levies payroll taxes to pay for contemporaneous retiree benefit payments. The model does not distinguish federal from state and local government. Hence, in simulating with the model the elimination of income taxation in favor of sales taxation, we will, in effect, replace all state and local income taxes, as well as federal income taxes, with the sales tax. There is no money in the model and, thus, no monetary policy. There is, however, government debt, and the model can handle deficit-financed tax cuts. It can also handle gradual phaseins of one tax for the other.

Although the model handles a great number of complex processes, its predictions need to be viewed cautiously for several reasons. First, the model does not deal with several of the real-world distortions associated with the income tax that were mentioned above. For example, it doesn't distinguish corporate from noncorporate production, housing consumption from nonhousing consumption, different forms of corporate finance, different types of investment, or differences in capital gains and dividend tax rates. Nor does it permit the kind of tax arbitrage that is available to most tax-paying Americans through tax-subsidized saving accounts. Second, the model's agents are heterogeneous only with respect to their age. There are no welfare recipients or millionaires whose saving and work behavior might differ dramatically from that of the model's agents. Third, the model does not include saving for purposes other than retirement, such as bequests. Fourth, the model does not incorporate uncertainty with respect to either individual or macroeconomic outcomes. Fifth, the model ignores illegal tax avoidance, an issue that would certainly arise in implementing a national sales tax. Although the model abstracts from a significant portion of reality, it can, nonetheless, suggest the degree to which a switch from consumption taxation to income taxation might raise U.S. national saving.

Simulating the Switch from Income
Taxation to a National Sales Tax

In simulating the switch from income taxation to a national sales tax, I need to specify the economy's initial position as well as the way the tax change takes place. To begin, let's assume that the economy has a 15 percent proportional income tax and a 17 percent sales tax. The 15 percent income tax figure is based on the 1991 ratio of the sum of federal, state, and local personal and corporate income taxes to net national product. The 17 percent sales tax figure is based on the 1991 ratio of the sum of federal, state, and local sales and excise taxes to total personal consumption. These taxes are used to finance government consumption spending as well as pay interest on the government debt. The level of government debt is set at 50 percent of output. In addition to these features of fiscal policy, the economy is assumed to have a "pay-as-you-go" Social Security system with a 15 percent payroll tax rate.

FINDINGS

Table 6 shows the transition path of the economy that results from replacing in year zero the model's income tax with a national sales tax. I set the new national sales tax rate at the level needed, in conjunction with the preexisting 17 percent sales tax, to continue to finance the same level of government spending as well as pay interest on the stock of government debt. The first row in the table indicates the economy's initial (year zero) position. With no change in tax policy the economy would remain in this position through time. I measure annual saving rates, annual interest rates, and tax rates in percentage points. In the case of our economy's other variables, the units of measurement are arbitrary, so I describe each of these variables in terms of an index that has an initial (base year) value of one hundred.

The initial position of the economy features a 2.6 percent saving rate, a per capita capital stock of one hundred, a per capita labor supply of one hundred, a leval of per capita output of one hundred, a real wage rate of one hundred, a real interest rate of 9.4 percent, and, of course, a zero sales tax rate. The 2.6 percent saving rate is close to the current U.S. rate of saving, and the 9.4 percent real interest rate is close to the annual real rate of return that has been earned, on average, on the U.S. capital stock in the postwar period.

The remaining rows in table 6 show how each of these variables reacts to the introduction at time zero of the national sales tax. As row 1 indicates, the tax change produces an immediate and dramatic increase in the economy's saving rate, from 2.6 percent to 9.0 percent. Although the saving rate gradually declines

Table 6   Simulating an Immediate Switch from the Income Tax
                 to a National Sales Tax

Year	Saving Rate	Capital[a] Stock Index	Labor[a] Supply Index	Output[a] Index	Wage Index	Interest Rate	Sales Tax Rate
0	2.6	100	100	100	100	9.4	0.0
1	9.0	100	105	104	99	9.7	23.1
2	8.5	102	105	104	99	9.6	22.5
3	8.1	105	105	105	100	9.4	21.9
4	7.8	107	105	105	100	9.2	21.5
5	7.5	109	104	105	101	9.1	21.1
⋮							
10	6.2	117	103	106	103	8.5	19.5
⋮							
20	4.5	127	101	107	106	7.9	17.9
⋮							
60	3.7	131	101	108	107	7.8	17.3
⋮							
90	3.2	134	101	108	107	7.5	16.8
⋮							
150[b]	3.2	134	101	108	107	7.5	16.7

[a] The capital stock, labor supply, and output are per capita measures.
[b] The year 150 represents the economy's final steady state.

after year one, it remains above 6 percent through the tenth year of the transition. The long-run (year 150) value of the saving rate is 3.2 percent—23 percent larger than the year zero value.

The increased saving produces a concomitant increase in investment. As a result, the capital stock rises. Indeed, the switch in tax regimes leads, eventually (by year 150), to a 34 percent increase in the per capita capital stock. The increase in the capital stock is gradual; only about one-quarter of the ultimate increase occurs in the first ten years of the transition. The increase in the capital stock raises the productivity of workers and thus their real wage. The policy also lowers the return to capital. The real interest rate falls by almost two hundred basis points in the course of the transition.

Although the real wage ultimately ends up 7 percent higher than it would have been without the tax change, for the first few years of the transition the real wage actually falls because agents respond to the prospect of higher real wages and higher short-term real interest rates by increasing their labor supply. In the short run, before the capital stock has had much of a chance to increase, there is an increase in the supply of labor relative to the supply of capital. As a result, labor in the first few years of the transition becomes relatively abundant, meaning that the price it receives in the market—the real wage—falls. Eventually, as interest rates fall, the incentive to work more in order to save more and receive higher rates of return on the additional savings diminishes. As a result, labor supply declines. In the long run, the supply of labor is only 1 percent greater than it is in year zero.

The changes in the supplies of capital and labor alter the per capita level of output. Between year zero and year one, there is a 4 percent increase in output. In the following ten or so years the switch in the tax structure raises the economy's growth rate by two-tenths of 1 percent per year. In the long run, the level of per capita output is 8 percent larger than it is at time zero.

The final variable to discuss is the national sales tax rate. The year one value of this tax rate is 23.1 percent But it declines through time, with its value in the long run ending up at 16.7 percent. The reason the tax rate can decline is that the growth of the economy permits a higher level of consumption and thus produces a higher consumption tax base. In addition, the reduction in the interest rate lowers required interest payments on the government's debt.

To summarize the findings in table 6, the simulation of a switch to a national sales tax rate produces a significant increase in saving, capital accumulation, the real wage, and the level of per capita income. Although the dynamics are nonlinear (eg., labor supply first rises and then falls), all the results make intuitive sense.

MAINTAINING A CONSTANT NATIONAL SALES TAX RATE

As an alternative to having the national sales tax rate decline through time, we might want to have a tax rate that is constant through time. I've used the model to simulate such a policy. I've found that if I set the tax rate equal to 19 percent, the model produces deficits in the short run because the additional tax revenue raised with the 19 percent tax falls short of the loss in revenue from eliminating the 15 percent income tax. But over time, the growth of output and the consumption tax base associated with the reform raise the amount of revenue collected by the 19 percent tax, permitting the full retirement of the additional debt that is issued in the short run. In this constant tax rate simulation the long-run capital stock and output levels are 32 percent and 7 percent higher than their respective year zero values. These long-run percentage increases may be compared with the 34 percent and 8 percent increases of table 6.

ARE THE RESULTS REASONABLE?

Given the size of the model's predicted response to a switch to a national sales tax, one might ask whether the results are plausible or whether they simply reflect some extreme assumptions about labor supply and saving behavior. The answer is that the labor supply and saving responses assumed in the model are quite conservative and well within the range of responses that has been estimated in the empirical economics literature. In addition, the life-cycle model being simulated is the basic bread-and-butter model of neoclassical economics.

There is, however, one feature of the model that may make the transition occur faster in the model than it would in the real world. This is the model's assumption that new capital can be immediately added to the existing stock of capital without the incursion of installation costs. As discussed in Auerbach and Kotlikoff (1987), the addition of such installation costs would slow down the transition but would not alter the size of the long-run change of any of the economy's variables.

Another issue, with which I have not yet dealt, is the progressivity of the income tax that is to be replaced. As mentioned, the AK model can handle progressive as well as proportional tax rates. In the case of a progressive income tax, whose degree of progressivity is roughly comparable to that now in the United States, the year zero position of the economy from which the transition begins features a 2.2 percent, rather than a 2.6 percent, saving rate, a per capita capital stock that is 18.1 percent smaller, a per capita labor supply that is 5.2 percent smaller, a per capita output level that is 8.6 percent smaller, a real wage that is 3.5 percent smaller, and an interest rate of 10.4 percent rather than 9.4 percent. Because the switch from this progressive income tax regime to a proportional sales tax produces the same long-run outcome as indicated in the law row of table 6, the saving, capital accumulation, and growth effects of the tax change are all magnified by assuming that the initial income tax is progressive. For example, the long-run increase in the per capita capital stock is 63.4 percent and the long-run increase in per capita output is 18.3 percent.[6]

THE IMPACT ON THE INITIAL ELDERLY

Although switching to a national sales tax has a lot to recommend it, it does not include the treatment of the initial elderly who, as mentioned, end up paying much more in consumption taxes than they would have paid in income taxes. For example, in the simulation of table 6, the oldest elderly in year one, those who are age fifty-five, suffer a 23 percent decline in their final year's consumption. There are different ways to avoid, or at least mitigate, this redistribution away from those who are old at the time of the switch in tax structures. One is to make additional transfer payments to the initial elderly by, for example, raising Social Security benefits. The problem with making transfer payments to the initial elderly is that these transfer payments will lead them to consume more, and this additional consumption will limit the increase in saving and capital accumulation.

Table 7 shows the transition arising from an immediate switch to a retail

Table 7   Simulating an Immediate Switch from the Income Tax
               to a National Sales Tax but Compensating Initial Elderly
               for Their Increased Tax Burden

Year	Saving Rate	Capital [a] Stock Index	Labor [a] Supply Index	Output [a] Index	Wage Index	Interest Rate	Sales Tax Rate
0	2.6	100	100	100	100	9.4	0.0
1	6.6	100	104	103	99	9.7	22.1
2	6.4	101	104	104	99	9.5	21.8
3	6.3	103	104	104	100	9.4	21.5
4	6.1	104	104	104	100	9.3	21.2
5	5.9	106	104	104	100	9.2	21.0
⋮							
10	5.1	111	103	105	102	8.8	19.9
⋮							
20	4.1	118	102	106	104	8.4	18.7
⋮							
60	3.0	122	101	106	105	8.1	17.8
⋮							
90	3.0	122	101	106	105	8.1	17.8
⋮							
150 [b]	3.0	122	101	106	105	8.1	17.8

[a] The capital stock, labor supply, and output are measured per capita.

[b] The year 150 represents the economy's steady state.

sales tax, but one in which the government makes transfer payments to all generations alive at the time of the transition to ensure that none of these generations
is made worse off from the tax switch. These transfer payments are, of course,
largest for the oldest generations alive at the time of the tax switch because they
do not benefit as much from the elimination of income taxes as do younger
generations. Although the provision of this compensation to initial generations
limits the additional saving generated by the sales tax, there remains, nonetheless,
a substantial saving response. According to table 7 there is a 22 percent increase
in the economy's long-run capital stock. Although this is less than the 34 percent
increase of table 6, it is still quite substantial. With the compensation scheme in
place, the long-run increase in per capita income is 6 percent (compared with 8
percent with no compensation). The fact that one can compensate initial generations in switching to a national sales tax and still make future generations significantly better off is reflective of the inefficiency of an income tax structure relative
to a consumption tax structure.

Summary and Conclusion

Our nation is facing a grave crisis with respect to its rate of saving. We are saving at record low levels; unless we start saving more, we will continue our slide toward second-class economic status. A shift to a national sales tax has the potential for dramatically increasing our saving rate. It would do so by improving incentives to save and redistributing from the elderly with high propensities to consume to young and future generations with low or zero propensities to consume.

In addition to raising saving and investment, consumption taxation would reduce many of the distortions of the current tax system. Indeed, the distortion of saving behavior alone is so great under our current system of income taxation that it appears we could switch to consumption taxation, fully compensate the initial elderly for their higher tax burden, and still end up with a much higher rate of saving, capital accumulation, and level of per capita income.

Notes

1. The net national saving rate is defined as net national product less the sum of household consumption and government purchases divded by net national product.

2. Domestic investment can, of course, also be financed by foreigners. Indeed, in the late 1980s foreign investment financed a large component of U.S. domestic investment. But over the long run, it appears that domestic investment is fairly closely tied to national saving.

3. These tables come from Gokhale, Kotlikoff, and Sabelhaus (1995).

4. To see this, suppose homeowners, owners of automobiles, and owners of other durables were forced to pay rent to themselves for their use of their homes, cars, furniture, and so on. At one level, this would be a wash because the person writing the check would also be the recipient of the check. But this requirement would raise households' taxable income, leading them to pay more income taxes. Does it make sense to think of, say, a homeowner as renting her house to herself? The answer is yes because, in occupying her house, the homeowner is effectively earning the rent on the house and then spending it on herself.

5. For a detailed description of the AK model, see Auerbach and Kotlikoff (1987).

6. Interestingly, as described in Auerbach and Kotlikoff (1987), almost the same final steady state arises if the switch is to a progressive consumption tax.

References

Auerbach, Alan J., and Laurence J. Kotlikoff. *Dynamic Fiscal Policy*. Cambridge, Eng.: Cambridge University Press, 1987.

Bradford, David F. *Untangling the Income Tax*. Cambridge, Mass.: Harvard University Press, 1986.

Congressional Budget Office. "Effects of Adopting a Value-Added Tax," February 1992.

Gokhale, Jagadeesh, Laurence J. Kotlikoff, and John Sabelhaus. "Understanding the Postwar Decline in United States Saving: A Cohort Analysis." Boston University, Department of Economics, April 1995. Mimeographed.

U.S. Treasury. *Blueprints for Basic Tax Reform*. Washington, D.C.: U.S. Government Printing Office, 1977.

11

The Economic Impact of Fundamental Tax Reform

DALE W. JORGENSON

Introduction

Tax policy for saving and investment is critical for stimulating U.S. economic growth because investment is the most important source of growth. To achieve a more satisfactory growth performance, the tax burden on investment must be reduced substantially. This could be achieved by fundamental tax reforms like the flat tax, proposed by Congressman Dick Armey, or the USA (unlimited savings allowance) Tax, proposed by Senators Sam Nunn and Pete Domenici. These tax proposals would have the effect of shifting the base for taxation at the federal level from income to consumption, while preserving the existing administrative structure of the income tax. An alternative approach for shifting the federal tax base to consumption would be to adopt a value-added tax, like that employed in Europe and Japan. A consumption-based value-added tax would eliminate investment from the tax base. The system for value-added taxation common in Europe is based on allowing credit for the value-added tax already paid on business purchases of goods and services. Adoption of this system for the United States would require a new structure for tax administration, based on auditing sales and purchases of all businesses.

A third approach to consumption taxation is a retail sales tax like that employed by many state governments and some local governments in the United States. The existing administrative structure established by state governments could be employed for federal retail sales tax collections, possibly by having these collections done by existing state agencies but financed by the federal government. To exclude investment from the federal sales tax base, such a tax would have to be levied only on purchases by final consumers—households and institutions—and not on purchases by businesses.

Current consumption tax proposals are based on well-tested economic ideas and could serve as an appropriate starting point for fundamental tax reform. An important advantage of the Armey flat tax and the Nunn-Domenici USA Tax proposals is that the resulting consumption tax systems would be administered in much the same way as the present income tax system. The traditional objection to a consumption tax is that it would be regressive rather than progressive, falling disproportionately on low-income taxpayers. Both the flat tax and the USA Tax would achieve progressivity by means of a system of personal exemptions.

The Tax Reform Act of 1986 is the most recent fundamental tax reform in the United States. This landmark legislation preserved income as the tax base for the federal revenue system. However, the federal income tax was substantially reformed by eliminating special tax provisions for a number of specific types of investment, such as the investment tax credit for investment in equipment. These reforms removed important barriers to the efficient allocation of capital. In this chapter I show that the 1986 tax act created nearly one trillion dollars in new opportunities for economic growth!

Although recognizing the significant achievements of the 1986 tax act, I show that this legislation fell far short of exploiting the available opportunities for stimulating U.S. economic growth through tax reform. Changing the tax base from income to consumption would have generated more than two trillion dollars in opportunities for economic growth! I conclude that adopting consumption as the tax base would have *doubled* the benefits from fundamental tax reform. Ironically, a consumption tax was explicitly considered and rejected in the debate that preceded the 1986 tax legislation.

In a 1977 study, *Blueprints for Tax Reform*, the U.S. Treasury had proposed two alternative approaches for shifting the federal tax base from income to consumption. The first of these is a value-added tax, like that employed in Europe and Japan. The second would eliminate investment from the tax base by permitting taxpayers to treat investment expenditures as a tax deduction like that for any other business expense. Because investment would be excluded from the tax base, all other deductions from capital income, such as deductions for interest expenses, would be eliminated. However, these approaches to tax reform were considered and rejected by the U.S. Treasury in a 1984 report that initiated the debate leading to the 1986 tax act.

Neutral cost recovery, recently passed by the House of Representatives as Title II of the Job Creation and Wage Enhancement Act of 1995, is an important step toward reviving the Treasury proposals of 1977. This system for recovering capital cost would provide depreciation deductions with the same present value as immediate "expensing" of investment. These deductions would be based on the recovery of capital cost over the lifetime of an asset, as under current law. However, the deductions would be increased annually to allow a return on capital of 3.5 percent a year and compensate for inflation. At a discount rate of 3.5 percent, these deductions would have the same present value as an immediate write-off of capital outlays.

Neutral cost recovery, like the Treasury proposal of 1977, would eliminate investment from the tax base. To complete the shift in the tax base to consumption, however, it would be necessary to eliminate other deductions from capital income at the same time, including deductions for interest expenses. Otherwise, the U.S. Treasury would be in the position of providing subsidies through tax deductions for taxpayers who choose to finance investment through debt rather than equity. These subsidies could stimulate a revival of the tax shelter industry that flourished before the Tax Reform Act of 1986.

The recovery of capital costs should be regarded as one component of a tax system based on consumption rather than income. Shifting the federal tax base from income to consumption, as recommended in *Blueprints*, would require deductions equivalent to expensing of investment. However, other deductions from capital income would have to be eliminated at the same time. Adoption of a consumption tax would create important new opportunities for U.S economic growth.

The 1986 Tax Reform

I will support my conclusions by first reviewing the achievements of the 1986 tax reform.[1] I have presented simulations of future U.S. economic growth under alternative tax policies in table 1. These simulations show that the economic impact of the 1986 tax reform was positive and substantial at rates of inflation prevailing at the time. As the rate of inflation has declined these benefits have grown substantially, reflecting the fact that capital cost recovery deductions under the 1986 legislation were not indexed for inflation. These deductions decline in present value as the rate of inflation increases.

More specifically, I have compared growth opportunities available to the U.S. economy under the 1986 tax act with those available under the preexisting 1985 tax law and two tax reform proposals advanced by the Treasury in 1984 and the president in 1985. The benchmark for comparison is the 1985 tax law at a 6 percent inflation rate. Table 1 presents the difference between growth opportunities under alternative tax reforms with those resulting from no change in tax policy and an unchanged rate of inflation. It is important to be explicit about the role of inflation because the 1985 tax law and the 1986 tax act omitted important

Table 1   Growth Opportunities Created by the 1986 Tax Reform
               (in billions of 1987 dollars)

Rate of Inflation (%)	Revenue Adjustment	1985 Tax Law	Treasury Proposal	President's Proposal	1986 Tax Act
0	Lump-sum tax	$724.0	$1,489.6	$1,691.4	$1,561.8
	Labor income tax	478.2	1,468.8	1,642.4	1,565.0
	Sales tax	400.3	1,452.9	1,614.6	1,558.7
	Individual income tax	374.5	1,456.1	1,619.1	1,563.1
6	Lump-sum tax	0.0	1,907.6	2,452.2	448.4
	Labor income tax	0.0	1,711.4	2,170.4	746.9
	Sales tax	0.0	1,600.1	2,104.9	901.2
	Individual income tax	0.0	1,595.8	2,007.9	999.4
10	Lump-sum tax	−477.1	2,060.4	3,015.6	−200.8
	Labor income tax	−333.7	1,791.6	2,584.7	267.3
	Sales tax	−285.2	1,623.5	2,356.4	517.0
	Individual income tax	−221.9	1,604.8	2,353.1	748.6

NOTE: In 1987, the national wealth (beginning of the year) was $15,920.2 billion dollars.

provisions for indexing the tax structure for inflation included in the Treasury proposal and the president's proposal.

In comparing U.S. economic growth under alternative tax policies I require that all changes in tax policy be revenue neutral, that is, revenue and expenditure of the government are the same as in the base case given by the tax law of 1985. This requires adjusting tax revenues to maintain the budgetary position of the government. A hypothetical "lump-sum" tax or subsidy does not add to tax-induced distortions of private decisions and serves as a standard for comparison among alternative tax policies. I also consider three alternative methods for adjusting government revenues. These involve proportional changes in taxes on labor income, sales taxes on investment and consumption goods, and taxes on income from both capital and labor.

Table 1 presents estimates of the growth opportunities created or destroyed by alternative tax reform packages; all estimates are in billions of 1987 dollars. Let me first be precise about the meaning of the term *growth opportunities*. The objective of government policy, including tax policy, is to enhance the standard of living of U.S. consumers now and in the future. The concept of growth opportunities is a summary measure of the present value of future increases in the standard of living. It represents the willingness of the present generation of taxpayers to pay for a change in tax policy that will affect their own standard of living and that of future generations of taxpayers.[2]

Turning to the impact of the 1986 tax act, we see that this fundamental tax reform produces a sizable gain in opportunities for future U.S. economic growth. For the revenue adjustments based on proportional changes in tax rates, these gains range from 746.9 billion 1987 dollars to $999.4 billion, or nearly *one trillion dollars!* There are important differences between results for a hypothetical "lump-sum" tax adjustment and adjustments based on changes in tax rates. However, the results do not depend significantly on which of the tax rates is used in maintaining revenue neutrality.

Although the Tax Reform Act of 1986 obviously generated substantial growth opportunities for the U.S. economy, the Treasury and the president's proposals would have done substantially more to enhance economic growth. For tax adjustments based on changes in tax rates to maintain revenue neutrality, the Treasury proposal would have produced growth opportunities ranging from 1,595.8 billion 1987 dollars to $1,711.4 billion. The president's proposal would have produced gains ranging from 2,007.9 billion 1987 dollars to $2,170.4 billion, or more than *double* the gains from the 1986 tax act! Nonetheless, tax policy makers should recognize the 1986 reform as a giant step in the right direction.

The estimates presented in the first column of table 1 also make it possible to isolate the effects of changes in inflation with no change in tax policy. The 1985 tax law, like the Tax Reform Act of 1986, was not completely indexed for inflation so that the tax burden increases with the inflation rate. By contrast the Treasury proposal and the president's proposal involved indexing the tax structure for inflation. With no change in tax law the results presented in table 1 show that an increase in the inflation rate from 6 to 10 percent would have imposed a loss on the economy in the range of 221.9–333.7 billion 1987 dollars. Reducing the inflation rate to zero would have produced a gain in the range of $374.5–$478.2 billion.

If we compare the Treasury and the president's proposals with the 1986 tax act at a 6 percent inflation rate in chart 1, we find that these proposals would have produced much greater gains in growth opportunities. Gains from the president's proposal would have been more than double those of the 1986 tax act, and gains from the Treasury proposal would have been 50 percent higher. However, at a zero inflation rate the two proposals and the actual 1986 tax legislation would have had similar economic impacts, resulting in gains in growth opportunities of one and a half trillion dollars. Under the 1986 tax act the gains shrink with increased inflation, but these gains actually grow with increased inflation under the two alternative proposals.

In summary, the Tax Reform Act of 1986 created almost one trillion dollars in growth opportunities for the U.S. economy. This demonstrates the potential contribution to growth from fundamental tax reform. As the inflation rate has gradually subsided, these growth opportunities have steadily increased. At a zero rate of inflation the impact of the 1986 tax act on U.S. economic growth would

Chart 1   Growth Opportunities Created by the 1986 Tax Reform

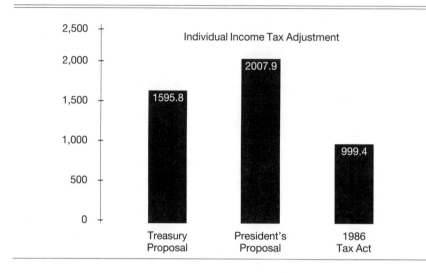

have been closely comparable to that of the Treasury proposal or the president's proposal. However, the 1986 tax act did not incorporate provisions from these proposals that would have largely insulated the U.S. tax structure from the impact of inflation.

Fundamental Tax Reform

In this section I consider the economic impact of a shift in the tax base for the federal revenue system from consumption to income. I also consider a number of alternative tax reforms. As in the previous seciton, I use the 1985 tax law with a 6 percent inflation rate as a benchmark. These alternative reforms focus on tax distortions induced by differences in the tax treatment of income from corporate, noncorporate, and household sectors and short-lived and long-lived assets. In the parlance of the 1986 tax debate, these are different ways of "leveling the playing field." As before, I achieve revenue neutrality for each proposal by adjusting tax rates to preserve the balance between revenues and expenditures.

Initially, I will focus attention on the seventh line in table 2. This is the consumption tax scheme proposed in the Treasury's 1977 *Blueprints for Tax Reform* and now embodied in the Armey flat tax and the Nunn-Domenici USA Tax proposals. Under these proposals the tax base for the federal tax system would be shifted from income to consumption by excluding investment from the tax base. In the business sector this would be achieved through deductions for in-

Table 2   Growth Opportunities Created by Leveling the Playing Field
               under the 1985 Law (in billions of 1987 dollars)

	Lump-Sum Tax Adjustment	Labor Income Tax Adjustment	Sales Tax Adjustment	Individual Income Tax Adjustment
Within sector interasset distortion	$ 443.9	$ 248.1	$ 168.7	70.2
Intersector distortion:				
C and NC sectors	−93.3	−416.7	−523.8	−715.5
Intersector distortion: All sectors	2,262.6	2,159.9	2,118.6	2,067.7
No tax distortion:				
C and NC sectors, all assets	326.4	69.2	−29.1	−169.7
No tax distortion:				
All sectors, all assets	2,663.7	2,603.9	2,572.4	2,547.2
Corporate tax integration	1,313.1	493.4	238.1	−274.5
Consumption tax rules				
(zero effective tax rates)	3,859.9	2,045.4	1,749.3	2,045.4
Consumption tax rules (zero effective tax rates; no sales tax on investment goods)	4,128.1	1,988.0	1,722.1	1,988.0

vestment outlays like those for any other business expenses. The eighth line of
table 2 is a more thoroughgoing version of this scheme that would eliminate sales
taxes on investment as well.

The introduction of consumption tax rules for capital cost recovery in 1986
would have generated growth opportunities of more than *two trillion dollars*. This
fundamental tax reform would have doubled the gains in U.S. economic growth
that resulted from the 1986 tax act. This is the consequence of leveling the
playing field among all economic sectors—households, noncorporate businesses,
and corporations. At the same time income from different types of assets—plant,
equipment, inventories, and land—would be treated symmetrically under the tax
law. The tax treatment of income from all assets employed in the U.S. economy
would be completely neutral under consumption tax rules like those proposed in
Blueprints.

The first line of table 2 is a hypothetical tax reform that would eliminate
differences in the tax treatment of different assets but would leave the existing tax
distortions due to differences in the tax treatment of corporate, noncorporate, and
household capital income unaffected. The second line would remove distortions
between corporate and noncorporate business but would not alter the treatment
of income from household assets, such as owner-occupied residential housing.
The third line extends this treatment to the household sector.

The fourth line would level the playing field among assets in corporate and
noncorporate sectors, while the fifth would extend this treatment to the house-

hold sector as well. The sixth would reduce taxation on corporate assets to those of noncorporate assets through "corporate tax integration," as proposed by the Treasury's 1992 report *Taxing Business Income Once*. Equalizing the treatment of income from assets in business and household sectors would create the greatest opportunities for U.S. economic growth, as indicated in the simulations summarized in the third and fifth lines of table 2.

An important advantage of consumption tax rules is that income from capital employed in the household sector, such as owner-occupied residential housing, would be treated symmetrically with income from capital employed by corporate and noncorporate businesses. An alternative approach to equalizing the treatment of all forms of capital income would be to try to include income from owner-occupied residential housing in the federal tax base. However, this would require such politically unpalatable measures as reducing or totally eliminating popular tax deductions for home mortgage interest and state and local property taxes.

As a practical matter, the inclusion of income from the services of owner-occupied residential housing in the tax base for income would he highly problematic. Although owner-occupied residential housing is an investment from an economic point of view, the services of this housing are part of both consumption and income. A possible approach to the taxation of this part of income would be to treat each owner occupier as a business owning a residence. This approach would involve an "imputation" for the rental value of housing as part of taxable income. European experience[3] shows that this approach is nearly impossible to implement.

A second approach to the taxation of income from owner-occupied housing would be to exclude the value of new residential construction from investment by disallowing a deduction for the purchase of a home along with all other housing-related deductions, such as home mortgage interest and state and local property taxes. In the Armey flat tax proposal the appeal of a low flat rate of taxation would help to offset the political consequences of eliminating these popular deductions.

A third approach to taxation of housing, employed in the Nunn-Domenici USA Tax proposal, represents a compromise between the existing income tax treatment and a full-scale consumption tax treatment. In this approach the current tax treatment of owner-occupied housing would be retained, while business income would be treated under consumption tax rules. This would nearly equalize the tax burdens on the household sector and the business sector. An important advantage of this compromise between income and consumption taxation would be to avoid complex transition rules for owner-occupied housing already in existence at the time of fundamental tax reform.

In summary, the principal conclusions that emerge from comparison of all

Chart 2   Growth Opportunities Created by a Consumption Tax

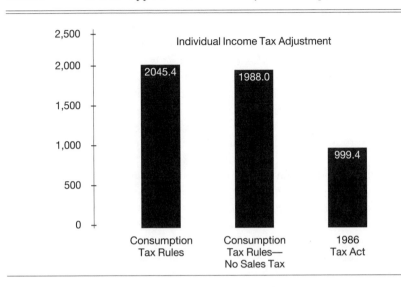

eight hypothetical reform proposals are illustrated in chart two. The most important opportunities for future growth of the U.S. economy would be created by the adoption of consumption tax rules for capital income. This would make it possible to reduce business taxes at both corporate and individual levels substantially. If this approach to tax reform had been adopted in 1986, the gains would have been equivalent to almost two trillion dollars, or *double* the gains resulting from the 1986 tax act.

Directions for Future Tax Reform

The purpose of the simulations of U.S. economic growth described in the preceding section is to compare actual tax reform proposals with the Tax Reform Act of 1986. The current tax structure retains many of the features that resulted from the 1986 reform. However, important changes in tax policy were incorporated in the Budget Enforcement Act of 1990 under President Bush and President Clinton's Omnibus Budget Reconciliation Act of 1993. Both of these budget agreements raised tax rates for upper-income tax payers, increasing the reliance on capital income taxes relative to those on labor income. These changes have created important new opportunities for generating economic growth through fundamental tax reform.

I next provide a more precise assessment of opportunities to contribute to the future growth of the U.S. economy through tax reform.[4] For this purpose I link tax-induced losses in economic efficiency directly to U.S. economic growth. I use a nondistorting tax system as a benchmark in measuring the loss in efficiency from taxation. In this tax system all revenue is raised by purely hypothetical lump-sum taxes that do not distort private decisions and involve no efficiency loss. By focusing on differences in losses among alternative tax programs, I am able to identify promising avenues for future tax reform.

My first conclusion is that the loss in efficiency imposed on the U.S. economy by the current tax system is very large. The efficiency loss is equivalent to 18 percent of government tax revenue. Each dollar of tax revenue costs the private sector a dollar of forgone investment or consumption and an additional loss in growth opportunities of eighteen cents. I refer to this estimate as the *average excess burden*, defined as the gain in efficiency that would result from replacing the whole U.S. tax system by a nondistorting system. Let me hasten to emphasize that this replacement is purely hypothetical.

The concept of efficiency loss most relevant to tax reform is the *marginal excess burden*. The marginal excess burden of the U.S. tax system is defined in terms of the efficiency loss *per dollar* for the final dollar of revenue raised. The marginal excess burden enables me to quantify one of the most familiar propositions in tax policy analysis. Because efficiency losses rise as tax burdens increase, the marginal cost of raising tax revenue is much greater than the average cost. I estimate that the marginal efficiency loss is 39.1 cents per dollar of revenue, more than double the average loss.

Most important, large differences in marginal excess burdens among different tax programs remain. For example, the marginal cost of raising a dollar through taxes on capital income at the individual level is 111.7 cents, while the cost of raising a dollar from labor income taxes is only 37.6 cents. For every dollar of tax revenue transferred from capital income to labor income, the U.S. economy *gains* 64.1 cents in future growth opportunities. This transfer would be revenue neutral and thus in perfect conformity to the Clinton budget plan of 1993. This provides a clear indication of important potential gains in future U.S. economic growth through tax reform.

I next describe the efficiency costs of various parts of the U.S. tax system in greater detail. For this purpose, I analyze the growth of the U.S. economy under reductions of tax rates for the following nine components of the U.S. tax system: (1) the corporate income tax, (2) capital income taxes at the individual level, including taxes levied on noncorporate capital income and taxes on individual capital income originating in the corporate sector, (3) property taxes on corporate, noncorporate, and household assets, (4) capital income taxes at both corporate and individual levels, (5) labor income taxes, (6) capital and labor income taxes, (7) the individual income tax, (8) sales taxes on consumption and invest-ment goods, and (9) all taxes.

Table 3 presents the average and marginal efficiency costs of all components of the U.S. tax system under the Tax Reform Act of 1986. The marginal efficiency costs of the whole U.S. tax system in the ninth panel of table 3 show that the marginal efficiency cost at rates prevailing under the 1986 tax act was .391, meaning that the loss in efficiency for each dollar of tax revenue raised was 39.1 cents. However, the average efficiency cost for the whole tax system was .180; thus replacing all taxes by a nondistorting tax would have increased opportunities for economic growth by an average of 18 cents per dollar of tax revenue.

The marginal efficiency cost of sales taxes given in the eighth panel of table 3 was .262 after the reform, while the cost of property taxes given in the third panel was .176. By contrast, the marginal efficiency cost of all income taxes given in the sixth panel of table 3 was .497. The efficiency losses were 49.7 cents per dollar of income tax revenue, only 17.6 cents per dollar of property tax revenue, and only 26.2 cents per dollar of sales tax revenue. A substantial increase in efficiency could have been realized by reducing income tax rates and increasing the rates of sales and property taxes. We conclude that the Tax Reform Act of 1986 did not successfully overcome the excessive reliance of the U.S. tax system on income taxes.

The structure of the income tax itself is completely out of balance with marginal efficiency costs of labor income taxes at .376, individual capital income taxes at 1.017, and corporate income taxes at .448. Substantial gains in efficiency could have been realized by further reductions in marginal tax rates on individual and corporate taxes on capital income, even at the expense of increases in mar-ginal tax rates on labor income. Considerable gains in growth opportunities for the U.S. economy could have resulted from reduced reliance on individual in-come taxes on capital income and more reliance on corporate income taxes.

Second, within the income tax there is excessive reliance on taxes on capital income at the individual level. Finally, existing taxes on capital income put excessive burdens on individuals, relative to corporations. Taxes on capital in-come at both corporate and individual levels are too burdensome, relative to taxes on labor income. Every dollar transferred to labor income taxes from capital income taxes at the individual level costs the U.S. economy 64.1 cents in lost growth opportunities. Reversing the direction of the 1986 reform by raising mar-ginal rates for high-income taxpayers has greatly increased the tax burden on capital income. This will be enormously costly in terms of opportunities for reviving the growth of the U.S. economy. These conclusions are summarized in chart 3.

In summary, the best way to create new growth opportunities for the U.S. economy would be to reduce the top rates of taxation at the individual level, not to increase these rates. This could be financed by cutting back on tax expenditure

Table 3   Efficiency Costs of U.S. Tax Revenues after the Tax Reform Act of 1986

		REDUCTION IN TAX RATES (%)										
		5	10	20	30	40	50	60	70	80	90	100
Corporate income	MEC [a]	.448	.435	.418	.397	.379	.363	.348	.334	.322	.310	.301
	AEC [b]	.448	.442	.431	.421	.412	.404	.397	.391	.384	.379	.374
Individual capital income	MEC	1.017	.989	.951	.904	.853	.812	.767	.727	.688	.650	.613
	AEC	1.017	1.003	.977	.953	.928	.906	.884	.863	.842	.822	.803
Property value	MEC	.176	.174	.171	.168	.164	.160	.157	.153	.149	.145	.142
	AEC	.176	.175	.173	.171	.169	.168	.166	.164	.162	.160	.158
All capital income	MEC	.675	.650	.616	.573	.533	.498	.466	.435	.407	.382	.359
	AEC	.675	.663	.640	.619	.600	.582	.566	.551	.537	.524	.512
Labor income	MEC	.376	.358	.333	.303	.276	.253	.237	.216	.201	.190	.183
	AEC	.376	.367	.350	.334	.320	.307	.296	.285	.275	.266	.259
1 + 2 + 5 = 4 + 5	MEC	.497	.462	.414	.355	.301	.254	.212	.175	.142	.114	.091
	AEC	.497	.480	.448	.418	.391	.366	.343	.323	.304	.287	.271
Individual income	MEC	.520	.490	.449	.396	.349	.305	.265	.229	.196	.167	.140
	AEC	.520	.505	.477	.451	.426	.403	.381	.361	.342	.325	.308
Sales value	MEC	.262	.259	.254	.249	.242	.236	.230	.224	.218	.211	.205
	AEC	.262	.261	.257	.254	.251	.248	.245	.242	.239	.236	.232
All tax bases	MEC	.391	.356	.308	.249	.197	.151	.113	.082	.063	.048	.040
	AEC	.391	.374	.342	.312	.285	.260	.238	.220	.204	.190	.180

[a] marginal efficiency cost
[b] average efficiency cost

Chart 3   Efficiency Costs of U.S. Tax Revenues (%)

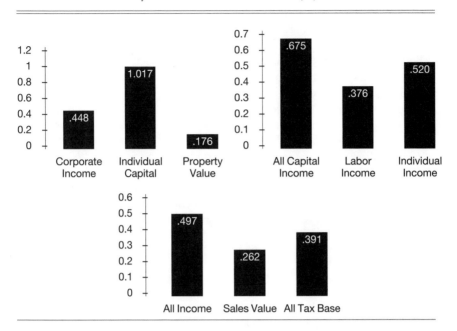

programs such as deductions for mortgage interest and state and local property taxes. President Bush's Budget Enforcement Act of 1990 and the Clinton Omnibus Budget Reconciliation Act of 1993 have substantially increased taxes on capital income at the individual level. A growth-oriented tax policy requires reinforcing the basic thrust of the Tax Reform Act of 1986 by reducing differences in the marginal excess burdens imposed by different parts of the U.S. tax system.

Conclusion

My first overall conclusion is that increases in tax rates for upper-income taxpayers in 1990 and 1993 have nullified many of the growth opportunities for the U.S. economy created by the Tax Reform Act of 1986. It is important to underline this conclusion because the recent emphasis on "soaking the rich" has increased reliance on capital income taxes relative to those on labor income. This will be enormously costly in terms of future consumption for growth of the U.S. economy. Future tax reforms should strengthen rather than weaken the basic thrust of the Tax Reform Act of 1986.

Second, neutral cost recovery is an important contribution to the debate over tax reform. This tax proposal would introduce provisions for recovery of capital costs that are equivalent to the expensing of investment expenditures required under consumption tax rules. However, neutral cost recovery must be combined with other tax reforms, such as the elimination of deductions for interest expenses, to enhance the neutrality of the federal tax system. Achieving neutrality in the taxation of income from all assets in the U.S. economy is the most important goal for future tax reform.

Finally, changing the federal tax base from income to consumption is an idea whose time has come. This change will create important new opportunities for growth in the standard of living of all Americans. The traditional objections to consumption as a base for taxation on grounds of fairness have been successfully addressed in the Armey flat tax and the Nunn-Domenici USA Tax proposals. These proposals would create substantial new growth opportunities for the U.S. economy. Both are based on well-established economic ideas and could serve as a point of departure for tax reform legislation.

Notes

1. This review is based on my paper "Tax Reform and U.S. Economic Growth," with Kun-Young Yun. The paper provides a more detailed appraisal of the Tax Reform Act of 1986.

2. Further details are given in my paper with Yun, "The Excess Burden of Taxation."

3. This experience is reviewed in my book with Ralph Landau, *Tax Reform and the Cost of Capital: An International Comparison.*

4. Here I draw on a second paper, "The Excess Burden of U.S. Taxation," that I have published with Yun.

References

Armey, Dick. "The Freedom and Fairness Restoration Act." Washington, D.C., 103d Congress, 2d Session, 1994.

Jorgenson, Dale W., and Ralph Landau, eds. *Tax Reform and the Cost of Capital: An International Comparison.* Washington, D.C.: Brookings Institution, 1993.

Jorgenson, Dale W., and Kun-Young Yun. "Tax Reform and U.S. Economic Growth." *Journal of Political Economy* 98, no. 5, part 2 (October 1990): 151–93.

——. "The Excess Burden of U.S. Taxation." *Journal of Accounting, Auditing, and Finance* 6, no. 4 (fall 1991): 487–509.

Nunn, Sam, and Pete Domenici. "The USA Tax System." Alliance USA, Washington, D.C., 1994.

Smith, Nick. "Neutral Cost Recovery Act of 1995." Washington, D.C., 104th Congress, 1st Session, 1995.

U.S. Deaprtment of the Treasury. *Blueprints for Tax Reform*. Washington, D.C.: U.S. Government Printing Office, 1977.

——. *Tax Reform for Fairness, Simplicity, and Economic Growth*. Washington, D.C.: U.S. Government Printing Office, 1984.

——. *The President's Tax Proposals to the Congress for Fairness, Growth, and Simplicity*. Washington, D.C.: U.S. Government Printing Office, 1985.

——. *Taxing Business Income Once*. Washington, D.C.: U.S. Government Printing Office, 1992.

Index